Parting Gifts of Empire

Parting Gifts of Empire

PALESTINE AND INDIA AT THE DAWN
OF DECOLONIZATION

Esmat Elhalaby

UNIVERSITY OF CALIFORNIA PRESS

University of California Press
Oakland, California

© 2025 by Esmat Elhalaby

All rights reserved.

Cataloging-in-Publication data is on file at the Library of Congress.

ISBN 978-0-520-38926-7 (cloth)
ISBN 978-0-520-38927-4 (pbk.)
ISBN 978-0-520-38929-8 (ebook)

GPSR Authorized Representative: Easy Access System Europe,
Mustamäe tee 50, 10621 Tallinn, Estonia, gpsr.requests@easproject.com

34 33 32 31 30 29 28 27 26 25
10   9   8   7   6   5   4   3   2   1

For ANJALI

And for R and L

Contents

Acknowledgments *ix*
Note on Translation and Transliteration *xv*
Map *xvii*

Introduction: Decolonization and Its Forms of Knowledge *1*

1. Empire *28*
2. Islam *53*
3. Asia *77*
4. Nonalignment *104*
5. Area *127*

Epilogue *161*

Notes *169*
Bibliography *211*
Index *237*

Acknowledgments

More than 410 days into a genocide in Gaza, I must acknowledge—at the outset—that this work is not particularly urgent. This book is about ideas and writing, and the social conditions, or social history, of intellectuals in the colonized world. Those conditions today are being transformed. For hundreds of intellectuals in Gaza, their condition now is simply a shallow grave or rotting beneath the rubble of their own homes. It is impossible to account for the family, friends, and colleagues killed by Israel. There is not, probably, enough paper in the world. But I cannot begin to thank all the people who made this book possible without first acknowledging at least those in my immediate family who were recently murdered by the Israeli state in Gaza: Sahar Abushaban, Mohammad Abushaban, Rana Abushaban, Nabila Elhalaby, Hani Aqeela, Ashraf Abushaban, Essam Abushaban, Adly Elhalaby, and Basheer Alashi. Until liberation.

. . .

I must thank my teacher Ussama Makdisi, who patiently allowed me to figure out what it was I wanted to do and has always supported me despite my run-ins with George Bush Jr., Avi Dicthter, and other, lesser criminals (and my own criminality). I would not be in a position to write this book if it were not for Ussama's regular encouragement and generous critique. Tani Barlow taught me how to read Soviet and Asian Marxisms. Betty Joseph was generous with her time and ideas, even on short notice. Thanks especially to Manan Ahmed, who tutored me, before I even got to grad school, in the many genres of scholarly writing and the mores of a hostile academy. Cyma Farah, Nate George, and Suraya Khan offered respite. Sunil Agnani's fortuitous appearance at Rice reminded me that I wasn't crazy. Hosam Aboul-Ela, Leena Dallasheh, Fady Joudah, Abdel Razzaq Takriti, and Hicham Safieddine offered camaraderie and ruthless criticism on and off the Rice plantation. At UCLA, Nile Green, Robin D. G. Kelley, Vinay Lal, Saree Makdisi, and Susan Slyomovics aimed me in the right direction. I was lucky to spend time in Haifa at Mada al-Carmel, Arab Center for Applied Social Research, where I learned important lessons from Khaled Furani and Areej Sabbagh-Khoury. Waleed Hazbun facilitated my seat at the microfilm machine in Jafet. Rosie Bsheer facilitated my squatting in Widener. Durba Mitra always asked the right questions and offered characteristically clear answers, regarding this book and much else. Omnia El Shakry's interest in and support for my efforts were and remain invaluable.

I spent most of grad school on the run from Houston. Enormous gratitude to friends in Beirut, Cairo, Amman, New York, London, Lucknow, Delhi, and up and down the California coast. Thank you Jehad Abusalim, Wael Abd El-Fattah, Zuleikha Ahmedani, Nader Atassi, Tawfik Bseiso, Javier Arbona-Homar, Mansour Aziz, Sohaib Baig, Kaoukab Chebaro, Raph Cormack, Ziad Dallal, Hardeep Dhillon, Ahmed Elamine, Nasser Elamine, Muniera Hoballah, Aaron Jakes, Hazem Jamjoum, Alex Jreisat, Sumayya Kassamali, Cynthia Krecheti, Naeem Mohaiemen, Hussein Omar, Tanjil Rashid, Laila Riazi, Nadya Sbaiti, Majd Al-Shihabi, Samhita Sunya, Pelle Valentin Olsen, and Adam Waterman. Hana Sleiman always kept me grounded. And I might have become a lawyer, or worse, if it wasn't for Suleiman Hodali.

I finished this book in Toronto, among friends and enemies. I am lucky to have arrived in Toronto at the same time as Adrien Zakar, who quickly became my most important interlocutor and critical reader. Aamer Ibraheem shared my—let's say—enthusiasm—for Israeli Orientalism, and sundry other things. Chandni Desai, Muhammad Ali Khalidi, Dania Majid, Nada Moumtaz, and Alejandro Paz, my comrades at Hearing Palestine, entered the fray fearlessly. Robyn Maynard and Nisrin Elamin embody solidarity. In crucial moments, Bhavani Raman articulated what I was trying to do far better than I could. Natalie Rothman is probably the best department chair one could ask for. I consider myself extremely lucky to be in Toronto with so many sharp and generous people, including Ahmed Abushaban, Tamara Abdul Hadi, Safia Aidid, Doris Bergen, Katherine Blouin, Frank Cody, Kevin Coleman, Rebecca Comay, Deborah Cowen, Sanchia deSouza, Anver Emon, Cindy Ewing, Rachel Goffe, Kanishka Goonewardena, Anup Grewal, Connie Guberman, Rick Halpern, Atiqa Hachimi, Malavika Kasturi, Whitney Kemble, Uahikea Maile, Max Mishler, Shahrzad Mojab, William Nelson, Melanie Newton, Leila Pourtavaf, Shozab Raza, Rakesh Sengupta, Omar Sirri, Jesook Song, Nhung Tuyet Tran, and Alissa Trotz. Students in my seminars "Transnational Asian Thought" and "Intellectuals and Decolonization" helped me think through many of the ideas in this book. In addition to being excellent students, Salma Serry and Ajwa Zulfiqar provided crucial research assistance, often on short notice.

I am grateful for all the comments and criticism I have received on this work as I shared it with audiences at UC Berkeley, Columbia University, Yale University, McGill University, UCLA, Universidade NOVA de Lisboa, UCR, UC Davis, NYU Abu Dhabi, Harvard University, Cambridge University, Simon Fraser University, the

National University of Singapore, and Oxford University, as well as the meetings of the Middle East Studies Association, the American Comparative Literature Association, and the Arab Council for the Social Sciences. Thanks also to the three reviewers for UC Press, whose comments and suggestions improved this book immeasurably. For interest in this work, and moral and material support over the years, my thanks also to Cemil Aydin, Sara Farhan, Amal Ghazal, Peter James Hudson, Youssef Ismail, Alexander Jabbari, Suad Joseph, Darryl Li, Abdulla Moaswes, Pedro Monaville, José Neves, Timothy Nunan, Jemima Pierre, Mezna Qato, Michael Reyes Salas, Ahmad Shokr, Sherene Seikaly, Mohammed Al-Sudairi, Manuela Ribeiro Sanches, John Willis, and Ather Zia. Niels Hooper's enthusiasm for this book from the outset, and encouragement near the end, made it happen.

I did receive some funding from various bodies to do some of the research in this book, although I could have used more. For the Critical Language Scholarship that took me back to Lucknow for further Urdu study one summer, I am obligated to thank the State Department of the United States. It is my hope that this study does not serve American imperialism and its ancillaries in any way. I must also thank Rice University for funds provided while I was a graduate student there, mostly archives that have no bearing on the present study, but I did learn a lot digging in the crates. Funds from NYU Abu Dhabi and UC Davis allowed me to travel and acquire much-needed books. Thanks also to the University of Toronto for its largesse, especially the Connaught Fund. I am most grateful to the librarians and archivists who facilitated this research. My gratitude also to those who got in my way; after all, haven't American academics done enough? Eyad in Beirut always had something I was looking for. To friends who ferried contraband books in their luggage at my behest, many thanks. At the British Library I must thank Daniel

Lowe and Nur Sobers-Khan for showing me the basement. Thanks to Phong Tran at the Library of Congress for his interest. Enormous thanks to the anonymous many who digitized countless documents, books, and periodicals.

Immense gratitude to Nora Boustany for sharing documents with me about her grandfather, taking me up to Dibbeyeh, and chatting with me about her life and her family. Thanks also to Mandakranta Bose for sharing her memories of her own extraordinary father. My thanks to Sandipto Dasgupta for connecting me to Mainul Abedin, who kindly granted me permission to use his father's incredible artwork on the cover of this book. Zainul Abedin was commissioned by the Arab League to travel to Jordan's Palestinian refugee camps in 1970. His paintings were subsequently printed in Arab League publications, like those discussed in chapter 4.

I am obligated to thank Duke University Press for kind permission to republish material from my article "Nonalignment and Its Forms of Knowledge," *Comparative Studies of South Asia, Africa and the Middle East* 43, no. 3 (2023): 386–97. And also to Cambridge University Press for permission to republish material from "Empire and Arab Indology," *Modern Intellectual History* 19, no. 4 (2022): 1081–1105.

Even though researching and writing this book has meant I don't get to see my parents nearly enough, I hope this book may serve as some modicum of restitution. My parents, Palestinians from a Gaza that remains colonized until this very hour, taught me how to be in this world, how to dwell in it in Arabic, and how to work for others. Rawan has been a selfless and patient sister; I owe her more than she knows. Youssef and Kuku are my family. I cannot overstate how essential the moral and material support of my parents-in-law has been over the course of writing this book. And Rishi and Luna produced, more than once, the conditions for this book's creation. But this book, and much else, would simply not exist without Anjali Nath, who has lived with it as long as I have. And I probably would have never started writing this book if it wasn't for R, and probably wouldn't have finished it if it wasn't for L. May this world be yours someday.

Toronto, November 20, 2024

Note on Translation and Transliteration

Words and names from Arabic have generally been transliterated according to the style of the *International Journal for Middle East Studies*, but without diacritics, except for the ʿayn and ʾhamza, and usually only in titles, the notes, and bibliography. So in the text, *ulema* is used, not ʿ*ulema*. Proper names, however, include *ayn* or *hamza* in the text when dropping the diacritics might indicate a different or inaccurate name, at least in the first instance, for example, Wadiʿ al-Bustani, not Wadi al-Bustani. In other cases, like the name Said, as in Karima al-Said, the diacritical is dropped. Names with the Arabic definite article *al-* are written in full on the first appearance, but the *al-* might be dropped thereafter, as is common in everyday speech. So al-Bustani at first, but simply Bustani later. Individuals with standard, well-known transliterations for their names in English are rendered with those transliterations in the text and notes, so Anouar Abdel-Malek throughout, not ʿAnwar ʿAbd al-Malik. The titles of Urdu texts, and names without standard English renditions, are transliterated according to the standards of the ALA-LC, without diacritics. Names or titles drawn from English or French sources are written according to those sources. My own name is transliterated according to decisions made by own family, without reference to any academic system, revealing plainly the limits of these efforts. "Water binds you to my name," as Darwish put it. All translations are my own unless otherwise stated.

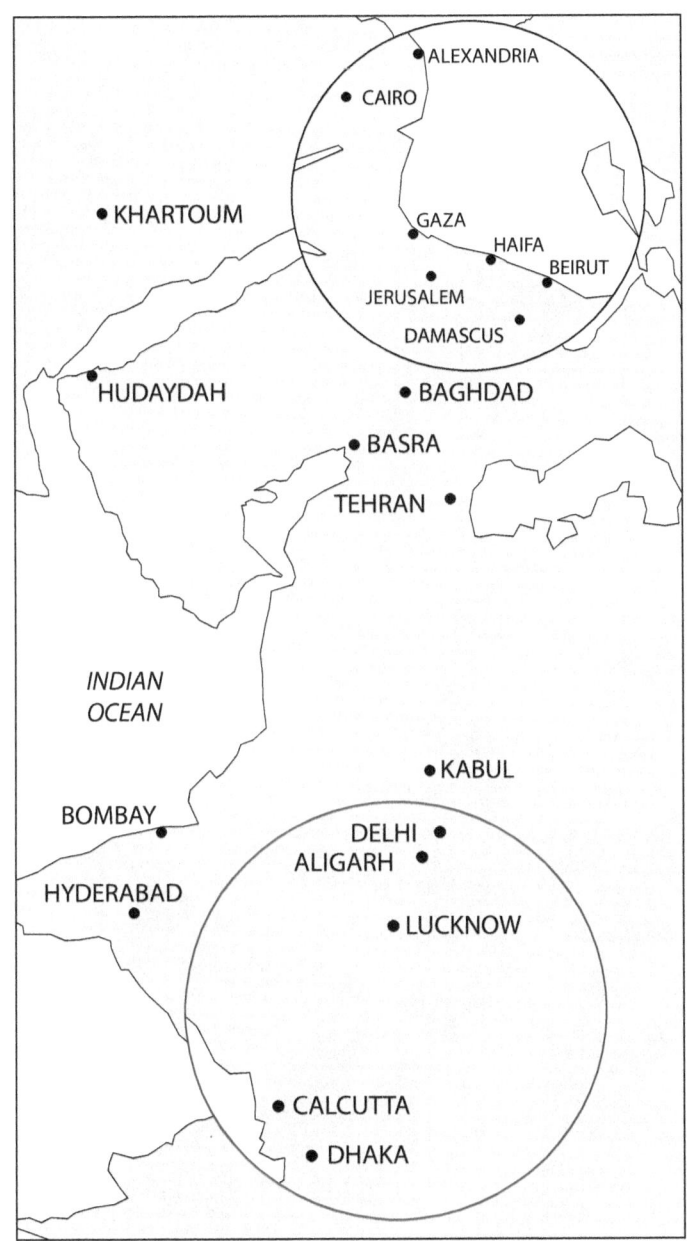

MAP 1. Significant cities in the history narrated in this book. Map produced by Nessie Nankivell.

Introduction

Decolonization and Its Forms of Knowledge

Over the course of the last few centuries of human history the world was transformed by capitalism and imperialism. Slowly, but decisively, the world was split in two. The specific mechanisms and political implications of Europe's proverbial expansion are the subject of considerable debate, but history's idioms attest undeniably to a profound change in the hierarchy of geography.[1] This history of land robbery, labor exploitation, and political domination was accompanied—indeed supported—by a vast apparatus of knowledge production.[2] Well known to us today are the many volumes that justified the enslavement of Africans and the immiseration of Asians on the basis of religion, science, and culture. "Thus," Edward Said wrote in 1977, "a marriage was made between modern science and imperialism whose consequence was untold catastrophe, human misery beyond count, oppression unlimited, disaster unqualified."[3]

With this edifice of imperial knowledge well accounted for, we may begin to examine the depths of its underside. This book is an account of what we may call anti-imperialism's forms of knowledge, postcolonized social science, and Third World study. In what follows, I search for the history of those attachments, affiliations, solidarities, movements, meetings, and revolutions made under the banners of Asia, of Africa, of the colored races and peoples, of the three continents, and the damned of the earth. I argue that we must pay close attention to the intellectual project of decolonization, not only because it may serve us still today, but because it was indeed foundational to anti-imperialism. This is not to say that the decolonization of the mind was the primary or principal motive of those movements for national liberation that moved Africans and Asians in the twentieth century. Those efforts were not simply natural expressions of some primordial attachments or carefully concocted communist conspiracies, as hostile contemporary observers often put it; rather, they emerged from and alongside ideas of liberation and solidarity produced under conditions of international collaboration. As historians of ideas from Amílcar Cabral to Hayden White remind us, the first step toward action is in the imagination. The popular rebellion that characterized the confrontation with imperialism in the first half of the twentieth century and the profound transformation that decolonization promised at its middle point were as much a challenge to imperial epistemology as they were to imperial politics. Indeed, the colonized invested in knowledge itself as a site of liberatory promise. The visions and aspirational infrastructures of anti-colonial thought, I argue, reached across India to Palestine, and Palestine became critical to a global imaginary of liberation. In fact, the colonization of Palestine, then as now, represented a potent challenge to both imperialism's self-image and decolonization's promises.

One of the ironies of empire was that it produced the conditions for its demise. Between the Mediterranean and the Indian Ocean—the primary space of this study—the conditions for the rise of anti-colonial internationalism were the emergence of a new class of workers and coterie of thinkers distinct from those merchants and clerics who had long traversed that space. "Europe," as Victor Kiernan put it, "was throwing the other continents together, sending Indian sepoys to China, Chinese coolies to South Africa, African slaves to Brazil. In one sense these peoples were being brought closer, in another sense more deeply divided."[4] This book considers what those people on the periphery thought of each other and how their ideas of each other were constricted by, mediated through, and built around or against Europe. Ultimately, I show how this history moved decisively beyond Europe, its languages, and its institutions. European imperialism transformed the terrain of non-European interactions indelibly. New kinds of people were able to cross these spaces, and new forms of knowledge were forged. It is important to note at the outset that attention to these connections does not necessitate an affirmative history of colonialism. Every history of modernity must contend with the financial and military power of Europe. But in this period of profound arrogance, corruption, intolerance, and violence—the characteristics and program of colonial rule—new types of relationships between the colonized become possible. Colonialism's unintended consequences—the vigor and imagination of anti-colonialism most especially—are the subject of this study. Geographically, this book elaborates on the intellectual links across one less-than-Third-World space, that long connected stretch of land and sea between those areas now known as the Middle East and South Asia.[5] This was a space fundamentally transformed by the partitions of British Palestine and British India at the middle of the twentieth century. In South Asia more than twelve million people were displaced in the event and its aftermath. At least one million souls perished. In Palestine, partition represented the culmination of a sectarian movement of colonial settlement that dislocated, and sought to destroy, an indigenous society. Partition haunts this book, but it is not a history of partition; rather, I seek to study some of partition's opponents and account for some of partition's effects.[6]

How can this history be written? There are cynical approaches, histories that foreground the failures of decolonization while disregarding the disorder and tyranny of imperialism. The rhetoric and conclusions of such accounts, which remain popular today, bear a striking resemblance to the imperial sources on which they most often rely. Certainly there are also romantic histories of decolonization, nostalgic or even naïve about who is excluded in their promethean accounts of liberation, whether women, or minorities, or so-called separatists, or card-carrying communists. But there is a critical historiography too. Indeed, the first critical histories of anti-colonialism and decolonization were produced in the crucible of revolt itself. The decolonization of knowledge, then, was part and parcel of the social and political activities of the day. It was in the midst of the struggle for Mozambique that Edouardo Mondlane wrote his *The Struggle for Mozambique*, in which he not only accounted for the activities of the Mozambique Liberation Front but also found space to critique the forms of knowledge propping up the Portuguese Empire. "It has been customary among Europeans and Americans," he wrote, "to conceive of all human thought as deriving from the western mind."[7] This study moves beyond the standard accounts of decolonization as an account of great men. Rather than seek a novel political theory out of the materials studied herein or sketch a concept history of decolonization, I offer a social history of ideas, attuned to a set of marginalized, untranslated, undigested intellectuals and their location in a history of political decolonization that has been caricatured and maligned. This study is attuned to poets, academics, and autodidacts whose work has gone largely uncirculated and unacknowledged. For the feminists I study, their position, already at the edges of colonial society's institutions of knowledge, only sharpened the foundations of their thought. This book tries to capture the omnivorous reading practices and relentless, pragmatic attachments to social, cultural, and political activity that characterized anti-colonial and nationalist intellectuals who sought to serve an international cause.

Scrutinizing this intellectual history can reveal forms of knowledge that might still be salvaged from decolonization and Third Worldism's irretrievable political past. More than simply recounting the events of decolonization—the grand accumulation of solidarity, the limits of which were subsequently revealed—I bring our attention to the *ideas* of decolonization. Considerable attention has been paid in the last two decades to how knowledge can be "decolonized." This effort, and its associated neologism "decolonial," has focused principally on questions of methods. The academic quest for methods has come to supersede the older inquiry into the relationship between theory and action. What is method, in the absence of a project, without grounding in the world? Many methods—means, tactics—can lead to the same outcome. This is not to say that we should eschew methodological, tactical, or even epistemological problems. In his well-known inaugural address at Liberia College, Edward Wilmot Blyden proclaimed, quite simply, "The African must advance by methods of his own."[8] Obviously there are non-Western modes of thinking profoundly at odds with the imperial view, ideas with "a power distinct from that of the European," as Blyden would assert. But seeking liberation (or worse, novelty or salvation) in the West through ideas pulled piecemeal from the wreckage of Western imperialism, without a serious reckoning with the context in which those ideas were made, is a heedless task. We may note that perhaps the earliest use of a phrase akin to the now popular imperative to "decolonize the mind" appears in a report on Cairo's first Afro-Asian Women's Conference in 1961. Under the heading "To De-colonise Minds," the French communist journalist Yvonne Quilès wrote that the liberation of women "is an inspiring idea, capable of winning both men and women once de-colonisation of minds has been achieved, for the interests of the whole nation is at stake."[9] The decolonization of the mind, in this instance, is a collective project, not an individual pursuit. And its emphasis is not textual nor its location academic, but rather conceived as a necessary part of an internationalist project of national liberation staged by feminists in the Third World.

Focusing principally on the content of thought at the expense of its conditions, both the conditions of its production and the conditions of its distribution, produces in the end a woefully incomplete picture of decolonization's relationship to knowledge. Such efforts recall Sigfried Kracuer's indictment of those "run-of-the-mill investigations which make you think of predatory raids into the past."[10] American theorists, for example, who posit the Egyptian radical intellectual Sayyid Qutb as the paradigmatic Arab critic of Western mores and American imperialism, do so without asking how Qutb—at the expense of countless other intellectuals of his generation from across the Arab world—arrived to them in English in the first place.[11] If they did, they might learn that Qutb's *Social Justice in Islam* was the very first book published by the American Council of Learned Societies' (ACLS's) Near Eastern Translation Program, which aimed to make Americans "aware of the concepts and ideologies by which the thinking and attitudes of the various peoples of the Near East are molded."[12] The ACLS's efforts were funded by the Rockefeller Foundation and "made possible by Aramco's commitment to buy enough copies to cover the costs."[13] Any history of decolonization's ideas must, most would agree, seek sources beyond those directly forged by the infrastructure of American imperialism.

The impulse to decolonize nevertheless remains a necessary one. Rather than attempt to decolonize knowledge by exposing, again, the Eurocentrism of European thought, I seek to narrate decolonization's forms of knowledge on their own terms. At bottom, this book is a history of the kinds of ideas—imperfect, incomplete, and largely forgotten—associated with the long and ongoing political decolonization of the world. These were not necessarily radical ideas. Indeed, in some cases they were patently reactionary. But bringing attention to their political and social role is indeed the point. Only when we have a proper understanding of non-Western ideas can we begin to criticize or utilize them in our own efforts. The decolonization of knowledge today cannot be premised merely on the critique of colonial knowledge or the impossible recuperation of the premodern, but on a sustained conversation with those efforts to decolonize knowledge amid the decolonization of society. I am not proposing we cease our search for an epistemology capable of confronting our present, but that we practice some humility in our demands on the past. The anthropologist Talal Asad issued this warning in 1980: "There is no guarantee that 'indigenous paradigms' will be any better.... It is not the origin of given theories, methods, and explanations which will tell us whether they are more suitable."[14] In the following I offer a history of those ideas that animated efforts to decolonize, principally in West and South Asia, during the course of the twentieth century. I track the political and social transformations that brought us from the colonial disciplines of the nineteenth century to the imperial areas of the twentieth. I seek to narrate this intellectual history through the lives of the colonized. This book highlights, critically but honestly, the distance between knowledge for liberation and knowledge for domination. Recall Immanuel Wallerstein's realization, upon arriving in anticolonial Africa, the different mentalities of European colonials and their African subjects. "It did not take long," Wallerstein wrote in the introduction to the tome that emerged from his travels with the African revolution, "to realize that not only were these two groups at odds on political issues, but that they approached the situation with entirely different sets of conceptual frameworks."[15] In what follows, I trace the roles played by missionary institutions, colonial administrators, and imperial formations in shaping anti-imperialist thought. I track efforts by Asian intellectuals to build a language, then ideas, and finally institutions of solidarity. I also reveal how ideas of race and caste, or continent and nation, inspired and impeded efforts to build solidarity against imperialism. I try, in the end, to confront the profound challenge of solidarity and affirm its worth.

Partitioning History

Between the publication of the first and second issues of *al-Urwa*, its editor, H.F. al-Hamdani, left the newly created state of India for the newly created state of Pakistan.[16] *Al-Urwa* was the bilingual Arabic and English journal of the Indo-Arab Cultural Society of Bombay, first published in July 1947, a month before Partition. Hamdani, as editor and general secretary of the society itself, was a key part of the organization's intellectual and institutional foundations. He was, at the time of the society's founding in December 1945, a professor of Arabic at Ismail Yusuf College in Bombay. Having completed his PhD in Oriental studies at the University of London in 1931, he was the first in his family of Ismaili *ulema* to study in Europe and write in English.[17] His particular background was common among the other members, the latest incarnations of a porous and prosperous community of merchants and scholars that was slowly disappearing. The society was composed of academics, enthusiasts, and Arabo-philes. Its membership, activities, and journal are a testament to the forms of cultural and geographical affiliations that had circulated across West and South Asia for centuries.

The society's first elected president was Tariq al-Lafi, Lebanon's honorary consul general to India in Bombay. Lafi was a graduate of the American University of Beirut, and although he, like Hamdani, was the descendent of a long line of sufis and sheiks, his vocation was business, not scholarship.[18] Nevertheless, he had imbibed the cosmopolitanism of Bombay, a coastal city perhaps not altogether different from his native Beirut. In his first presidential address to the society on December 14, 1946, he identified Arabic as one of the key unifiers between those cities. He added that the stereotypes that may have reigned in the past, of an Arab bedouin in the desert or a turbaned Indian "promenading on an elephant," could not contribute to a new Indo-Arab unity. Only "mutual confidence and belief in the necessity of mutual co-operation . . . [will] pave the way to building up a better society with new civilization which will liberate mankind from its present complications."[19]

Al-Urwa's opening editorial laid out the society's plans and principles. First and foremost was an emphasis on "continuous historical and cultural connections" between West and South Asia, a trope that will be repeated in the pages that follow. These connections were the basis of a necessary interdependence, for "self-sufficiency, in our opinion," the editors wrote, "is neither possible nor desirable."[20] Among the targets of the editors' criticism was the "decadent condition" of Arabic education in India, ensconced as it was in the *madrasas* and detached from the transformations in Arabic literature occurring in the Middle East, a central concern of Muslim reformist movements in early twentieth-century South Asia.[21] Besides the journal's scholarly essays and regular lectures on topics of concern—early guests included Muhammad Asad (Leopold Weiss) and Asaf Ali Asghar Fyzee—the society proposed the establishment of a reading room and a book series.[22] Its first issue was dispatched across South Asia and the Middle East, to Aden, Aleppo, Baghdad, Beirut, Cairo, Damascus, Jerusalem, Mecca, and farther afield.[23] *Al-Urwa* published an idiosyncratic mix of news, reflections, reviews, and essays covering themes modern and ancient. It is a pleasure to read. Its contributors included learned members of the society in Bombay, but were more often prominent scholars located elsewhere in the subcontinent or Europe and the United States. The well-known Lebanese American Arabist Philip Hitti contributed a short and playful piece, "A Perfect Day in Arabic," which introduced the impact of

Arabic on common English words. And despite the society's membership being overwhelmingly Muslim, Islam was not the focus of the journal's attention. Topics covered included Maimonides on India, Arabs and the Hindu numerals, and modern Libya. But Bombay's Indo-Arab society and its eloquent journal could not survive the partition of the subcontinent in 1947. The tides of nonalignment, however, raised a new Indo-Arab partnership. A decade after the first Indo-Arab society was born on the eve of South Asia's partition, a second was inaugurated in the same city. The conditions of its birth and therefore the contours of its organization and content of its thought were markedly different.

On October 7, 1954, Jawaharlal Nehru inaugurated the new Indo-Arab Society on a grand stage in Bombay's opulent Western India Turf Club.[24] Crowded with dignitaries from the Indian government and the Arab states, the stage sat beneath many flags. India's tricolor flew at the center, while the Arab flags flanked it on either side. Messages of support were received from heads of state across the Middle East, from the Saudi king to Nasser. The new society's stated principles and goals were not so different from its ancestor's: the belief in a common bond between the regions, the promotion of cultural exchange, the fostering of trade, the publication of texts, and the arrangement of meetings, were all delineated. Although the general secretary of the society, Rafiq Zakaria, came from the same Bombay Muslim milieu as the late Indo-Arab Cultural Society—in fact, as a graduate of Ismail Yusuf College he may very well have been a student of H. F. al-Hamdani—the flags and politicians marked a departure from that world. Indo-Arab relations was no longer a reflection of historical mercantile or scholarly networks, but an arena of global politics and trade. Kamaladevi Chattopadhyay, a veteran internationalist who had long evinced an interest in Arab affairs, was the president of the society. In her remarks at the inauguration, she laid bare the organization's relationship to nonalignment, whose goal, in the rhetoric of its leaders, was nothing less than world peace in the face of two contending powers.[25]

In 1960 a cognate organization was founded in Cairo. Bandung in 1955 had been a grand stage on which to introduce a vision of nonalignment to the world. In a year's time a meeting in Tito's Belgrade would officially institutionalize the sentiment. Cairo, newly the capital of Nasser's experiment in federalism, the short-lived United Arab Republic (UAR), was one of the movement's key nodes. Therefore, for the launch of the Arab-Indian Friendship Association, the Egyptian city's "top businessmen, writers, lawyers, and journalists gathered in the mirror-studded Prince's Room of the swank Nile Hilton Hotel."[26] The chairman of the state-owned Suez Canal Authority was the association's president. The Cold War had made the stakes of reconnecting those ties between West and South Asia cut by centuries of colonialism—a common refrain, that night voiced by Rajen Nehru, wife of R. K. Nehru, the Indian ambassador to the UAR—higher than ever before.

Although *culture* disappeared from the names of these new societies after Partition, cultural efforts themselves did not. If the activities of intellectuals have receded from view, I want to bring them to the front. While our political histories of Indo-Arab relations remain woefully unfinished, this intellectual history seeks to inject politics into a global history resting comfortably on the ruse of connection. While the twentieth century would witness an unprecedented scale of planetary solidarity from South Asia to South America and beyond, the links between South and West Asia have a special significance due to their proximity and age.[27] The solidarities occasioned by the tricontinental struggle against an intransigent imperialism were powerfully new, but those forged between the Arab world and the Indian subcontinent had to contend with thousands of years of contentious history. This shared history of travel, translation, war, imperialism, religion, and politics, which linked Arabs and their neighbors just to the east, was rewritten and continually reimagined for the demands of decolonization.

Palestine from the Outside In

To focus on Palestine, or even Palestinians, is to impose serious limits on the global history of Palestine. Faiz Ahmed Faiz, after leaving Beirut, said that "after all these years I spent with the Palestinians, I became one of them."[28] It is this radical notion—in the face of constant stream of utterances proclaiming Palestinian's inhumanity or nonexistence—that Palestinianness is constitutive of a set of values and practices related to a struggle for freedom that is echoed in the work and writing of Jean Genet, Francoise Kesteman, Rosemary Sayigh, and Eqbal Ahmad. A Pakistani intellectual, Ahmad was a scholar of Arabic and of Arab politics. As a graduate student and afterward he spent years with North Africa's workers and writers (his PhD dissertation at Princeton was on politics and labor in Tunisia).[29] Later he was a relentless critic and comrade of the Palestine Liberation Organization. At a 1994 meeting in Gaza, Ahmad said to the Palestinians assembled: "In the marvelously universal terms in which Arab patriots defined Arabism, I should be counted as an Arab.... [R]ecall the century-old definition offered at the outset of the Arab national movement: All those who are Arab in their language, culture, and feeling are Arab.... In this age of sectarian and exclusionary nationalism, this was an open invitation I could not resist. So, meant this way, I am an Arab and entitled to making harsh judgements on the man-made disaster that pile on us."[30]

Ahmad's position exemplified his friend Edward Said's dictum, "never solidarity before criticism."[31] Ahmad in fact arrived in the Gaza Strip to replace Said, who couldn't attend. He was there to address the Strip's first conference on human rights, during that interregnum between one intifada and the next when Palestine's future was mortgaged to dishonest brokers. In addition to his own expression of solidarity, Ahmad took the opportunity to describe the larger history that preceded him. "At the dawn of decolonization," Ahmad announced, "Palestine was colonized. I recall my utter confusion at this irony of history."[32] Ahmad's words alert us to the intimacy of Middle Eastern and South Asian pasts. And as this study seeks to demonstrate, the impossibility of narrating them separately.

Palestine plays a key role in the history that follows. Although the defense of Palestine, the project of Palestinian liberation, and the constitution of a Palestinian idea were never the projects of Palestinians alone, recent global histories have largely ignored or caricatured Palestine. So how might we begin to approach Palestine's global history? One could trace the travels, the dislocations, and the collaborations of Palestinians thrown into the world. They were forced to navigate new international regimes for the displaced, to cultivate patrons, to articulate a political theory and a social language for a dispersed collective, a dismembered community. But the mere incorporation of Palestinian voices, of diversity, equity, and inclusion, does not suffice as a method for writing history.

The global history made in Geneva, or Berlin, or Cambridge, England, or Cambridge, Massachusetts, is often hostile to Palestinians, is ignorant of Arab history, and centers the political vocabulary of the North Atlantic. Michael Goebel's *Anti-Imperial Metropolis: Interwar Paris and the Seeds of Third World Nationalism*, which largely ventriloquizes the reports of those French police officers who chased down Asians, Africans, and South Americans across the city, exemplifies this approach. He goes so far as to characterize North African anti-colonial opposition to the Zionist colonization of Palestine in plainly Islamophobic terms: "The association's pan-Islamic tenets predestined its members for antisemitism."[33] Indeed, Pan-Islam has an almost mythical explanatory power when it comes to Palestine. In an article on Israeli development aid in India, the historian Benjamin

Siegel argues that Israel needs "to navigate the complexities of its uncertain status in the global community." "The incipient networks of global Pan-Islamism," Siegel concludes, "made these challenges most pronounced in countries with sizable Muslim populations."[34] That people in the colonized world might oppose Israel for reasons other than purported Islamic solidarity seems lost on Siegel. No surprise, then, that Israeli colonialism is scarcely mentioned and that Siegel's account of the kibbutzim's rise elides their role in dispossessing Palestinians from their land and driving Palestinians out of the labor market.[35] In this effort of elision and obfuscation, Siegel is not alone. An increasingly desperate body of work has sought to discount the analytical purchase of colonialism in the study of Palestine's colonization.[36] It seems when talking about Palestinians or Arabs or Muslims, the secular methods of historiography are abandoned for claims of predestination and the easy shibboleths of imperial historiography.

While the political and intellectual work of Palestinians informs this work, I seek to write Palestinian history from the outside in. The study of Palestine, whether constituted by the Palestine Liberation Organization, the Institute for Palestine Studies, Anglo-American universities, or Israel's colonial social science, has never been contained by the land of Palestine.[37] The expulsion and exile of the Palestinians has demanded a global view. So too has the frequency and intensity of the debate over Palestine—either directly or as parable—on the global stage. Work written at the acme of the Third World's revolution, like Asʿad ʿAbd al-Rahman's *Al-Tasallul al-Isra'ili fi Asiya* or G. H. Jansen's *Zionism, Israel and Asian Nationalism*, was attentive to Palestine's place in Asia's Cold War.[38] And recent work demonstrates that the archives and conventions of diplomatic history can hardly contain the depth of this past, characterized as it is by a revolutionary social and intellectual history.[39]

In thinking about this recent accounting of transnational Palestine, we may return to Ibrahim Abu-Lughod's 1981 article "The

Pitfalls of Palestiniology." When some forty years ago Abu-Lughod concluded that the "social and cultural evolution of the Palestinians in modern times is in desperate need of study," he was lamenting the overwhelming focus on European imperial records and the historical prerogatives of the Israeli state.[40] We have decisively moved on from that situation. Digital resources, institutional archives, book series, fellowships, and professorships—the study of Palestine has become remarkably rich and dynamic, if still dwarfed by the sovereign power of Israel studies. At the core of Abu-Lughod's lament was the overwhelming impact of those abundant distortions of Palestinian history written "from the perspective of the outside": the Israeli way of seeing Palestine, the American view, the British perspective. In his own remarkable essay on Palestinian history, Edward Said would write similarly that "our history is written by outsiders, and we have conceded the battle in advance."[41] But which outside and which outsiders? Certainly there is a world, the West or the North, that is hostile in its accounting of the Palestinian past. But there is a much larger world, the South, that has historically embraced Palestinian history and Palestinians, which has seen itself in Palestine and vice versa. That outside is the global that our scholarship has yet to account for. Generally the case for the global in histories of modern thought is made by making Europe one dyad in—to use a popular metaphor—an "encounter" with the rest of the world's peoples and texts. Mere mention of the world beyond Europe propels the provincial into the global. From this view, the global is inevitably imperial; it amounts to a rewriting of European history with attention to its international locations and colonial pursuits. These are accounts of the global from above, from a privileged place in an unequal geography. The intellectual production and the social conditions of non-European thinkers, therefore, remain largely absent in this global past. Histories of South Asia and the Middle East, however, can lay claim to the global merely on the argument that most of humanity lives there. It would be prudent for historians to consider the note June Jordan appended to her 1985 collection of essays *On Call*. "Given that they were the first to exist on the planet and currently make up the majority," Jordan wrote, "the author will refer to that population usually termed Third World as the First World."[42] Jordan's inversion is instructive. Today, we should take seriously—to think about the historiographical implications of—the "global" in global South. "Europe," Fanon famously wrote, "is literally the creation of the Third World."[43] So too the global cannot be thought of without its south.

Meeting Colonialism Firsthand

Decolonization demanded new knowledge. By the twentieth century, the subjects of imperial knowledge had become increasingly exasperated by the forms of knowledge that demeaned their history and aimed to determine their future. Meetings of intellectuals offered opportunities to think together and offered new social and political opportunities. Across the Third World intellectuals convened national and international meetings as they sought to configure their intellectual projects in relation to the demands of new political projects and the imperial frame that was still determining them. Just as imperial knowledge was increasingly produced through the collaboration of governments and corporations, of spies, academics, philanthropists, and thieves, so too was anti-imperial knowledge. This knowledge emerged in a haphazard way at first, and not always with state patronage. There was a conscious effort to think across the borders and beyond the boundaries of empires and nations. Pan-Africanism, Pan-Asianism, and Pan-Islamism did not recede from view in the wake of the Second World War and the efforts of a new formalized system of North Atlantic domination to make nation-states the primary unit of rights and exploitation on the global scale. When intellectuals convened on their own, they did so with rules of their own making.

Conferences have been relatively understudied by scholars despite the outsized role they have played in the professional life of academics.[44] Diplomatic historians and specialists in international relations have paid some attention to international meetings, especially those that resulted in treaties of some kind. So we have some literature on the activities of heads of states and their representatives as they transpired across Europe, from London to Lausanne. There also exists a quasi-scientific literature on the organization and management of conferences, seeking to prescribe the ideal conditions of conferencing, like the preferred number of attendees, the methods of preparing a program, and the proper use of space. Conferences were a fundamental part of twentieth-century political, intellectual, and economic life. The party congress and the university seminar were regular fixtures of collaboration and knowledge creation. From the Congress of Toilers of the Far East to Bretton Woods, meetings were the literal stages upon which new types of relationships could be enacted. By the middle of the century, yearly almanacs of conferences delineated thousands of meetings on every conceivable topic. Studying a meeting closely can effectively emplot ideas in a precise place and time. Recent work has begun to consciously attend to the quotidian life of conference-going in the intellectual history of the twentieth century. Maha Nassar and Rossen Djagalov have documented how meetings of Afro-Asian writers provided opportunities for intellectuals to meet who otherwise couldn't do so.[45] The memoirs of conference-goers, press accounts of the meetings, and correspondence of conference organizers reveal details often missing from the proceedings or otherwise obscured in the creation of individual pieces of writing.

Many meetings are mapped herein. From Lucknow to Bandung (twice), Edinburgh, Delhi (twice, at least), Cairo, Algiers, and Rabat, conferences, for empire and against, are considered closely. We begin now in France—and move shortly to Syria—to map some of the links and raise some of the questions that occupy this study. In September 1956 *Présence Africaine*, the Pan-Africanist magazine of the Senegalese writer Alioune Diop, convened its first Congress of Black Writers and Artists. Delegates from across Africa and its diaspora arrived in Paris for four days of debate and discussion. The attendance of a good number of Americans at the event—and the infamous absence of others, namely W. E. B. Du Bois—marks it now as a key battle in the cultural Cold War then raging. Richard Wright, an editor at *Presence*, appealed to the National Association for the Advancement of Colored People and the State Department for American delegates to attend the gathering, making his case in explicitly political terms. "The situation with *Presence Africaine* is as follows," Wright wrote to NAACP chair Roy Wilkins, "The Communists are making a play for the control of the magazine."[46] In the lead-up to the conference, the Congress for Cultural Freedom promised Wright that they'd underwrite a jazz performance by Dean Dixon.[47] But the "Bandung Spirit" had been summoned a year earlier, and the growing shadow of the Algerian Revolution meant that no imperialism, European or American, was left unchallenged by the Black intellectuals assembled in Paris.

From Cairo, the Egyptian communist intellectual Anouar Abdel-Malek reported on the conference with great interest, publishing an article on the Congress in *al-Risala al-Jadida*, one of the new state journals of postrevolutionary Egypt. It was edited by the prolific writer, former aristocrat, and military officer Yusif al-Seba'i, whose influence in Egypt would earn him the sobriquet "the general of the army of letters," or in the words of Abdel-Malek himself, "the inept Colonel."[48] Seba'i's magazine was the first in a series he would edit in the next two decades. But it was part of an intellectual project that far exceeded the edicts and boundaries of Nasser's Egypt.

The literary culture produced by the local bourgeoisie and authoritarian empires of the nineteenth century could not serve the needs of decolonization in the middle of the twentieth.

Established to replace *al-Risala*, which was once the most important Arabic weekly of its day, the first issue of *al-Risala al-Jadida* (the *new Risala*, the new message) was published in April 1954. In his opening editorial for the magazine, al-Seba'i wrote that the new journal would continue the project of the old and that the name was a tribute to *al-Risala's* distinguished editor Ahmad Hasan al-Zayyat. As literacy has expanded, so too has interest in literature and literary journals, Seba'i argued. But the yellow pages of solid text that once characterized literary journals were no longer sufficient for the needs of the day. Writers, al-Seba'i continued, must write clear prose intelligible to all, published in well-illustrated journals. Moreover, literary magazines must open themselves up to new writers, rather than publish the same well-known names.[49] Al-Seba'i's editorial hints at the tenor of the populist cultural policy he was tasked with in the decades to come and the types of literature he would champion. A writer of realist short stories himself, al-Seba'i would also have a hand in patronizing another major Arabic realist, Naguib Mahfouz, whose great novel of the 1919 revolution, *Bayn al-Qasrayn* (*Palace Walk*), was serialized by the *al-Risala al-Jadida* starting with its first issue.

In discussing the first Congress of Black Writers and Artists, Abdel-Malek confronted two questions that would concern him for decades, and that concern me here: What is the relationship between knowledge and imperialism? And what does decolonization entail? In the 1960s—as he completed his essential study of Nasserist Egypt and his dissertation on Egypt's *nahda* at the Sorbonne—Abdel-Malek wrote a series of critical essays for French journals on imperial knowledge and colonial society, most famously "L'orientalisme en crise" in UNESCO's *Diogenes*. His concerns and those of the people assembled in Paris in 1956 correspond strongly. Allione Diop would announce at the opening of the conference, "History with a capital 'H' is a one-sided interpretation of the life of the World, emanating from the West alone."[50] Later in the proceedings the impositions of "White geographers" were questioned by Louis Achille.[51]

Abdel-Malek's essay was published on the eve of his exile from Egypt. An active member of Egypt's communist movement—he had only been released from prison a few months earlier—Abdel-Malek would eventually leave for Paris in 1959, evading Egypt's prisons as the communist Left and Nasser's government negotiated their coexistence.[52] For the most part, Abdel-Malek doesn't offer much in his account that isn't already known; unfortunately, he wasn't actually in attendance. We can safely assume that Abdel-Malek's account was based on *Presence Africaine*'s own report on the congress.[53] But some of his inquiries and points of emphasis are worth considering. For example, he speculates about whether any Sudanese were involved in the conference.[54] Most interesting, however, is his highlighting a convergence of events that has not previously been remarked upon: the first Congress of Black Writers and Artists and the second Arab Writers Congress convened on overlapping days in 1956. The meeting in Paris took place September 19–22, and the Damascus, Syria, meeting September 20–25.

As star-studded as the Paris meeting, the Damascus conference has nevertheless received scant critical attention. Held on the grounds of Damascus University, its delegates were among the region's most prominent intellectuals, including Taha Hussein, Badr Sakr al-Sayyab, Nazik al-Maliki, Mikhail Naimy, Constantine Zurayk, Suhail Idress, Raif Khuri, Hussein Mroueh, Amina al-Said, Wadad Sakakini, and Khalil Mardem Bey. Only one delegate attended the Damascus conference from the Sudan, Professor Abid Abd al-Nour. Al-Seba'i was Egypt's chief representative. In his address he would claim that "Nasser is the greatest believer in literature's importance."[55] Like its counterpart in Paris, the Arab conference produced a call "from the

Arab writers to the writers and thinkers around the world." The bulk of their statement concerned pressing political matters. The Suez Canal had been nationalized only a few months earlier. "We ask you to join us in our just cause," the statement read, "the return of our stolen land to the Arab people expelled from Palestine, the defense of Egypt's right for the use of its land, support for the Algerian people in their war against colonialism, and for the liberation of all the Arab states that suffer under the yoke of colonialism."[56] The synchronicity of these two meetings speaks both to the sheer concentration of conferences in the second half of the twentieth century and to the significance of this moment for intellectuals poised to make political demands as a group.

Such gatherings had their internal limits and external enemies. At the 1968 Cultural Congress of Havana, C. L. R. James (present at Paris in 1956) articulated an ambitious role for such gatherings and in doing so called attention to their limitations in relation to mass movements. "The function of this Congress," James would announce in his remarks, "is that intellectuals should prepare the way for the abolition of intellectuals as the embodiment of culture."[57] Also in Havana, two years earlier, Amílcar Cabral reminded his tricontinental audience that "we are not going to eliminate imperialism by shouting insults against it."[58] The co-option of some intellectuals, the abandonment of others, and the assassination of others still are fundamental to colonialism and anti-colonialism's intellectual history. What I narrate in this book are some of those efforts to produce knowledge and solidarity under conditions of genocide and partition. And some intellectuals, conscious of Cabral's warning, attempted to do so within the boundaries of their vocation. To be sure, decolonization in the face of American imperial ascendance was no easy task. Ruth First, assassinated by the South African police in 1982, articulated the situation plainly 1970: "If left-wing forces led the independence movement, then the Americans would sustain collaborationists if possible, or a colonial power if necessary. Decolonization was a move to shore up 'stabilizing' forces in restless regions, rather than a recognition of the right of peoples to the independence and the freedom that the phrases of the United Nations so eloquently embodied."[59]

The intransigence of imperialism, the complexes of the Cold War, the challenges of an inherited tradition—of the nahda and the freedom struggle—the exigencies of the state, the diktats of a party, the inertia of institutions, the passions of the clique, the demands of a magazine, all determined the course of the history I relate in this book. Abdel-Malek's position, as an exilic, critical, and communist intellectual, is not unique. Every individual and group studied in this book navigated the spaces between empires and nations; indeed, they built those spaces themselves.

Anti-Colonial Thought

We may, then, begin to identify the characteristics of anti-colonial thought. I think there are probably three key elements. First there is a realization, recognized from the moment of colonization and elaborated ever since, that imperial knowledge is a lie. In a 1939 essay, C. L. R. James concluded simply, after cataloging some of the myths propagated about Africans in Western histories, "All of this, from beginning to end, is lies."[60] Nearly every effort of historical reconstruction emanating from the colonies would be prefaced by a similar maneuver—would by necessity elaborate such a criticism. This was an abolitionist project, an effort to abolish the epistemology of colonialism. Sometimes this was done systematically or with regard to a specific thinker or body of knowledge. We may draw a straight line from Jamal al-Din al-Afghani's rebuttal to Ernest Renan in *Journal des débats* (1883) to Abdallah Laroui's critique of Gustave Von Grunebaum in his *Crisis of the Arab Intellectual* (1974).[61] Often this critique of European knowledge was haphazard, not necessarily in response to a scholarly argument, but a political proposal or a legal claim. It could even be a handful of verses in a newspaper, like Wadiʿ al-Bustani's 1918 response to the Balfour Declaration, printed upon the front page of a Palestinian newspaper. Beyond the scholarly convention of rehearsing earlier works' limits or flaws, the Third World intellectual was inextricably bound to activities beyond the page. As Walter Rodney would put it in relation to the bourgeois historical interpretations of the Russian Revolution: "This is not a mere academic debate—it is a matter of life and death."[62]

So how did they counteract those spurious theories and histories? The answer was often in their own institutions, their own periodicals, departments, institutes, and colleges. The second characteristic of anti-colonial thought was this constructivist project to build a new world. This is not to say that institutions for the elaboration and propagation of knowledge did not exist before Europe. There are deep traditions of philosophy, philology, history, and geography across Asia and Africa. We were bequeathed, quite reluctantly, and at the cost of our own institutions, a set of schools and institutes attached to the Christian missionary enterprise and the companies, armies, and states of the European capitalists. Beginning in the nineteenth century, and accelerating in the middle of the twentieth, a concerted effort was made to produce new knowledge beyond the imperial frame. In Beirut, Butrus al-Bustani's National School and, in Jerusalem, Khalil Sakakini's Constitutional School, were deliberately conceived alternatives to the sectarian missionary schools in their midst.[63] Meetings provided the opportunity to make these efforts collaborative. If the Congress of Berlin in 1878 and the Paris Peace Conference of 1919 represented the high points of imperial arrogance and the profound exclusion of the world majority, Afro-Asian conferences, like the aforementioned Congress of Black Writers and Artists, modeled a different relationship. At the opening session of the 1955 Asian-African Conference in Bandung, Khaled al-'Azm, then Syrian foreign minister, registered this difference: "International conferences have become a daily occurrence, but this conference of ours is unique in the eyes of history. By its very nature, by its very objectives, and by its very name our conference stands without parallel and without precedent.... Here is an assembly that meets, not to establish a balance of power, not to divide spoils and not to draw new maps for homelands or people. We come to bury the evils, not to praise them."[64] Sites of study came to be conceived in internationalist terms, too. The first Afro-Asian Solidarity Conference in Cairo in 1958 recommended that an "international university for Afro-Asian studies" be established.[65] "We need an Institute of African and Oriental Studies right in the heart of Port-of-Spain," George Lamming demanded in *The Pleasures of Exile*.[66]

Finally, the major distinction, the fundamental one, is an explicit attachment between the scholarly enterprise and a political and social project, whether it be nationalism, anti-imperialism, communism, Pan-Africanism, or nonalignment. While white social science has sought to deny the ways it serves imperialism, anti-colonial knowledge has not had such a complex.[67] The building of an infrastructure for knowledge production was not simply for the sake of knowledge production itself, but for genuine liberation. The real or imagined politics of anti-colonial knowledge has lasting implications for how historians of the non-West practice their discipline today. Satish Chandra offered this sober, if damning, assessment from Delhi in 1972: "To an extent area studies programmes have tended to perpetuate the notion that Afro-Asian countries are 'patients' in the field of history, and that the history written by the historians of the area are somehow inferior, being tainted by the 'nationalist' bias, whereas it is presumed that the writings of historians from metropolitan countries, i.e. the former colonising powers would be free from the 'Imperialist' bias. This tendency to attempt to continue the colonial situation in the field of history in the name of the centre and the periphery is bound to have harmful repercussions."[68]

The activities of Israeli academics in the Afro-Asian world—in, but not of it, due to Palestine's conquest—are particularly useful for examining this score. Israelis, famously excluded from Bandung in 1955, were present in considerable numbers at two more academic meetings that were nonetheless politically significant: the 1963 Africanist Congress in Accra and the 1964 Orientalist Congress in Delhi.[69] Israeli reports on the events are revealing. A month after the congress, at a meeting of the Israeli Oriental Society in Jerusalem, Uriel Heyd, an Israeli diplomat turned Ottomanist from the Hebrew University, presented his reflections. Published later in the society's journal *Hamizrah Hehadash*, or *The New East*, Heyd's remarks register the persistence of colonial condescension. "Convening a Congress of Orientalists in an Eastern country has merits," Heyd remarked, "such as the opportunity to see an Eastern country up close. . . . [H]owever, one should not ignore the great shortcoming arising from this either . . . in India there was quite a large number of amateurs among the Indian lecturers, people with a good traditional education, but pre-scientific, whose lectures sometimes had an apologetic tone."[70]

Heyd expands upon this point: "We have largely adapted to Western research methods. Compared to many people from Asian and African countries, we are freer from an excessive emotional attachment to the subjects of our research." Heyd here raises a common and persistent charge with considerable roots in the colonial archive. Other participants in the meeting emphasized that their contributions were considered the best and complained about their exclusion from the organization of the congress and the lamentable inclusion of Arabs in the Orientalist Congress's secretariat. In his report for *Hamizrah Hahedesh* on the Accra Congress, Pessah Shinar, an Arabist from the Hebrew University, expounded at length on the presence of Arabs and Muslim Africans at the conference, and complained also about what he saw as their defensive positions.[71] Israeli intellectuals distanced themselves from their anti-colonial neighbors, for good reason. And distance toward them prevailed in turn. Reporting on the conference for *New Outlook*, Amnon Kapeliuk observed that "a certain 'coolness' prevailed towards the Israelis as a body" during the Delhi meeting.[72] The forced disappearance of the political, perhaps the principal aspiration of Cold War social science in the global North, served to mask a political opposition to projects of liberation, including projects of knowledge production, located in the global South. Historical studies of the social sciences in the non-European world have focused principally on their enlistment in two distinct political projects: colonial conquest itself and nationalist state-making. In departing from the colonial archive and national space, this book seeks to narrate how the locations and formations of scholarly inquiry were marked by global conditions and internationalist political movements.

Non-Western thought emerged in the context of a concentrated struggle for political autonomy from imperialism and political unity against it. It also was couched in the effort to counteract both the ideas and institutions of European and American knowledge. Khalil Nakhleh and Elia Zureik's preface to their important 1980 volume *The Sociology of Palestinians* provides a succinct riposte to colonial social science: "Unlike Western-generated, 'normal' sociology, a sociology of the Palestinians is a native or indigenous sociology, it must be attached, committed, and action oriented.... It must anchor itself in the persistent re-examination and demystification of Western-generated conceptual frameworks towards groups, communities and societies who do not subscribe to the dominant mode of thought.... It is not merely a sociology of domination, but an analysis of methods and theories of dissolving domination."[73]

Nakhleh and Zureik demand a form of knowledge capable of contending with the present rather than serving a status quo premised on dispossession from their land and disappearance from history. "Thus," they conclude, "a sociology of the Palestinians at this juncture in history must be a sociology of radical socio-cultural change, however violent and abrupt it may prove to be."[74] This book, like any other, is an attempt to grapple with our present as much as it seeks to reveal how we arrived here. I seek to do justice to anti-imperialist thought by critically evaluating its promises and limits. At a meeting of the UN Commission on the Status of Women in 1949 in Beirut—geographically and chronologically at the center of this book—ʿAnbara Salam al-Khalidi asked a question with which we still contend. "Will the women, we may wonder . . . meet with a greater measure of success, where men have failed, to draw the nations closer together . . . to put an end to the policies, whose foundations rest on racial philosophies and whose objectives centre on exploitation and oppression?"[75] Salam al-Khalidi articulated the same demand as many other intellectuals in this book, feminist and not. That her questions remain relevant now and could be posed to many of the other intellectuals discussed in this book is a testament to both her brilliance and the work that remains to be done.

Throughout the chapters that follow, I move from the colonial furnace of the early twentieth century to the trials faced by ostensibly postcolonial states in the 1970s in order to follow the journey of ideas as they are deployed over the course of political decolonization (and not). The first chapter maps empire's new grounds for solidarity, and the second throws a wrench in our story from the outset, as I am wont to do, in tracking the history of Pan-Islamism. The third chapter turns to the Asian idea, including interlopers and opponents. Chapter 4 tries to resurrect the popular history of nonalignment and some of its Arabic idioms. The final chapter turns to the study of areas, this time from the areas themselves. Each chapter takes an idea, spatial and political, and tracks its voyage through texts, events, and individuals, large and small. Lessons, and warnings, abound.

1   *Empire*

"Oxford is my goal; a foul or a fall; a failer or a fool; I want to know more and become more. I may be hung; I may be stabbed; I may be smashed and ground to earth; but starvation can never be a cause to my death."[1] Thus wrote twenty-three-year-old Wadiʿ al-Bustani from Cairo to John Lubbock, a science popularizer and confidant of Charles Darwin in London known officially as Lord Avebury. Bustani was in Cairo at the time, working for the British in the Public Works Department, Eastern Division. "Dear sir," Bustani wrote:

> It is a critical moment—but my beats and throbs are as regular as ever. "To be or not to be, that is the question." Whether I should stick to my present post of £10 per 1 moon's revolution, and continue to live on the figures (only Ten in shape I add and register—and die when Death knocks . . . or bid this routine together with colleagues, friends and relatives farewell, and entrust myself to the sear, with the sole hope of one-day anchoring on the British Isles with the twofold ambition of shaking hands with the author of "The Uses of Life" and "On Peace and Happiness" and of challenging that day's circumstances.[2]

Bustani, the young romantic poet, was unsatisfied with his bureaucratic duties in Egypt and longed to be a part of another world. He was writing to Lubbock because he had nearly finished translating *On Peace and Happiness*, one of Lubbock's books, and wished to have a photo of its author for the frontispiece. When his translations were complete, Bustani made his way to London, where he finally met his guru.³

Bustani was born to a Maronite family in 1886 in the small mountain town of Dibiyye, in today's Lebanon. His intellectual inheritance is important to note at the outset. He came from perhaps the most prominent family of the nahda, the Arab renaissance of the nineteenth century. Butrus al-Bustani—a foundational figure in the history of Arab ideas and the founder of the first secular school in the Levant—is his most famous relative. And though Butrus died three years before Wadiʿ was born, Sulayman al-Bustani, Butrus's nephew and the translator of the *Iliad* into Arabic, had a profound personal impact on Wadiʿ.⁴ Arguing that the young Wadiʿ's Arabic was weak, Sulayman once implored him to memorize the Qu'ran, so Wadiʿ did. He went on to study English and French at Syrian Protestant College, now known as the American University of Beirut, graduating in 1907. Following Bustani's career from Mount Lebanon, through British Egypt, British India, British South Africa, and finally British Palestine, produces a subterranean map of colonial politics and colonial ideas. With it, we can register Bustani's transformation from colonial subject to anti-colonial "agitator."

John Lubbock's books amounted to guides on how to become a certain kind of English gentleman: liberal, humane, and literate. He was popular globally, like his friend Darwin, and in the early twentieth century his books were being translated across the world into a number of non-European languages, from Armenian to Gujarati.⁵ Bustani would eventually translate three of Lubbock's works into Arabic: *On Peace and Happiness*, *The Uses of Life*, and *The Pleasures of Life*. These were the first Bustani translated from English in what would become a long career of translation. In the preface to

The Pleasures of Life Lubbock writes of the importance of a particular set of Oriental texts: "The Ramayana and the Maha Bharata... are not only interesting in themselves, but very important in reference to our great oriental Empire."[6] Lubbock lists the hundred books one must read. Besides the two aforementioned Sanskrit epics, he includes three other non-European texts among his canon: the Qur'an (which Bustani had already memorized), Kalidasa's *Shakuntala*, and the *Rubaiyat of Omar Khayyam*.[7] In the nineteenth century Eastern texts reinvigorated European intellectual culture. Literature, high and low, was infused with a corpus of lauded non-European classics. By the early twentieth century, Lubbock's list was as predictable as it was common.

This canon was indelibly imperial in its making. The European colonization of the world; the rise of the new historicist philology; and the hegemony of romantic visions of human, nation, race, and world all occasioned the emergence of two related and parallel discourses by the middle of the nineteenth century: world religions and world literature. Sanskrit texts like the Mahabharata (including the Bhagavad Gita) and the Ramayana sat at the confluence of these new ideas, representing both ancient Hinduism and ancient India. The celebration of these works in Europe was regularly—indeed, by requisite—accompanied by the denigration of contemporary Hinduism and India. "Decline" was the historiographical trope of choice.

From their perch, the Orient appeared as the principal site of *Weltliteratur* for the European peninsula's philologists. And although ideologically and institutionally Pan-European, the primacy of the British Empire in Asia made Great Britain a central location for the elaboration of these new ideas and English a key vehicle for their export. By 1900, a century of philology, translation, collection, collation, and theft had produced a world canon—Oriental in progeny—that was exceedingly well-known and widely read. The place of empire in the constitution, proliferation, and distribution of a literary canon intelligible to British citizens (at home) and British subjects (abroad) has been thoroughly examined.[8] The colonial conditions of canonicity are impossible to deny. For example, the works in Max Muller's Sacred Books of the East Project—which "effectively defined the parameters of the 'major religions of the world'" according to Tomoko Masuzawa—may have been published by Oxford University Press, but the project was funded by the India Office itself.[9] In addition to texts like Lubbock's, Bustani was reading this growing corpus of Orientalism and its related projects. On his trip to London to visit Lubbock, he also traveled to Oxford to see David Margoliouth, doyen of Arabic studies in England, whom he would write about enthusiastically.[10] Aamir Mufti argues that the emergent intelligentsia of nineteenth-century India was "in a strong sense schooled in Orientalism, which constituted for it the very horizon of modern and Western humanistic knowledge."[11] Bustani was no different. His understanding of India was inextricable from his reading of European Orientalism.

In 1912, a year after publishing his Arabic translation of *The Pleasures of Life*, Bustani published the first translation of the *Rubaiyat* in Arabic. In Bustani's Arabic rendition of Edward Fitzgerald's infamous English "translation," the *rubi'yat* of Khayyam become *sabi'yat*. That is, rather than quatrains, Bustani's version is in stanzas of seven lines, a common Arabic poetic form. With his new translation, Bustani was joining the "Omarians" of late nineteenth-century Europe, or what John Yohannan called "the cult of the Rubaiyat."[12] Having translated the syllabi of British imperial culture, Bustani began to execute their assignments. In his introduction to the translation he provides a biography of the elusive poet and rehashes the familiar debates about the quatrain's authenticity and Khayyam's life story. Bustani also contributes his own dubious theory about Khayyam's origins. He argues that Khayyam—the name refers in Arabic to one who sews tents—was of Arab origins and that his family must have migrated to Persia, for Persians in the eleventh century did not use tents as Arabs did.[13] This fact, Bustani argues, is but one more reason that Khayyam's verses must be read in Arabic. World literature therefore, as Yaseen Noorani has argued in the case of Sulayman al-Bustani's translation of the *Iliad*, is presented to "the Arabic reading public as a repository of national self-discovery."[14] Bustani's Arabized Khayyam was part of a larger national discourse. As enthralled as he may have been with the world literary enterprise being promoted by imperial Europe, accounting for Bustani's intellectual activity demands a consideration of the colonial frame he worked within and the currents of nationalist and anti-colonial thought he encountered.

When Bustani traveled away from Mount Lebanon and its environs, he was entering a world transformed by colonialism. In 1909 Bustani would follow the ever-tighter routes of capital and empire to Yemen. A job as a translator in the British consulate there took a young Bustani out of the American missionary enterprise he had long occupied and into another—undoubtedly related—colonial initiative in the East. This was his first experience of life under the Raj, which by then covered nearly a quarter of the globe. As the historian John Willis has written, "Aden and the Aden Protectorate constituted one of the westernmost parts of India."[15] From there he went to Cairo under British occupation, and finally in 1912, Bombay. Bustani recalls reading Monier Williams's verse translation of Kalidasa's Shukuntala on a Bombay beach, which inspired him later to render his own poetic rendition of the text into Arabic.[16] But in India he was not simply engaged in the entangled web of Orientalism and empire he had come to know. Bustani was employed as a bookkeeper by a well-known pearl merchant from the Persian Gulf, connecting him to those older histories of trade and family that had long characterized Arab and Indian interactions. Bustani was an addition to the scene.

While in India, he traveled to Bengal to visit Rabindranath Tagore at his school in Shantiniketan, or Dar-as-Salam, the Abode of Peace. Long internationalist on his own accord, Tagore was thrust by the Nobel Prize in Literature into world consciousness in 1913. His visits to Egypt (in 1926) and Iraq (in 1932) were major political and intellectual events.[17] By the 1930s, translations of and commentaries on his writings could be found in all the major newspapers, journals, and textbooks of the Arab world. In 1941 one prominent Egyptian journal confidently announced that Tagore "was the most translated foreign writer into Arabic."[18] Bustani himself translated Tagore's play *The Gardener* into Arabic in 1916, giving the Arabic reading public their first taste of the Indian intellectual's writing. Bustani's translations of Tagore's poetry and drama traveled quickly across the nahda's global network of journals and writers. As Ilham Khuri-Makdisi has noted, journals like *al-Hilal* and *al-Muqtataf* "represented particularly powerful spheres that conferred legitimacy on ideas and discourses in the late nineteenth century and early twentieth in Beirut, Cairo, and Alexandria, but also beyond, including within the Syrian diaspora in the Americas."[19]

In May 1918, Bustani's Tagore arrived in New York City. The first Arabic literary magazine in North America, Nasib Arida's *al-Funun*, published Bustani's translations of Tagore's poetry.[20] A month later Mikhail Naimy, one of *al-Funun*'s most frequent contributors, reflected on the task of the translator in an article about Bustani. He began by arguing for the need for more Arab writers and translators. Translators, Naimy argued, connect readers with humanity by opening up new oceans of knowledge to them.[21] But translation, he admitted, is a tricky task. He took up the example of Bustani's Tagore translations. Bustani, Naimy argued, made a major contribution to Arabic by translating these poems and must be praised for doing so. But his translations failed to capture the rhyme and music of Tagore's verses, in Naimy's estimation.[22] Naimy, who spent decades in the United States, was fluent in English and therefore able to read the English versions of the Tagore poems Bustani translated. Despite this criticism, the very presence of and spirited engagement with Bustani's translations in *al-Funun* speaks to the size of the intellectual world Bustani himself trafficked in. His own itinerary may have been determined by his location inside the British colonial frame, but Bustani's work traveled further, across the Arab nahda's own world of print.

Bustani aimed to introduce Arab readers to India's past and present generally. In 1916 he published a series of articles about India and Indians in *al-Hilal*. Among them was "With Rabindranath Tagore," in which he described his visit to Tagore's residence and school in Bengal in July 1914, only a few months after the announcement of the Nobel Prize. "I ate and drank and sat with Tagore."[23] "His eyes," Bustani went on, "show his wisdom and his speech is sweet." Bustani wrote about the character of Tagore's school, where, on his visit, he lectured the students on the state of Egypt and Syria. But the most profound and original section of the article is Bustani's intervention into the Arabic language and Arab understandings of Hinduism. He wrote: "He [Tagore] is 'hinduwi,' that is, an Indian who is not a Muslim. Arabs call all Indians who do not believe in Allah idol-worshippers. So I have decided to use 'hinduwi' and the plural 'hinduwiyyun' to avoid confusion or ambiguity. Most of our writers refer to them as 'hindus' the translation of the English and French words using the letter 'seen' which is not how you make a plural in Arabic. The word 'hindi' or 'hinud' means all those living in India."[24] While it is impossible to separate Tagore's fortunes from his entanglements with the British or English role across British imperial space, Bustani's engagement here offers insight into his larger literary and historical commitments.[25] It is clear that Bustani's intellectual investments were not simply bounded by European tastes. His dissatisfaction with the existing Arabic lexicon and attempt to dispel misunderstanding are a testament to his scholarly orientation toward the representation of India in Arabic. Without the civilizational condescension or imperial largesse that buttressed Europe's Indologists, Bustani approached his study of India seriously.

Tagore himself occupied this imperial space. Famously a denizen of Calcutta, he exclaimed in an early poem, "Duranta Asha" (Wild hopes): "I would much rather be an Arab Bedouin." His journey to Iraq was one of his very last trips in a lifetime of travel. Tagore wrote that despite not feeling physically up for it, having received the invitation to go to a Bedouin camp, he could not say no. "It occurred to me then," he wrote in his travelogue, "that if I did not get a taste of what I wrote in my imagination so many years ago then I might live to rue my decision."[26] As a Bengali, "nurtured by a network of rivers," Tagore reflected on the differences between him and his desert-inhabiting hosts. "How contrasting," he pondered, "the two races, the Bedouins and the Bengalis, are." He was unimpressed by their music and dance, but for their toughness he had the highest of scientific praise: "These people are the finest specimens of this natural selection as survivors of the ruthless tussles of life, leaving behind the weaklings who perished."[27] Tagore's words would not have been out of place in the writings of Gertrude Bell herself, imbued as it was with the language of race. But Tagore's empathy with the Arabs was of a different register than that of Bell and other "agents of empire [and] friends of the Orient" as Edward Said called them.[28] For Tagore, British imperialism in Iraq was indefensible.

Tagore was deeply concerned with the implications of Britain's presence in Iraq. Tagore's trip to Persia and Iraq was only the second time he traveled by airplane, and it is perhaps for that reason that the British rule from the sky so disturbed him. He wrote with awe and concern of the power and peril of human flight, describing the Dutch pilots of his airplane as "the personification of energy." But in his condemnation of British "air control," the policy of pacifying and governing wartime and Mandate Iraq through the terror of aerial bombing, Tagore spared no words. With characteristic verve and biblical locution, he wrote that the Iraqis killed by the British bombs "meet their fate by decree of the upper region of British imperialism,—which finds it so easy thus to shower death because of its distance from its individual victims. So dim and insignificant do those unskilled in the modern arts of killing appear to those who glory in such skill! Christ acknowledged all mankind to be the children of his Father; but for the modern Christian both Father and children have receded into shadows, unrecognizable from the height of this bombarding planes; for which reason these blows are being dealt at the very heart of Christ himself."[29]

While in Iraq, an Air Force chaplain asked Tagore for a message to give his pilots, whose mental state was in disarray. As Priya Satia has noted, the sky above the desert "was not a place for empathy but for total physic breakdown, apparently."[30] Tagore wrote an impassioned plea against apocalypse: "If in an evil moment man's cruel history should spread its black wings to invade that realm of divine dreams with its cannibalistic greed and fratricidal ferocity then God's curse will certainly descend upon us for that hideous desecration and the last curtain will be rung down upon the world of Man for whom god feels ashamed."[31]

Tagore saw the implications of air power even beyond the Iraq before his eyes. The poet was prescient when he wrote that "if the measures of the aeroplane view were to become our normal standard, we should be living in another world altogether."[32] Caren Kaplan dissects precisely this confluence of measurement and world making from above. She notes that Iraq "became one of the most heavily mapped regions in the world" and how that mapping was premised on a sophisticated and systemized system of aerial photography.[33] These ways of seeing are now commonplace. Tagore witnessed this view from its birth in conquest. While he observed the scene from above, thousands of his fellow countrymen were involved on the ground, where until this day many Indian soldiers lie buried. Indeed, the graves of Indian soldiers stretched across the world, among them Palestine, another one of Great Britain's new colonies, and where Bustani himself would make his name.

Ecumenical Palestine

"Thus he entered the arena of battle," wrote ʿAbd al-Rahman Yaghi of Bustani's first poem in Palestine.[34] Bustani arrived in Jaffa in the last week of November 1917. He came to Palestine to work as an assistant in the British administration, again moving along those routes made by empire. Bustani left India in 1916 and stayed in South Africa for a year thereafter, partly in the employ of the British at Transvaal. While there, in the midst of the Great War, he wrote and published a slim volume of poems, the *Quatrains of War*. Dedicated to the "South African Overseas Contingent," the martial poems ask their readers to repeatedly "Arise! March on, and Falter not! Respond!"[35] Some quatrains are explicit about which side of the war Bustani champions: "Join the Chorus of the Mighty Brave / Whose Bleeding Hearts encore 'GOD SAVE THE KING.'"[36] Two years later, upon his arrival in Palestine, Bustani's tune quickly changed. Written in the immediate wake of the Balfour Declaration, his first poem from Palestine declared his concern over British intentions. Bustani's Indian career turned out to be instructive, and the germ of the disenchantment with the British that would lead to his resignation from the colonial government two years later can be discerned. In "The Infant State" (al-dawla al-radiʾ) he wrote: "We have opened our chests to you / outstretched our hands / but I fear you shall betray us / I know the Indian road."[37]

In Palestine, Bustani's fealty to the worldly culture cultivated by the British Empire was stretched to its limit. He spent the rest of his life in Palestine, mostly in the port city of Haifa, an important point on the map of war and trade that the British were forging between the Indian Ocean and the Mediterranean Sea. While Bustani continued to work on his translations of hinduwi texts, his fortunes and intellectual activity were increasingly tied to the politics of the British Mandate and the European Zionist colonization of Palestine. Bustani was thrust out of the literary world he had inhabited for the first half of his life and poured himself into the service of an Arab nation, the anti-colonial struggle in Palestine in particular. The imperial culture that determined the global itinerary of his youth proved illusory. Despite his political and intellectual efforts, Bustani came to realize that respect for the lives and lands of people like him were not on the British agenda. His first foray into organized political activity is emblematic of the ethos he would carry in all his efforts. Bustani was one of the founders of the Muslim-Christian Association in Haifa, an important but short-lived organization across Palestine.[38] These associations were an early organized source of opposition to the British policies in Mandate Palestine that the historian Laura Robson has rightly characterized as sectarian. The British constructed, according to Robson, "a colonial administration that assumed the political centrality of communal identifications."[39] Robson describes how Palestinian Christian intellectuals nevertheless embraced an ecumenical way of thinking, a form of knowledge that fundamentally marked the Arab nahda according to Ussama Makdisi.[40] The British, keen on facilitating Zionist goals and wary of the Arab nationalist resistance such ecumenical organizations could engender, changed the landscape of Muslim-Christian political cooperation in the Mandate by introducing new sectarian institutions like the Supreme Muslim Council.

As the Mandate dragged on, Bustani's poetry continued to pose a challenge to British activities in Palestine and European colonialism in general. His verses evinced an ecumenical spirit and anti-colonial instinct. In 1925 he published a poem titled "We Are All Muslims" (kulina muslimun) in the Egyptian magazine *al-Zahra'*.[41] That same year, Syrians revolted against the French Mandate government. The French response was draconian and included the bombing of Syrian villages and cities. Regarding this violent retaliation, one French general said "you need to terrorize people," and the then British consul in Damascus described it as "a sustained policy of frightfulness."[42] This campaign culminated in the devastating bombardment of Damascus in October 1925, which lasted for forty-eight hours, led to the death of at least a thousand people, and garnered global attention. In his poem, Bustani summons the image of the incendiary bombs destroying the Syrian city. "Oh fragrant Damascus, what will we call you," Bustani asked, "after you have been burned and destroyed / and your river has flowed with blood."[43] The core of the poem's message is not Bustani's lament over Damascus, but a call for Arab unity in the face of colonial violence: "Wake up o Arabs! Hear the sound of justice! / There is no such thing as Druze or Christian, there is only the land of Syria and the land of Iraq / In the doctrine of the West, we are all 'Muslims.'"[44] Bustani understood that for the French, being "Muslim," even if you were not, made you a killable subject. Bustani, nourished by an Arab nationalist project, flips what he recognized as an Orientalist label: being Muslim, for him, only underlined the necessity for solidarity.

The many poems Bustani wrote over the course of his time in Palestine were collected in his diwan, *al-Falistiniyyat*, published in 1946. "As far was we know," Khalid Sulaiman wrote of Bustani, "he is the first Arab poet who published a collection of poems on Palestine."[45] In the introduction to *al-Falistiniyyat*, Bustani called himself a Lebanese Palestinian: "I was born in Lebanon, but am Palestinian by homeland."[46] Bustani's ideas were forged under global, imperial conditions. In Palestine, Bustani was becoming increasingly aware of the unequal geography that structured the world. By the 1930s, Bustani was also writing verses—undoubtedly inspired by Tagore—in celebration of the East. "The Easterner will return to the Westerner his faculties of reason," he wrote in one poem, "for the Easterner possesses more care and reason."[47] Attention to these elements in his work and the context of their creation challenge conventional understandings of Islam and politics in British Palestine. An example is the occasion of the Indian activist Muhammad Ali Jouhar's funeral in Jerusalem on January 23, 1931, when Bustani recited a poem to the assembled. His verse possessed the same ecumenical and anti-colonial spirit as his other poems. Both Muslims and Christians, Bustani wrote, mourn Jouhar. And the "greedy" British, unnamed but implied, arrived in Palestine, as in India, "to light a fire." His poem was originally published alongside other speeches and poems from the event a few days later in the newspaper *al-Jamiʿa al-ʿArabiyya*. In the notes he appended to the poem in *al-Falistiniyyat*, Bustani claims he was the first Christian to deliver a eulogy on the grounds of al-Haram al-Sharif.[48] Though a difficult assertion to verify, it would certainly reflect the spirit of the age. Only a decade earlier, the Coptic priest Qommus Sergius had famously preached from inside Al-Azhar's mosque during the heady days of 1919. In contrast to the repeated invocations of Sergius's sermon in accounts of Egyptian national unity, Bustani's presence in Jerusalem that day has been eclipsed in a historiography that adopts wholesale British colonial preoccupations with Pan-Islam. Jouhar's funeral in Jerusalem, therefore, has only been narrated in those terms. It was indeed Amin al-Husseini, the mufti of Jerusalem and head of the Supreme Muslim Council in Palestine, who arranged for the burial to take place in his city. In a series of overtures to Muslims worldwide, culminating in the World Islamic Congress convened in December 1931, al-Husseini aimed to cement Jerusalem's place among the sites and institutions of the "Muslim World."[49]

Whatever the designs of al-Husseini, Bustani was not drawn to the Maulana because he wanted a place on the Pan-Islamic stage, but rather because of a shared commitment to anti-colonial nationalism. He wrote that Jouhar was in London, "with the Hindu (hinduwi) leader the Mahatma Gandhi, in the service of the Indian Nation (umma)."[50] Bustani knew Jouhar and had met with him repeatedly years earlier when he lived in India. Confident assertions of the funeral's singularly Pan-Islamic appeal ignore both Bustani's presence and the kind of politics he represented. The authors of a recent article on the event, which focuses on al-Husseini's role as a "propagandist," mention only in passing that a "Christian Arab poet read a poem composed especially for the funeral," without further comment or elaboration.[51] Moving beyond colonial rubrics and taking seriously the activities of anti-colonial internationalists, whose utterances are suffused with local, ecumenical appeals, reveals connections like those forged by Bustani.

Palestinian writers have been particularly attuned to this aspect of Bustani's oeuvre. In a recent book on the poetry of Mandate Palestine, the Haifawi literary critic Suleiman Jubran writes that Bustani's poetry—packed as it is with references to the Islamicate past and the colonial present—"is not just Lebanese-Palestinian poetry, it is Christian-Muslim poetry, it is the first to address colonialism-Zionism in Palestine."[52] Here, Jubran echoes the judgment of the Palestinian writer Ghassan Kanafani, who in his well-known study of the 1936 revolt in Palestine praises Bustani, the anti-colonial poet: "He was the first to warn against the Balfour Declaration and its challenges, the very month it was issued." Kanafani argues that the poetry Bustani wrote in the 1920s was one of the most important influences on the multitude that moved in the 1930s. Bustani's insurgent poetics and ecumenical impulse are exemplified in a remarkable exchange with the British Mandate authorities, which Kanafani recounts:

[On] March 28th 1920, [Bustani] had himself led a demonstration, which chanted a song that he had composed himself. He was summoned to an inquiry, and the following appears in the records of the inquiry conducted by the Public Prosecutor:

PUBLIC PROSECUTOR: Statements have been made that you were carried shoulder-high, and that you said to the people who were following behind you: "Oh Christians, Oh Muslims."

THE ACCUSED: Yes.

PUBLIC PROSECUTOR: And you also said: "To whom have you left the country?"

THE ACCUSED: Yes.

PUBLIC PROSECUTOR: Then you said: "Kill the Jews and unbelievers."

THE ACCUSED: No. That violates the meter and the rhyme. I could not have said that. What I said was both rhyming and metrical. It is called poetry.[53]

Bustani's political activities during his time in Haifa were not limited to what the historian A. L. Tibawi called his "distinct poetical gifts."[54] In June 1923, at the Sixth Palestine Arab Congress held in Jaffa, Bustani asked the gathering to adopt a resolution stating that "taxation without representation" was not consistent with the democratic principles adopted in Great Britain itself, and therefore a boycott should be called.[55] Despite regularly confronting British colonial rhetoric and practices in Palestine, Bustani nevertheless thought Arabs could reason with the British Empire. But the British simply did not uphold the principles they espoused.

In June 1936 Bustani published in English and Arabic a salvo against the Balfour Declaration and the Mandate System as a whole, *The Palestine Mandate: Invalid and Impracticable*.[56] Bustani demonstrates, with meticulous detail, how the British Mandate in Palestine violates the principles of international law specifically and the ethos of British liberalism generally. Even within the uneven and unjust Mandate system, the situation in Palestine is an aberration, Bustani argues: "To this the Palestine Arabs revolted in 1920, in 1921, in 1924, in 1929, in 1933 and it is in the midst of the 1936 revolt that the present study is made."[57] "This study," he writes later, "is merely a hurried but honestly motivated effort to expose facts and merits."[58] He quotes at length from official League of Nations documents, the Balfour Declaration, and the work of the Mandate's attorney general, Norman Bentwich, annotating and introducing their utterances to explicate his case. He criticizes Britain's policy and rhetoric, exposing its autocratic approach to the "Palestine Problem" and endless obfuscation of the reality on the ground, including the British habit of ordering hapless commissions of inquiry. The book was submitted to the high commissioner for Palestine and the colonial secretary in London to little effect, like many of the diplomatic efforts Palestinians undertook in the years before 1948. But the Arabic edition was enthusiastically received by Pan-Arab journals like *al-Mashriq* in Beirut and *al-Hilal* in Cairo.[59]

Bustani had more success in the courtroom. In addition to his poetry and his regular contributions to the burgeoning nationalist press, Bustani worked in the Mandate's courts in an effort to defend the lands of Palestinians. He studied law in Jerusalem, at the school established by the British for that express purpose.[60] As was the case with lawyers in much of the colonized world, many of the Arab law graduates became heavily involved in the Mandate's politics. Bustani was no exception and quickly added the law to his repertoire of political activity after graduating from the program. His most notable legal victory was the designation of a large tract of land in the Ghor-Beisan area as public land and therefore off limits to the Jewish Agency. Bustani argued that this land had long been under the dominion of the Arabs who occupied it. Though this may not have been entirely accurate in light of the particular forms of property rights that reigned during the Ottoman period, it served Bustani's larger political project. In his valuable study of how land law was transformed in Palestine from the mid-nineteenth century until 1948, the historian Munir Fakher Eldin argued that "Bustani's emphasis on local autonomy ... had a definite purpose to serve: to downplay the reality of Ottoman sovereignty in favor of a normative claim of an original Arab national sovereignty."[61] Bustani's activist lawyering drew the ire of the British authorities and the Zionist movement. In his autobiography, Chaim Weizmann expressed great disdain for Bustani's success in defending the Arab right to this particular tract of land.[62] Indeed, Bustani's activities in Palestine garnered him quite the reputation among the British authorities and the Zionist movement. He was described variously by his critics as "the worst scoundrel in the place," "an excitable, energetic young demagogue," a "notorious agitator," "a man of very excitable disposition," and "an active extremist."[63] In all the comments of his vociferous critics, Bustani's Indology was unmentioned.

Liberation Philology

In March 1947, a journalist from Cairo's *al-Risala*—the Arab world's premier literary weekly—met Bustani at the city's Grand Continental Hotel. Bustani was on his way back to Haifa from London, where he had just been on a political mission. The Arab Higher Committee was still trying to make its case to the British authorities. Bustani took advantage of the sojourn to do some research in that entrepôt of global knowledge, the library of the British Museum. The journalist asked Bustani about the stack of papers he carried with him, manuscripts of his translations of hinduwi epics. Bustani was in the midst of translating the Ramayana and the Mahabharata into Arabic. In the interview, Bustani mentions his reasons for translating these particular Sanskritic texts: "The translations of India's epics into European languages opened new doors in fiqh al-lughah, 'al-philologiyya.' Today, if you look at any comprehensive English language dictionary you will see that many English words have their origins in Sanskrit. If we translate these texts into the Arabic language we will notice the same thing."[64] Such a philological project lays bare the sheer boldness of Bustani's undertaking. But Bustani did not labor under conditions of his own choosing. Between April 23 and May 22 of that inauspicious year of 1948, thirty-three members of Haganah occupied Bustani's house on the sea in Haifa. Despite this, Bustani—like Emile Habibi—remained in Haifa. When the soldiers left, they took him and briefly imprisoned him. Upon returning to his home, he quickly packed up his precious manuscripts.[65] They ended up with his son Fuad, who with the help of Palestinian fishermen would periodically make his way down from Beirut to check on his parents. Bustani's was a philology under colonialism, not colonial philology.

There has been a search, since Orientalism was knocked from its summit, for noncoercive, nonhierarchical approaches to the study of the other. How does one study from within an exploitative system? In a series of erudite essays, Sheldon Pollock has recently sought to rehabilitate philology, despite its sordid past. In what he has variously referred to as "liberation philology" and "comparison without hegemony," Pollock has argued that philology can offer "one important way out of the dead-end area-studies model of language labor as merely producing the raw data for the Lancashire mills of self-universalizing Western theory."[66] Inspired by the work of Baruch Spinoza, Antonio Gramsci, D. D. Kosambi, and Edward Said, Pollock calls for a critical philology, attuned as much to political texts as to the literary. Any history of this scholarship must attend to those intellectuals from the colonized world who studied and translated old texts—however imperfectly—in the crucible of anti-colonial revolt. Some accounts of comparative literature's origins begin provocatively with the German Jewish philologist Erich Auerbach's exile in Istanbul, where he wrote *Mimesis* while estranged from Europe and its libraries during the Second World War.⁶⁷ He recounts on the final page of his study a number of topics he "should have liked" to have included, had circumstances been different.⁶⁸ In a striking parallel, Bustani, writing at roughly the same time in Haifa, makes a similar admission in the prologue of his Mahabharata. He intentionally calls his text a prologue or preamble (*dibaja*) rather than an introduction (*muqaddima*) because, according to him, an introduction would be impossible to write from his present location. But Bustani was writing from his besieged home, not from exile. "My books are as far from me now as India is, and then further. They are in the hands of my children outside of Israel, and I am in the grip of Israel. Between us is fire and steel and certain death."⁶⁹

If we look at scholarship forged through a shared history of colonial rule and anti-colonial revolt, rather than the scholarship produced in the process of subjugation and exclusion, a different kind of writing emerges.⁷⁰ What does the study of a region look like when it is produced under conditions of geographical proximity, cultural affiliation, and political solidarity, rather than distance, judgment, and domination? Bustani's life and work begin to reveal what the study of the not so distant other—who is also close, but is not a compatriot—can look like.⁷¹ Such intellectual practices, forms of south-south knowledge, should be instructive. At the very least they can bring into relief the methodological, disciplinary, geographical, and political presuppositions that the social sciences and humanities in the West inherited from colonialism.⁷² Bustani himself brings the same commitment to careful reading—and the same investment in liberation—to his excoriation of British rhetorics of rule that he does to his elucidation of those texts he believes to be irreducibly Indian. In both cases, having jettisoned from his reading practice any conscious devotion to British imperial precepts, he seeks to project a vision for an egalitarian future, free of domination and communal discord.

Bustani's Mahabharata, the only one of his Arabic translations that he prepared for publication before his death, was published in 1952, a collaboration between the Alumni Association of the American University of Beirut and the publisher Dar al-Ahad. Albert Hourani described Sulayman al-Bustani's Arabic *Iliad* as "a book of a kind which had never appeared in Arabic before: a handsome, well-produced volume of 1,260 pages, with an introduction, a running commentary, indexes and illustrations."[73] The Mahabharata translated by Wadi' al-Bustani was similarly monumental in form. The cover spells out the title in an Arabic script that mimics the Devanagari of Sanskrit, and the book is full of color illustrations borrowed from Indian editions of the epic text. Bustani subtitled the book "al-malhama al-Hinduwiyya, kubra' al-malahim al-'alamiyah." The Hindu Epic, among the greatest epics in the world.

Bustani had studied Sanskrit during his time in India, but not to the extent needed to translate the epics he was interested in. His translation, or Arabization, comes from the Indian civil servant and historian Romesh Dutt's 1898 English verse translation of the Mahabharata. Bustani is explicit about his role in the endeavor: the title page reads that the translation (*tarjama*) of the text from Sanskrit is Dutt's, and he is the one who has put it into Arabic poetic form ('*arabiyyaa sh'ariyyan*). However, Bustani does do more than simply render the text into Arabic. Unlike Dutt, who aimed to produce a modern, literary Mahabharata for modern Indian readers like himself, Bustani's project was more than just one of belles lettres.[74] Introducing a new text to Arab readers, he sought to produce both an aesthetically beautiful piece of poetry and a scholarly edition. Therefore, in addition to Dutt's poetic version, Bustani drew on a number of other editions of the Mahabharata in English and French; hence his trips to London. Bustani's nearly hundred pages of original endnotes—Dutt's edition contains no notes—are evidence of this larger project. Some of the notes refer readers to different episodes and characters within the epic, while others provide context, offer alternative translations, or explain specific concepts.

Bustani writes that while he was translating the Mahabharata from Dutt's English translation, he heard the Lebanese poet Shibli Faris utter on the radio that there "is no sectarianism in culture."[75] After hearing this, Bustani said "ameen"—like the English amen—which he compared to the Sanskrit "om." Bustani writes: "We took from the Jews so there is nothing wrong with taking from the Indians." "The Prophet," he continues, "took from the Torah, so there is no problem taking from India" and he cites that famous hadith that implores believers "to seek knowledge even unto China."[76] Bustani then makes an explicit comparison, arguing that the ethos found in a Quranic verse that says that God is with the weak and the patient is shared with the Mahabharata. Bustani simultaneously argues that the Mahabharata is both an instructive text for his contemporary political context, on the one hand, and parallels Arabo-Islamic principles, on the other. Beyond the discussion of his own circumstances, his introduction is suffused with the political. Gandhi gets repeated mentions, as freedom fighter and inheritor of the Buddha's teachings. Bustani notes that he completed his translation of the Bhagavad Gita the day after Gandhi was assassinated. He sent a copy to G. D. Birla, the Indian businessman who had been hosting Gandhi in his home at the time of his murder. Bustani dedicated the translation to the "soul of the Mahatma, in the name the Arabs of Palestine."[77] Bustani went on to write that Dutt, who died in 1909, could never imagine India's independence.[78] Dutt's introduction to his Mahabharata, which Bustani translated, is devoid of any political discussion.

As his citations and ideas reveal, the precise sources of Bustani's readings of Hinduism and India were often the voluminous works of European Orientalists. Bustani's imagined readers, however, were not the same, so his points of emphasis, sources of comparison, and method of address differ markedly from the likes of Muller or even Dutt. One of his unpublished manuscripts, "Akhbar al-Ahala" (Divine chronicles), is a collection of quotations and commentaries testifying to the monotheistic origins of Hinduism.[79] The manuscript contains passages from Hindu texts, quotations from secondary sources, and Bustani's own interpretations and explanations. The book also serves as a general introduction for Arab readers to a series of Hindu concepts and characters: Vishnu, Brahma, Agni, Lakshmi, karma, *ananda*, and many others. He also explains the chronology of Hindu mythology. Bustani's specific form of address through comparison continues throughout the text. "Brahma," he writes, for example, "is to Hinduism, what 'Allah' is to Arabs."[80] Certain ideas present in Bustani's works can be found in both the many-centuries-old Arabo-Islamic corpus and the writing of modern European Orientalists. The notion of Hinduism as monotheism that captured Bustani so strongly is shared between these two bodies of knowledge. In his famous book, Al-Biruni himself repeatedly notes the monotheistic roots of Hinduism.[81] Bustani goes on to write that readers will be skeptical of his claim that Hinduism is monotheistic, but nevertheless it is the truth.[82] It is clear then that Bustani was writing into an already established sense of what India and Hinduism are thought to represent in Arab thinking. His writing was nothing short of an attempt to transform the terms and attitudes of Arabs' India. And although he did so in the spirit of solidarity and in the interest of dispelling myths, Bustani's India was an invention that did not reflect the reality of difference or diversity in the land of Hindustan itself. Like the India of Orientalists like Max Muller or nationalists like Jawaharlal Nehru, Bustani's India was his own, tied inexorably to his particular place in an unequal colonial geography.

In the end, Bustani's neologism *hinduwi* never caught on, and the impact of his Indology is difficult to account for. In 1966, the Indian Council for Cultural Relations (ICCR) published an edition of his

Shukuntala based on the manuscripts Bustani's family donated to the Indian government.[83] In 2012 the ICCR and Abu Dhabi's Kalima Project finally published an edition of his *Ramayana*, unveiling the book at the Jaipur Literary Festival in January 2013 (although mention of the text has now been scrubbed from Kalima's website).[84] The rest of his unpublished manuscripts, including a translation of *Kalila wa Dimna*, remain in the library of the ICCR. Copies of Bustani's 1952 Mahabharata are unfortunately quite rare. The only citation of the text I have tracked down is quite notable, however: an article by the great Bahraini poet Ibrahim al-'Arayyed in *al-Abhath*, the journal of Faculty of Arts and Sciences at the American University of Beirut.[85] Al-'Arayyed himself was an important link between modern Arabic literature and India. Born in 1908 in Bombay, he studied Urdu at Aligarh and translated Persian and Urdu poetry into Arabic. He merely quotes from the translation, but its presence in his hands reveals at least some of the text's capacity to travel. In 1947 *al-Risala* had enthusiastically reported on Bustani's efforts in the months before their aforementioned interview with him in Cairo. The editors lamented that what they know today of India comes to them from Orientalists (*al-mustashriqin*), despite the long, well-documented history of Arab and Indian knowledge production from at least the Abbasid period.[86] Bustani, they argued, should be praised for bringing Indian knowledge into Arabic on their own terms. Bustani represents, then, the very possibility of producing knowledge of the other outside the confines of colonial formations.

Partition

After 1948, despite remaining in Haifa, Bustani resigned from the political activities he had been a part of in the preceding years. In one Israeli intelligence report from February 9, 1949, Moshe Yitah, the director of the short-lived Ministry of Minorities in Haifa, wrote that Wadi' "remained living in his home, even though most of the Arabs in Haifa moved in accordance with the decree of the military authority to Wadi Nisnas, and in his home there was for a long time a base of the Haganah. He is not engaged in public or political activity and is involved, as his acquaintances say, only with issues of rich literature."[87] Bustani's position, like all Arab inhabitants of the new Israeli state, was precarious. Obviously weary of his fate, he wrote to thank the Ministry of Minority Affairs for not expelling him or confiscating his property: "This has all become possible thanks to my presence here, with all my books and manuscripts for which the authorities in Israel have been thanked and will always be thanked in contrast to the memory of our friend Azra Haddad retains of the Iraqi authorities who robbed him of his Hebrew translation of Omar Khayyam."[88] While his manuscripts would later be smuggled out of the country, the mention of Azra Haddad is telling. Haddad, one of Baghdad's most prominent Arab nationalist intellectuals, had just reluctantly arrived in the new state of Israel, along with more than one hundred thousand other Iraqi Jews. Bustani must have felt a certain kinship with Haddad, not only because they had both cut their teeth in the Pan-Arabist press of the early twentieth century, but also because he himself had translated Khayyam into Arabic. In 1953 the tragic fortunes of the Arab world's Jews were becoming increasingly clear. The world of translation and intellectual exchange that Bustani had tried to foster was collapsing around him.

But Bustani was not entirely without hope. As his health waned, Bustani finally left Haifa and spent the last months of his life in Lebanon. In one of his final poems, published shortly before his death, India served as a negative example. The poem praises Camille Chamoun, the second president of independent Lebanon. In it, Bustani juxtaposes the case of South Asia, in which partition occurred—while also celebrating the role of Gandhi, who opposed partition and upheld the ethics of the great Hindu epics—with the case of Lebanon, a model of ecumenism in the Arab East. He writes of the new, multisectarian state:

> Of those devout among us, there are those who read the Bible and those who read the Quran
> My homeland is my heaven on earth until god takes me to his heaven in the sky
> Lebanon is the homeland of thought and culture, if our East surveyed its nations
> The East would want Lebanon to be a lighthouse filling humankind with light, so it has become so.[89]

Despite the political passion of his life, Palestine, being gone, and his intellectual passion, India, being dismembered, Bustani remained committed to a vision of Eastern unity and pluralism. Global transformations birthed in Bustani a worldly imagination. The itinerary of his life and the content of his writing were inseparable. Each of his narrations of the Indian past was indelibly marked by the conditions and ideas of his Arab present. Bustani, it can be said, was a product of empire. His life and work reflect a history of imperial connections beyond those of administration and exploitation: an intellectual history of philology and solidarity. After 1948 Bustani's thinking was certainly guided by the language and conditions of the postcolonial nation-state. Lebanon, the land of his birth, became his final refuge, but his dreams of another, unpartitioned, world were not foreclosed.

2 *Islam*

Most historians of the subject have rightly highlighted Pan-Islam's chimeric character. Wilfred Cantwell Smith put it simply some years ago when he wrote that "Pan-Islam is, and has always been, primarily a sentiment of cohesion. It is not cohesion itself, nor any institutional or practical expression of it."[1] Pan-Islam was the name for Islam in a time when Muslim sovereignty was disappearing and the world was being made over in Europe's image (and for Europe and its ancillaries' profit). It was a response to a new international order. I turn to Pan-Islam now in order to reveal its limits, both as an idea summoned by its enemies and adherents and as the backdrop to a set of relationships that take place in its shadow. Partisans of Pan-Islam were confident of their faith's place in this new world. "A League of Nations," wrote the editor of the influential Hyderabadi journal *Islamic Culture*, "has been started to try to do a part of the work Islam has done, to bring the varying nations into unison and frame a code of international law conducive to peace and progress."[2] Islam, in this rendering, was international *avant la lettre*: the West was just catching up. Some visions of Islamic cooperation laid bare the extent to which this new idiom was more a reflection of a new age than a radically new Islamic political theory. "The fact is that whether a Musalman openly styles himself a Pan-Islamist or not," the Indian scholar and organizer Mushir Hosain Kidwai put it in 1908, "he is in spirit and at heart a Pan-Islamist and is sure to be ready to serve the cause of Islam and even to spread it howsoever he can."[3] In a time of global capital, world empires, and universal history, Islam was always already Pan-Islam.

India has served a crucial function in Pan-Islam's imagination and articulation. The subcontinent was seen as a source of the funds and bodies necessary for Islam's defensive role in the modern world. The peripatetic intellectual and pioneering Pan-Islamist Jamal al-Din al-Afghani's famous 1885 appeal to the Ottoman sultan Abdulhamid II was largely concerned with India's Muslims, whose "great numbers are mostly holders of property and wealth, and are extremely firm in Islam and are affected in the defense of the faith and the millet."[4] Indian interest in Ottoman affairs long preceded the Khilafat movement of the twentieth century, which despite its name, as Gail Minault has demonstrated, was far more interested in the struggle against the British in India than in the maintenance of the Ottoman caliphate.[5] Beginning with the Russo-Turkish War of 1877, Muslims in British India raised huge amounts of funds in support of the Ottoman Empire. Although the Ottomans sought to raise funds in India, it was philanthropy emanating from Indians themselves that constituted the bulk of the money remitted.[6] And during the Balkan Wars of 1912–13, Indian medical missions were dispatched to support the Ottoman soldiers on the front. But Indian money was not just flowing to Istanbul. New commercial networks forged by colonialism followed historical religious routes, distributing funds across the Ottoman realm, refurbishing shrines in Najaf, and facilitating travel to Mecca.[7] Despite this financial largesse, not all Indian Muslims were supportive of a modern Islam that placed too much authority in the hands of the Ottomans. No less than Sayyid Ahmad Khan, one of the most prominent Indian Muslim intellectuals of the period, put it simply: "Even taking for granted that the Sultan of Turkey is the Caliph, we say that if he is the Caliph, he is the Caliph only in that country which he governs and for those Mohammedans only who owe him allegiance."[8] Khan's pro-British alliances in India certainly betray some of the reasoning behind his position. Indeed, the intellectual reaction against him, from people like Shibli Numani, was sometimes coupled with expressed support for the Ottoman sultan.

While Pan-Islam's Ottoman or Arab expressions, *ittihad-i islam* or *al-wahda al-islamiyya*, have unique intellectual genealogies, the idea is also a European one. The British especially, but also other European empires, were both participants in and observers of Pan-Islam.[9] At key moments in the British conquest of India they expected a hardly sovereign Ottoman Empire to cooperate in matters Islamo-political. In the midst of the failed Ottoman campaign to regain territory against Russia in 1787, for example, Tipu Sultan's emissaries arrived in Istanbul seeking support against the British, but the Ottoman sultan Selim III did not dare antagonize his allies and advised the leader of Mysore to cooperate with the invaders.[10] Indeed, the British would explicitly ask the Ottomans to say so. Perhaps the most infamous example of this dynamic is the Ottoman reaction to the Indian revolt of 1857. The rebels sought support from the caliph but were rebuffed. The British, however, secured permission from the Ottomans to transport their troops through Egypt to help suppress the revolt and secure their territory. More striking was their success in procuring a proclamation from the Ottoman sultan, which was read aloud in Indian mosques, imploring Muslims not to fight against the British.[11] Cemil Aydin has read this incident as emblematic of the imperial world order that reigned until the end of the nineteenth century, when the racialization of Muslims inaugurated a more explicit attachment to Pan-Islam among Muslims and non-Muslims alike.[12] Any account of Pan-Islam must reckon with the extent to which it was shaped by a colonial situation. Colonialism helped determine the relationship between colonized Muslims with other Muslims around the world and with non-Muslims who may have polemicized against their beliefs, facilitated their travel, and exploited their labor or land.

Besides imposing its will on the Ottomans on an imperial stage, the British Empire famously characterized itself as a Muslim empire. Unlike other European powers, which adopted an Islamic idiom in their appeals to Muslims, the British had enormous control over a large Muslim population. Napoleon's declaration that he had come to Egypt to defend Islam or the European fascist courting of anticolonial Muslims during World War II cannot be compared to Britain's supremacy in numbers. "Unquestionably," the British imperial theorist Valentine Chirol would announce at the beginning of his 1906 lecture on Pan-Islam, "no sovereign counts amongst his subjects so many millions of Mahomedans as King Edward. The total number of Mahomedans in the world is approximately estimated at some 250,000,000." Only a tenth of that number, Chirol continued, "owe direct allegiance to the Sultan of Turkey" while many millions more could be found in "our Indian Empire [and] scattered about our possessions and protectorates."[13] Ideas of Britain's Muslim empire circulated widely. For the London illustrated weekly the *Graphic*, G. F. Morrell produced a map of Africa and Asia centered on the Indian Ocean, with British-ruled territories shaded in black. At the bottom of the map stand three turbaned and bearded figures, representing the British, Turkish, and French Empires. The figure labeled the "Mohammedans of the British Empire" towers over the other two, representing a population 96,237,000 strong. Beneath the confident veneer of British propaganda, however, was a serious anxiety over their meddling in what they deemed to be Islamic affairs. The colonial archive from the period is full of speculation about and extensive surveillance of Indian Muslim opinion regarding British actions across the Middle East.

Pan-Christianity against Pan-Islam

Muslim numbers were a major source of anxiety for Christian missionaries as well, who in the heyday of Pan-Islam agonized over real and imagined conversions to "in a sense, the only anti-Christian religion."[14] Islam's claim to be a successor to Christianity and its theological imperative to seek converts made it a greater enemy than other, nonmissionizing faiths. Muslims, moreover, posed a global demographic threat to Christendom. Their capacity to reproduce their already significant numbers was particularly worrisome. "It is not a problem of 200 million, more or less, the present population of the Muslim world," an American missionary in Egypt clarified, "but that it is a problem of these to-day, and their children and their grandchildren—well-nigh a billion human souls before the close of the twentieth century."[15] Muslims did not respond lightly to missionary activities and European imperial Christianity more generally. The official Ottoman response was to dispatch its own missionaries. Abdulhamid II's efforts to consolidate his rule by emphasizing his title as caliph and attempting to strictly control what forms of Islam where practiced in his domain included the dispatch of state-sanctioned shuykh from the Hanafi madhab (the school of Islamic jurisprudence favored by the Hamidian regime). "Abdulhamid," the historian Selim Deringil has noted with regard to this particular practice, "was attempting to do precisely what he feared the British and French would do to him, that is use Muslims of French or British allegiance as a potential fifth column."[16] Like Christian missionaries, Abdulhamid's' project of conversion focused on Africa. Beyond the Ottoman imperial center, Arabs and Indians responded to missionary advances—largely in the form of institutions like orphanages, hospitals, and schools rather than conversions, which were few and far between among Muslims—with their own welfare and education institutions.[17] Writing the history of colonialism necessitates attention to how colonial ideas are distributed. Not every reaction to colonialism is anti-colonial. Colonialism produced an uneven geography, demarcated by typologies of color and caste and hierarchies of labor and faith.

From January 18 to 23, 1911, some 160 missionaries, representing more than fifty boards, societies, and churches, convened in the north Indian city of Lucknow. In the preceding centuries it had been one of the great sites of Indian poetry and music, rivaling the Mughal capital of Delhi as the center of Islamic culture in India. For that week in January, however, Lucknow played host to the General Conference on Missions to Muslims, since its Muslim sovereign had long been deposed and the region was then firmly under the rule of the British Raj. The delegates met in secret at Isabella Thoburn College, as "it was deemed wise to restrict admission to approved visitors only." "Great care," the organizers noted, "was also taken to prevent leakage of news to the secular press until the Conference had finished its sessions."[18] The meeting was convened by a group of missionaries with the express purpose of responding to the Pan-Islam that was challenging their ability to convert Muslims in particular and heathens generally, given what they understood as Islam's missionizing aims and abilities. The gathering came in the wake of two related conferences in the previous decade, at Cairo and Edinburgh. The Cairo conference in 1906 had inaugurated a discussion over the pooling of missionary resources to study the misunderstood nature of Islamic doctrine and practice among European and American missionaries. The Edinburgh Conference, held a year before Lucknow in 1910, established the larger framework under which the missionaries working among Muslims would collaborate. Edinburgh inaugurated a new ecumenical era of mutual cooperation among the many Christian churches of the West.[19]

The Lucknow conference exhibited all the usual missionary anxieties over Pan-Islam. The evangelists gathered in the spirit of collaboration, which they announced was a necessary response to their dire situation. The conference was analogized to the Meccan pilgrimage: "As the Muslim Hajj makes for the spirit of unity and Pan-Islam, so must Christian unity make all our policy and strategy: there must be one united front and in all great moves, the forces at work must move in concert."[20] The often acknowledged impact of missionaries on Islamic reform here witnesses a reversal: the real or imagined march of Islam inspires a new and lasting ecumenism among the Christian evangelists. Realizing that the sheer force of the Gospel would not be enough to turn the heathens into saved men and women, Christian missionaries adopted a new approach, turning to each other's expertise and Orientalism's substantial corpus in order to professionalize their activities in unison. The resolutions passed at the conference aimed to concretize the missionaries' lofty ideals and always grand ambitions. First and foremost was a resolution calling for renewed attention to be placed on the continent of Africa, "the region upon which our present efforts must be chiefly concentrated to meet the advance of Islam."[21] Another expressed missionary commitment was "to strengthen the work among animistic tribes, pagan communities, and depressed classes."[22] Perhaps most significantly, however, was the resolution prescribing the establishment of a training college for missionaries in Cairo. The American missionary and missiologist Samuel Zwemer, mastermind of the Lucknow conference, moved to Cairo in 1912 and played a crucial role in the school's establishment and functioning. Christened the Cairo Study Center, Zwemer's project would become a central hub for missionaries to train in the Arabic language and familiarize themselves with the peoples and places of Islam. Heather Sharkey notes that Zwemer "also became an organizational dynamo behind the ecumenical project to develop Christian literatures for Muslims."[23] This endeavor required more than just translating texts from European to non-European languages. The racial science and

Orientalism forged under colonial conditions combined to reify the differences between the missionaries and the Muslims they wished to save. At Lucknow, one missionary, lamenting their failure to garner conversions, argued that their Christian liturgy was not intelligible to the "oriental mind." If success is to be found in their errand into Islamdom, their own Christian texts and practices "must be orientalized, to say the least."[24] The archbishop of Canterbury had put it even more plainly about a decade earlier: "We Westerners never shall convert the Mohammedans. I am afraid it is hopeless. . . . They must be approached by Oriental missionaries."[25]

While a number of delegates arrived in Lucknow from their posts in Egypt, Syria, Palestine, and the Persian Gulf (Zwemer was then working in the Arabian Mission in Bahrain), the only Arab in attendance was one Paul Dimishky (there were a handful of other "Orientals" at the meeting, Indian converts to Christianity). He was a member of the Society for the Propagation of the Gospel's (SPG's) mission in Bombay, the purpose of which was to convert the western Indian city's heathens—Mohammedan, Hindu, and otherwise—into Christians. Dimishky's focus was the Muslims in particular, on whom he was a kind of expert. In an article published in the months after the Lucknow conference, Dimishky produced an ethnic and sectarian taxonomy, "The Moslem Population in Bombay." In it he clarified the differences between Shaiks, Sayids, Moghuls, Konkanis, Arabs, and Pathans, as well as those between Bohras, Khojas, Maimans, and Julhais.[26] The first group was among those Muslims in the city of "foreign extraction" and the latter four of "Hindu descent." Beyond this initial, pernicious ascription of difference, each individual group is described with regard to its distinct history, social characteristics, and style of jurisprudence and worship. Sayids, for example, "are truthful, honest, sober, idle, fond of pleasure and thriftless." The Khoja is "a good hater," and they "are neat, clean, sober, thrifty, ambitious, and in trade enterprising, cool and resourceful."

Such ethnographic typologies were fairly common by the beginning of the twentieth century, amalgamations of Orientalist and missionary knowledge. Readily circulated in missionary and scholarly tracts, the purportedly accurate and even scientific knowledge of distinct tribes, sects, and races was, as a now large body of critical work will attest, printed, circulated, and displayed. Journals, first of Oriental studies and then those specifically concerned with the "Muslim world," were widely read and distributed among the relevant missions. The very journal Dimishky wrote in, the *Moslem World*, was a product of the collaborative efforts initiated at Cairo in 1906, and its first number was published in the month of the Lucknow conference. The English-language journal, published in London for the Nile Mission Press, joined the shelf with *Revue du Monde Musulman* and *Der Islam*, both founded in the preceding decade.

At the end of the article Dimishky—like so many missionaries before him—registered his frustration over the lack of Muslim conversions. While missionaries failed, Dimishky lamented, Islam's false teachings—through the efforts of a growing number of reformist associations—flourished, "reinforced every day by hundreds of co-religionists from almost all parts of India and Arabia." Missionaries were keen observers of Islamic reform. At the 1910 Edinburgh conference, W. H. T. Gairdner, a prominent missionary in Cairo, relayed with alarm the rapid spread of what he called "Neo-Islam" from West Asia across the Caucasus. "For ideas are like electricity," he warned, "they move fast, especially when the metals of a railway line conduct them."[27] New methods of print and new opportunities for movement certainly played a central role in the proliferation of Islamic reform. Dimishky's lament, therefore, was not entirely unwarranted. His enemy, so to speak, had the same weapons his own camp had.

Paul was the son of Hanna Dimishky, who was born in al-Lyd in 1847 and ordained a deacon by the bishop of Jerusalem in 1889. As his name implies, Hanna's family originally hailed from Damascus.

Hanna's father, Joseph Antoine Safi, was himself an early Arab convert to Protestantism who moved to Palestine in the 1830s.[28] The elder Dimishky was an enthusiastic pastor who for many years ran a school in al-Lyd that much excited visiting European missionaries. In 1887 one observer was impressed by this "very energetic Native Agent" who "throws great life and spirit into the work."[29] Sometime later, the Reverend Doctor George Adam Smith, while traveling through Syria on his way back home to Scotland from India, stopped by Hanna Dimishky's school. Upon witnessing him expounding on the Gospel to his young students, Smith wrote that there was "no more important a station in Palestine" than al-Lyd.[30] When Paul joined the family business, he had quite the reputation to live up to.

The younger Dimishky graduated from Syrian Protestant College in 1902.[31] After working as a deacon in Beirut and Haifa, Paul was ordained as a priest in 1906 and made his way to Bombay shortly thereafter. He quickly learned Urdu/Hindustani, a helpful language to master if one was going to save the souls of Indian Muslims. But his relationship with others in the mission were strained from the beginning. "The Arab Dimishky is a brave fellow," wrote Bishop of Bombay Edwin James in 1909, "but grossly tactless and self-assertive. Why on earth was he brought here?" Dimishky's Arabness had seriously disrupted the racial order of the mission. Dimishky and his wife, Jones continued, "are certainly not like any Indian ever born, but the Indians resent their taking up the attitude of Europeans towards them."[32] For Indians as for Europeans, Dimishky's race posed a problem. In another letter, Jones spelled out the concerns clearly: "I think the difficulty is this, he is not an Englishman and is not an Indian, but is employed by you as a member of the European staff. He insists of his position more violently than any Englishman would do. The Indians regard him as an Oriental, and will not take from him what they would readily take from an Englishman."[33] Dimishky's race was further demarcated by his salary, a European's of £200 a year.³⁴ This financial arrangement lays bare the implications of Dimishky's place in the mission's racial order. As Stuart Hall once put it, race is the "modality in which class is 'lived' [and] the medium through which class relations are experienced."³⁵ To be paid more is to be worth more, and by one calculus Dimishky was worth as much as a European. Nevertheless, despite his salary and faith, his being a non-European was inescapable. This racial anxiety—coupled with his family's history in the missionary enterprise—no doubt contributed to his self-conception and social relations.

That Dimishky's race posed such a problem for the mission reveals the limits of the missionary project, a limit that some missionaries were well aware of. "A Muslim," one of the Indian delegates at Lucknow said, "who has read and knows the history of Islam well, will never tolerate the race distinction made within the Christian Church."³⁶ Imbibing Pan-Islam's own rhetoric of racial unity, the missionary reasoned that Muslims could not abide by the racist system consecrated in the evangelical project by the end of the nineteenth century. This point must have come to the Indian delegate easily as the subject of a colonial regime of racialization himself. But the thread running through the entirety of the Lucknow conference proceedings that exposes the sheer irony of Dimishky's positon is the importance of Arabic fluency for evangelism among India's Muslims. "I often feel," one participant put it frankly, "that a missionary working among Muslims without knowledge of Arabic is a contradiction in terms."³⁷ Dimishky's fluency in Arabic, therefore, should have been seen as a major and indispensable asset to the mission. Moreover, as an "Oriental" fluent in the Christian liturgy, he embodied precisely the combination those gathered at Lucknow wished to produce in their literature in order to more successfully evangelize.

It is telling also that Dimishky's documented quarrels always occurred not with those European members of the diocese who held him in such contempt, but with Indians. In 1908 Dimishky's feud with an Indian deacon bearing the surname Mukherji led to a reprimand from Bombay's bishop. Mukherji had accused Dimishky of adultery, a not uncommon charge wielded in the puritan confines of missionary settings.[38] Although Dimishky was absolved, he was sent to Delhi for a few months until things cooled down. In another episode, Dimishky was involved in an "affair of mutual misunderstanding and accusation" with a schoolmaster by the name of Ibrahim. Dimishky likely would have been sent away earlier if he had not been the only missionary in the diocese with knowledge of Urdu. By its own account, the SPG was alone among the missionary institutions in Bombay proselytizing to Muslims.[39] The Bombay mission pleaded with its North Indian counterparts in Lahore and Delhi for an Urdu-speaking replacement to Dimishky, to no avail.

By December 1910, Edwin James had had enough: "The Mission has been a hotbed of intrigue and slander for 4 or 5 years now, and the only remedy is that all the persons who have taken part of this horrible pasttime [*sic*] should go." Six months later, Dimishky would be gone. At bottom, for the bishop of Bombay the Arab evangelist's flesh was the problem: "Dimishky is an Oriental with wild Syrian blood in his veins, and he must be judged as an Oriental, though he is paid by you as a European Missionary."[40] Dimishky had swallowed whole the racial ideology of missionary culture, but it had not embraced him back. The mission wanted Dimishky out, but he was set on staying in India. In a last-ditch effort, he pleaded with his superiors to find him a post somewhere, anywhere, in India: "India is the place where I would like to concentrate all my energy and strength in this present stage of its unrest. In fact I would give up anything rather than quit India, and would spend the very utmost of my life in helping to bring this vast empire to the foot of the Cross. I shall, therefore be most grateful to you[r] Lordship for any help you can render to keep me in India."[41] What explains Dimishky's zeal for converting Indians? Part and parcel of his being European was a celebration of, in his own words, "western civilization and missions."[42] By the early twentieth century, Europe's sense of itself was inextricably tied to the global space where its power was felt. It seems that for the beleaguered Dimishky, to be civilized was to spread civilization. Dimishky's efforts against Pan-Islam, however, were encumbered by his own place in the racial-religious order of the mission.

Weeks before he left Bombay, the tone of Dimishky's letters turned desperate: "Could you not, for GOD'S sake, try to relieve me from this terrible anxiety by finding me a suitable post in India outside Bombay? Where am I to go during the monsoon with my dear wife and two little ones?"[43] His appeals went unheeded, and he was promptly sent off by the diocese's secretary, E. Philip Comber. On June 10, 1911, four and a half years after he had arrived in the city to faithfully serve the SPG mission, Dimishky set off from Bombay toward Port Said. As a kind of consolation for his dismissal, Dimishky was given a lump sum of £150 to compensate for the furlough pay he would have received had he stayed in his position for another three years. In his article for the *Moslem World* published at the end of his Bombay tenure, Dimishky mounted a subtle defense of his work and a critique of the mission's management. The SPG in Bombay, Dimishky argued, had "rather antiquated methods ... strongly in contrast with the splendid Delhi Mission of the same society."[44] The mission was not well equipped to do the work of preparing for the Lord's second coming, lacking both staff and facilities. Had it been, Dimishky confidently claimed, "the results would have been incalculable." Dimishky described the necessary qualifications a missionary needed to succeed in Bombay: "For working among the Moslems in Bombay the missionary must know Urdu and Arabic. It may also be useful if he has acquired some knowledge of Gujarati." He goes on to argue that Urdu "is easily picked up by Europeans" when it is printed in the Roman script, not mentioning that he himself was not a European, and had most certainly learned Urdu in its Perso-Arabic script. It is only in this postscript that his Arab origins are revealed: "This mission ... is represented by the writer of this article, whose mother tongue is Arabic." Dimishky, the perfect man for the job of resisting Pan-Islam, fluent in Arabic and Oriental mores, zealous in his defense of the gospel and distaste for Islam, was forced from his position. In the end, European missionaries wanted Arabic in India, in order to effectively challenge the energy of Pan-Islam, but not Arabs. This racist division of labor was buttressed by a substantial literature that natives, so to speak, contributed to assiduously. The breakdown of this order required both the undermining of Orientalism's power and the pursuit of solidarity beyond its commands. No easy task.

Between Al-Azhar and Ambedkar

On December 11, 1936, five Egyptians arrived by steamer at Bombay. They all hailed from the great mosque and seminary of Cairo, Al-Azhar, the resplendent. Founded in the tenth century by the Fatimids, by the early twentieth the school was the wealthiest and most prominent institution of higher Islamic learning in the Middle East and the world.[45] Students from across the world made their way to the school to learn *fiqh*, sharia, Arabic, rhetoric, and logic. Given its history and prominence, Al-Azhar was in a position to cultivate and export its own vision of Pan-Islam.[46] The *umma*, or community, that the Azhar of the early twentieth century sought to cultivate, a community of Muslims across the world—Sunni and Shia together—was to replace the diminished sovereignty of Islam's territorial empires. If Dimishky's case revealed the limits of Pan-Islam's opponents, this Azharite delegation revealed the limits of Pan-Islam itself.

In the twenty-five years between Dimishky's departure from Bombay in 1911 and the Azharite arrival in 1936, the world was indelibly transformed. A world war devastated West Asia. From famine to locusts to genocide, millions died in the Ottoman Empire and its environs. And in the wake of war, new struggles were born. A global anti-colonial revolt brewed as Europe faltered. The death of the Ottoman caliphate struck a blow to certain Pan-Islamic efforts while raising others. Among the currents that flowed in the war years and after—nationalist, anarchist, communist—Pan-Islam was among the most prominent. Its symbols and rhetoric adorned and inspired disparate movements. Europe's capitals became centers of clandestine activity, as colonial subjects sought knowledge, funds, and refuge. In a wartime memoir, the Indian revolutionary Har Dayal vividly described the scene in Germany, where many an anti-British agitator had taken refuge. Dayal had a low opinion of the Ottomans and Hamidian propaganda. Noting the case of an Indian Pan-Islamist who had abandoned everything to commit himself to the Ottoman caliph only to find himself destitute and without an avenue to support his cause, Dayal wrote, "I have come across several pathetic instances of waste of energy and enthusiasm due to the illusions of Pan-Islamism."[47] Reading the writing on the wall, Dayal's allegiances lay with the nationalist movements. "There is no such thing as Pan-Islamism," he declared.[48] Perhaps he was right.

So why did these Azharites go to India in December 1936? The answer has origins in both Egypt and India. I begin with the Egyptian case: ten years before the Azhari trip to India, Mustafa al-Maraghi was involved in the organization of the Cairo Caliphate Congress. The abolition of the Ottoman caliphate by the new republic of Turkey in 1924 elicited a huge amount of discussion and consternation on the part of the world's Muslims. In the empire's dying days, Muslims around the world, and in India especially, had sought to defend the caliphate's authority—and that of the Ottoman Empire as a whole—in the face of European war. The Khilafat movement in India however, collapsed like its cause. Its leaders and supporters took their talents and passions elsewhere. From this rubble, Muslim leaders across the Middle East and South Asia vied for the title of caliph, while Muslim intellectuals debated the nature and worthiness of the institution in their transformed world. Among those seeking to become the commander of the faithful on Earth was Egypt's King Fuad (the position was also coveted by other Muslim monarchs, like the nizam of Hyderabad). The announcement of the Cairo conference inspired a great deal of interest, as it offered an opportunity to exit the impasse that Muslims had found themselves in. The historian Mona Hassan has demonstrated how Muslim intellectuals, spurred in part by the Cairo conference, "began recording their ideas for the resurrection of the caliphate."[49] From Kabul and Istanbul to Java and Tokyo, Al-Azhar's forthcoming event was assiduously prepared for and highly anticipated.

However, when it became clear—thanks to criticisms first raised by anti-monarchical forces within Egypt—that King Fuad was angling for the position, suspicions grew that the conference was meant to be an occasion for anointing the Egyptian king, not an objective forum. Potential attendees expressed dismay over this state of affairs. The conference was delayed a year and its agenda altered to indicate that the selection of a specific caliph would not take place. When the conference was finally convened in May 1926, attendance was far sparser than initially anticipated. No official delegation was sent from India, for example, a scandalous absence. "Given the conference organizers' initial ambitions," Hassan concludes, "the low attendance and spotty representation of the world's Muslim population was both embarrassing and disappointing."[50] Some ten years later, with the caliphate question still open, the same reformist Shaykh Maraghi was made rector of Al-Azhar (his previous short stint in that position had been cut short in 1929 due to King Fuad's antipathy toward him).[51] Invested in the idea of an Egyptian caliph, Maraghi would play a pivotal role in promoting the newly installed King Farouk as the man for the job. Though not explicitly stated by Maraghi or anyone else involved, speculation swirled—chiefly among the British—that the Azharite delegation to India may have been a part of this ploy to make Farouk leader of the Muslim world.[52]

The immediate and explicitly stated reasons behind the delegation find their source not in the intrigues of the Egyptian state or in the longing for a lost caliphate, but rather in the activities of Bhimrao Ramji Ambedkar. B. R. Ambedkar, as he was known, was one of the most prominent intellectuals in India and one of the most important of the twentieth century. Trained at Columbia and the London School of Economics after being the first Dalit to enter Bombay University, Ambedkar's studies of the colonial economy, published in the early 1920s, included *The Problem of the Rupee* and *The Evolution of Provincial Finance in British India*. In the years that followed, as he became the most prominent leader of the Dalit movement, he published a series of political and historical studies of caste's place in Brahminical thought, past and present, including *The Annihilation of Caste*, *Riddles in Hinduism*, and *Who Were the Shudras?* Moreover, he actively organized the many millions in South Asia facing caste oppression. Ambedkar both articulated a political theory and galvanized a political movement that brought the demands of Dalits—the term he popularized for the various castes deemed "untouchable"—into Indian political debates as never before.

A year before the Azharite's mission, in October 1935, Ambedkar presided over a meeting of representatives of the depressed classes in Yeola in Southwest India. He advised the attendees to convert to any other religion besides Hinduism, specifically, to embrace a faith with an egalitarian structure. "Unfortunately for me," Ambedkar told the assembled, "I was born a Hindu Untouchable. It was beyond my power to prevent that, but I declare that it is within my power to refuse to live under ignoble and humiliating conditions. I solemnly assure you that I will not die a Hindu."[53] Ambedkar's statement caused quite a stir, scandalizing the nationalist Hindu elite and mobilizing

Buddhist, Christian, Sikh, and Muslim leaders eager to bring Dalits into their fold.[54] Some six months later in Bombay, Ambedkar gave another speech, further arguing that attempts to reform Hinduism appeared doomed and conversion was the only option. "The aim of our movement is to achieve freedom, social, economic, and religious for Untouchables. So far as Untouchables are concerned, this freedom can not be achieved except through conversion."[55] Muslims across South Asia sent messages to Ambedkar telling him that Islam was the best option for his constituency, including prominent Muslim leaders like Muhammad Irfan, of the Khilafat Central Committee, and Ahmed Said, head of the Indian Association of Ulema.[56]

Not long after he made them, Ambedkar's pronouncements and the hopes and desires they inspired made their way to the Arab world. In a series of articles in *al-Balagh* in 1936, Hamid al-Melaiji, the paper's bureau chief for the Eastern world, wrote about Ambedkar's statements and the possibility of many millions of Dalits converting to Islam. But interest in the Arab world did not stop there. Muslims, Arab and otherwise, reached out to Al-Azhar itself. In letter after letter, they asked, "What will you do?"[57] Muslims around the world sought Al-Azhar's leadership, as they had ten years earlier in the immediate wake of the Ottoman caliphate's dissolution.

In one of his articles, al-Melaiji quoted from a lecture by Muhammad Zakariyya Manyar (secretary of Bombay's Anjuman Tabligh al-Islam, a Sunni Muslim missionizing organization). Manyar said that the Azharites should not come to India, as the wealthy Hindu community had begun a violent resistance to the Azharitie project, hoping it would fail.[58] Others of course, were more encouraging. Some of the advice Al-Azhar received testifies to the breadth of its networks and the seriousness with which a potential mission from Al-Azhar was taken. Muhammad Iqbal, the prominent Indian poet and philosopher, sent a long letter to the Azhar with practical advice and philosophical reflection. He stated that the biggest challenge they would face was the diversity of languages in the subcontinent's south, all of which, he derisively added, could not express high religious ideas.[59] Among the most important consultants were the itinerant Tunisian intellectual Abd al-Aziz al-Thaʿalabi and the prominent Iraqi cleric Abd al-Karim al-Zanjani.[60] Both were prominent figures in projects of Islamic unity. Zanjani in particular was one of Al-Azhar's chief collaborators in the project of Shia-Sunni rapprochement. Some accounts claim that it was in fact Zanjani who suggested the mission take place and was tasked with organizing its program.[61] Thaʿalabi makes a strikingly similar claim about his own role.[62] The Azharites, however, while mentioning both men, do not credit one or the other as the single source of inspiration or support.

Despite his reservations, Maraghi decided that a mission should indeed be sent to assess the situation in India. It was determined that the delegation would comprise three scholars, a secretary with knowledge of English, and some Indian students already studying at Al-Azhar. The three scholars conscripted to go to India were Ibrahim al-Jibali, Abd al-Wahab al-Najjar, and Muhammed Ahmed al-Bedawi. Jibali was the most prominent of the three and had long evinced an interest in the world beyond Egypt, having been a key supporter of Ma Jian's translation of Confucius's Analects into Arabic in the early 1930s.[63] Muhammad Habib Ahmed, professor of Islamic history at Al-Azhar, was the English secretary. And a fifth individual, Muhammad Salah al-Din al-Najjar, would assist. Al-Najjar had studied engineering in Berlin and was an industrialist and diplomat as well as a professor at Al-Azhar. And he appears to have been less interested in converting Dalits to Islam than in growing his considerable wealth. In India, he hoped to cultivate the necessary relationships that would allow him to export Egyptian cotton to India and import to Egypt Indian cloth and jute.[64] Najjar's presence speaks to some of the ways this mission rests within a regional colonial frame, determined as much by religious solidarity (as in the case of the Islamic Congresses), nationalist collaboration (as in the connections between Arab anti-colonial activists and their Indian counterparts), and finally the flow of capital and labor. These conditions, political, religious, intellectual, and economic, are both global and granular in their significance. On the eve of the delegation's departure, the *Manchester Guardian* reported that the government of India was "believed to have tried to discourage the sending of this mission for fear of religious complications."[65] Al-Azhar, however, had responded by pointing out that countless other religious missions were allowed entry into India, so their delegation should be shown the same courtesy. And so the Azharites set out for India, a correspondent from *Al-Ahram* in tow.

The particulars of the mission are as follows. The Azharite delegation spent one hundred days in India. They inspected fifty educational institutions, including Jamia Millia Islamia, Nadwatul Ulema, and Aligarh Muslim University; they made thirty special visits with prominent figures, including Gandhi, Abul Kalam Azad, Zakir Hussien, and Muhammad Iqbal. Iqbal, they said, was very helpful during their trip, especially in Karachi and Lahore.[66] They gave thirty-two public lectures and a smaller number of private talks; they made it to twelve Friday prayers at ten different mosques, attended Eid prayers in Bombay and Calcutta, and visited twenty historic Islamic sites.[67]

The Nizam of Hyderabad, who had previously offered Ambedkar forty million rupees to convert to Islam, chartered an Imperial Airlines flight for the mission to return to Egypt via Baghdad. Muhammad Salah al-Din al-Najjar, the businessman, stayed behind in Karachi.[68] Shortly before leaving India, the delegation spoke with a journalist from the *Times of India* in Bombay. The group was described as a "goodwill mission," and the article surmised that the Egyptians were "not impressed with the industrial education being imparted in the country."[69] The question of Dalit conversion goes unmentioned throughout the article. Tellingly, given the aforementioned place of India in Pan-Islamic economics, Muhammad Habib

Ahmed defensively detailed Al-Azhar's financial situation to the journalist. "Some people believe," he said, "that we have come to collect funds in India, but the delegation affirms that this visit has nothing to do with securing financial assistance. Let me point out that Al-Azhar University is on a very good financial footing, and its annual expenditure is about Rs. 50,00,00 [sic]. The delegation has been financed with about 27,000, of which Rs. 20,000 was spent." Besides being thrifty, the delegation was well received, according to Ahmed. Indeed, they appeared to have been.

In the months after their return, the Azharitie mission released their findings in a series of articles in the seminary's journal, *Majjalat al-Azhar*, and in the newspaper *al-Balagh*, as well as publishing a more comprehensive account in a stand-alone report printed by Matbaʿit al-Hijaziyya in Cairo. The rhetoric and organization of the report reveal the religious and racial prejudices of the Azharite's Pan-Islamism. In one section, the Azharites discuss Ambedkar himself, whom they refer to as "Lincoln al-Hind," the Lincoln of India.[70] That is to say, the liberator. They write that they heard much about him everywhere they traveled. But they lament the fact that Ambedkar did not convert to Islam himself, a move they appear to have believed was imminent. Indeed, one gets the sense they felt somewhat betrayed, for despite their early praise of his political action, they go on to say that by not converting Ambedkar had let slip the Dalits from the embrace of Islam.[71] The official report includes a number of diagrams and charts delineating the demographic and linguistic makeup of India's Dalits based on the Indian census of 1931. It also includes a section laying out the history of India and Indic thought as it pertains to the making of the Dalits as a caste.[72] This is a decidedly invented history, which rests on notions of Indian life produced in large part by William Jones and his successors. It includes the history of the Aryan invasion and the so-called Laws of Manu, which was the first text Jones translated into English from

Sanskrit in order to return "Hindu"—that is "Indian" law—to the subcontinent.[73] The report also discusses the great waves of conversions on the subcontinent. It states that many Dalits converted to Islam among the other castes and that their status as Dalits became irrelevant once they converted. But before the modern period there was no active proselytization among Dalits, and now that must be remedied, it argues.

In the end, the research mission made only four substantive and relatively modest recommendations regarding Dalit conversion. They called for, first, the establishment of "cultural and information centers" across the subcontinent in Kerela, Surat, Dakka, Rangoon, Lahore, and Nagpur; second, the creation of scholarships for five Dalit converts to Islam in order to study at Al-Azhar; third, the providing of scholarships for twenty Dalit students to study at Nadwatul Ulema in Lucknow; and finally, the providing of money for the existing Tablighi organizations in India.[74]

But the bulk of the report does not actually deal with Dalits, the ostensible reason for the mission. After breaking down some of the particulars regarding who was part of the mission and when it happened, the report begins by noting that Indians saw Egypt as the center of the East's nahda. The report is front-loaded with praise for the researchers' country and institution. Al-Azhar in particular, for the Muslims of India, is the Kabba—that is their metaphor—of the study of Islam.[75] According to the report, the ulema of India believe "that the Egyptian system of education is the finest in the Muslim world, it is organized and ours is in chaos," they said. "We are always in disagreement," the Indian Muslims continued, "because of our many sects." They go on to include pages of testimony from India's most prominent Islamic educational institutions. Many of them spoke of the importance of Islamic unity and again of Al-Azhar's centrality in the Muslim world. Some of them, as in the testimony from the Arabophilic Nadwatul Ulema, spoke of their deep gratitude for the Azharite's travels and their disdain for the sorry state of affairs in India. Indian students, the Azharites also noted, desperately wanted to go to Egypt to study, because, unlike India, it was a place of enlightenment.[76]

After proudly rehearsing the history of India's Muslim conquest by Muhammad bin Qasim and Mahmud of Ghazni, in the pages that follow the Azharites go on to disparage the contemporary Indian Muslim intellectual scene.[77] All the sects in India, the Azharites argue, do not help the other sects and do not help the needy. They go on to state that "if only they were just one sect, they would not be in such a sorry state."[78] In the report, the denigration of Indian Muslims is relentless. One section begins quite bluntly with the sentence, "The Indians are underdeveloped in their learning."[79] They conclude that this sectarianism has prevented Indian Muslims from converting their Hindu compatriots.[80]

Indian reactions to these conclusions were to be expected. While in India, the Azharite contingent were warmly welcomed nearly everywhere they went, so it should come as no surprise that *Ansari*, an Urdu newspaper in Delhi, published an article regarding the Azharite report, "The Limit of Ungratefulness." "The deputation," read the article, "has broken the hearts of Indian Muslims by these base attacks."[81] In *Amrita Bazar Patrika*, the venerable Bengali daily, the sense of betrayal was even more pronounced. They wrote: "India is rather unfortunate in one respect; she receives with open arms every stray visitor or mission or deputation and tries her best to give them a good time; as a reward she is slandered right and left. This is understandable when the visitors concerned are whites but what pains us most is that, in the present instance, Indian Moslems have been attacked by their co-religionists in an Eastern country."[82]

In *Black Skin, White Masks*, Frantz Fanon famously wrote, "The feeling of inferiority of the colonized is the correlative to the European's feeling of superiority."[83] "Let us have the courage to say it outright" Fanon concluded. "It is the racist who creates his inferior."[84] It is prudent to ask, in the shadow of Pan-Islam, how particular forms of Islam are made inferior in the demand for unity. Mustafa al-Maraghi himself had advised the delegation before their departure to inquire about the state of India's Muslims in addition to studying the Dalit situation. He asked them to try, as much as they could, to remove the differences between the sects in order for them to be "mutually supportive brothers, for the cause of Pan-Islam [lil Wahda al-Islamiyya]."[85] He cited a verse from the Qu'ran (21:92) that reads, "This is your umma [community] a united umma and I am your Lord so worship me." These precepts allowed the delegation to mask their arrogance and condescension under the cover of a noble cause. The overwhelming impulse of the Azharites was to make sameness out of difference, to make Muslims out of Dalits, to cleanse Indian Islam of all its heterogeneity—in a sense, to make Indians into Arabs. That is to say, Muslims like them. While the Christian missionaries wanted Arabic without Arabs, the Azharites desired Indian Muslims without those practices or institutions that made them Indian. Their Pan-Islam, so profound within the walls of a Sunni seminary in Cairo eager to link with Shia Arabs, falls apart when stretched to Bombay. Connection, air travel, speed—those characteristics of the twentieth century that would imply access to solidarity, also reveal more readily the deep implications of difference. One can bring two souths together, but can't make them embrace.

3   *Asia*

On the afternoon of February 5, 1947, members of the Egyptian Feminists Union huddled in the bedroom of an ailing Huda Shaarawi, doyen of the Arab women's movement. A few days earlier the group had received an invitation to the Asian Relations Conference, and they were meeting to decide who would be dispatched to represent them. For the women assembled, the prospect of going to India was daunting. It was an unfamiliar place and would require a long journey by air. This scene is recounted in the memoirs of Hawaʾ Idris, a young cousin and mentee of Shaarawi's. Idris summons a familiar trope: Arabs and Indians had long had a close relationship, and now was the time to renew it. The conference, she wrote, was a dream come true. "The pioneers of the nahda," she exclaimed, "could not have imagined such an event would ever be organized."[1]

Although Shaarawi herself was too ill to travel, she had already resolved that the group would send representatives to the conference. A woman by the name of ʿIsmat ʿIssam was the first to volunteer, offering to pay her own way and hoping to inspire another woman to join her. The meeting, however, was quickly derailed. Idris wrote that one participant in the meeting objected to attending the conference altogether. The intentions of the organizers, the unnamed woman said, needed to be interrogated. The women noted that Muhammad Ali Jinnah, the leader of the Muslim League, had just been in Cairo and warned that the conference was being boycotted by Indian Muslims and its organizers were hiding their anti-Muslim prejudices.

A month and a half earlier, Jinnah had indeed stopped in Cairo on his way back from London. While there he met with prominent political figures, including the mufti of Jerusalem Amin al-Husseini and Muslim Brotherhood head Hassan al-Banna. Not everyone in Egypt was enthusiastic about his presence, however. The Wafd Party, long aligned with the Indian National Congress, recounted in its newspaper that Jinnah's "dependence on the British is not agreeable with Egypt's great national principles."[2] Jinnah stoked Pan-Islamic anxieties when he proclaimed that "it is only when Pakistan is established that Indian and Egyptian Muslims will be really free; otherwise, there will be the menace of a Hindu Imperialist Raj spreading its tentacles right across the Middle East."[3] A few days later, *Akhbar al-Youm* reported that Arab participation in the forthcoming Asian Relation Conference would mean "the virtual declaration of an Arab war on the Muslims of India!"[4] Jinnah's outrage had been sparked by Nehru's comments in the Indian Constituent Assembly days earlier that India "has become—let us recognize it—leaders of the freedom movement of Asia, and whatever we do we should think of ourselves in these larger terms."[5] Nevertheless, Idris was not convinced by Jinnah's declarations. She rebuffed the other woman, claiming that press reports were not evidence enough for such claims and that Jinnah himself was an unreliable source. Her opponent was outraged that Idris would challenge such a "great leader."[6] Shaarawi broke up the fight and decided that reliable information must be obtained before moving forward. She enlisted Idris to contact the Foreign Ministry and the Egyptian consulate in Bombay to find out if the conference was actually an anti-Muslim affair, as it had been characterized. The fact-finding mission determined that everything was sound. The Egyptian Feminist Union was heading to India.

. . .

'Abd al-Wahab al-'Azzam had himself long wished to go to India. He had a chance in the summer of 1939, when he was invited to attend a conference of Orientalists in Hyderabad, but the Second World War kept him away. After that lost opportunity, he recounts, his longing for India grew along with his "knowledge of its literature and languages."[7] Earlier in 1939, he had written a series of articles for the inaugural issues of the new Egyptian cultural weekly *al-Thaqafa*, titled "Islamic Literature of India," which introduced the magazine's readers to Mirza Ghalib and Muhammad Iqbal.[8] Indeed, throughout the 1930s he wrote articles about Indian literature generally and Iqbal in particular for *al-Risala*. Azzam was Egypt's premier Persianist and the founder of the Institute for Oriental Studies at Cairo University, where he had earned his doctorate in 1932 after receiving an MA at London's School of Oriental Studies. As part of his doctoral dissertation, Azzam published the first full-length translation into Arabic of Ferdowsi's epic *Shahnameh*.[9] In March 1947, after years of longing and study, Azzam finally had his opportunity to go to India. The roster of Arabs, then, was filling up. With the Egyptian feminists Hawa' Idris and Karima al-Said, Azzam joined two more Egyptians at the Asian Relations Conference, including Mustafa Momin and Mustafa Kamal (the Egyptian consul in Bombay).[10] A sixth Arab was also there, Lebanese politician Taqi al-Din al-Sulh, representing the Arab League.

Arabs therefore shared the stage with Nehru, Sarojini Naidu, and Mohandas Gandhi in 1947, when thousands gathered on the grounds of the Old Fort in Delhi to witness the forging of new Asian relations.

This Asian stage was already being shared by Arab feminists and their Indian counterparts in the years before the Asian relations conference. Arab women activists had participated in Indian Women's Conferences in the 1940s, to powerful effect. And Shaarawi herself was well known and beloved by Indian nationalist leaders and writers. Anti-colonial feminism was one of a number of overlapping and sometimes competing forms of social and political thinking that inspired the 1947 conference's participants. Arab and Indian women's activists regularly analogized their plight over the course of the twentieth century, in the face of a reticent international women's movement headquartered in the West.

Meetings of "Eastern Women," as they were known, took place throughout the first decades of the twentieth century. The days between the two world wars saw London, Paris, Brussels, and Berlin become hosts to many meetings Pan-African, Pan-Asian, and anti-imperialist in sentiment (some of them sponsored by the Comintern). But it was in those years immediately after the Second World War, accompanied as they were by the intensification of anti-colonial demands in the face of weakened, if belligerent, imperial powers in Europe, that postcolonial governments in waiting were finally able to collaborate on their own terms.

In his indispensable, if partisan, history of nonalignment and Afro-Asia, G. H. Jansen, a journalist and onetime press attaché for the Indian embassy in Cairo, recognized the Delhi conference as the beginnings of a new kind of Pan-Asianism. Indeed, he called it the "apex of Asianism." "Never again," he wrote, "would there be such a gushing outflow of the Asian spirit, pure and undefiled."[11] Despite this enthusiasm, however, the meeting seemed also to announce Asianism's limits. The conflict between the congress and the Muslim League revealed the limits of Asia in national affairs. "Thus," announced London's *Economist*, "the first consequence of a gathering theoretically aimed at promoting unity among Asiatics has been to add fuel to the flames of Indian civil strife."[12] Imperial observers were not the only critics. On the second day of the conference, after the fiery inaugural speeches, the great Indian Marxist and internationalist M. N. Roy released a manifesto casting doubt on the whole enterprise, titled "Asia and the World." "Representatives of resurgent Asia! May you deserve the distinction! But the demonstration of fictious solidarity will not be enough," Roy announced at the outset.[13] He was an opponent of the capitalist and undemocratic composition of Nehru's Indian National Congress. Nehru was, in Roy's words, "the pale-pink pseudo-socialist idol of which today poses as the would-be liberator of Asia."[14] Unlike Europe, Roy argued, Asia was not a cultural unit, Japanese imperialism being a case in point. The course of the proceedings themselves revealed the extent of the limits of Asia in world politics. Two controversies in particular soured the mood. First was China's disapproval of Tibet's being invited as an independent delegation, an affair with lasting implications. The second controversy was a flare-up over the question of Palestine, an episode that would place the Arab delegates at the very center.

The Sources of Occlusion

Taking place over ten days from March 23 through April 2 inside Delhi's Purana Qila—Old Fort—the Asian Relations Conference boasted a local audience in the tens of thousands and registered global comment. The presence of the Arab delegates at the meeting, however, has been ignored or explained away. This occlusion begins with the prevailing methodological nationalism of Middle East studies, which has left histories of events like the Delhi conference untold. More significant in this case, however, is that Arabs are reduced to agents of global Muslim sentiment, and Arab sympathy with the Muslim League's boycott of the conference is quickly—and on evidence not stemming from the available Arabic sources—assumed to be a matter of fact. Other interpretations are foreclosed as an assumed Muslim solidarity takes precedence. The goings-on of the conference and evidence contrary to such a narrative have not been closely considered. Reading Arab memoirs and the Arab press alongside the Indian and British archives produces a different picture of the conference than has previously been told.

Most accounts of the conference that mention the Arab dissension base their conclusions on the perspective of the India Office (or the Israeli archives). As evidence of a general Arab boycott, Cemil Aydin cites a letter written (in English) by the Muslim Brotherhood's Hassan al-Banna to Muhammad Ali Jinnah expressing Islamic solidarity and support for the Pakistan project.[15] But no historian has looked at the accounts of Arabs who attended the conference itself, despite the fact that their presence—small as it was—had a decisive impact on the proceedings. G. H. Jansen did not mention the Muslim League's impact on Arab nonattendance but did have an otherwise poor opinion of the Arab role:

> The only rational explanation for the absence of the Arab states is that, having suggested the conference in the first place, they were indignant at receiving their invitations late, so stayed away in a huff. But a less rational explanation is more plausible: they could not be bothered to attend; for Arabs have always been and still are, careless in their international public relations.... Nor did the few Arabs who did attend do much good. The Egyptian delegation was led by a member of the Muslim Brotherhood, which was fanatically anti-Indian, and the solitary observer from the Arab League, who was meant to represent the seven other Arab states, knew no English and so could have understood very little of what was said.[16]

None of the available evidence testifies to a general Arab boycott of the conference. Ironically, Jansen's condescending account may contain at least some truth. The Lebanese foreign minister informed the British consulate in Beirut, in response to their inquiries, that the Lebanese government, in concert with the Syrians, had refused their invitations to the conference "because they did not feel concerned in [sic] a conference composed of unofficial bodies."[17] Other sources of boycott or support, beyond disaffection and Islamic solidarity, have not been acknowledged. The American University of Beirut reportedly declined the invitation on account of its being a foreign institution.[18] Moreover, one Egyptian newspaper mentioned that the Arab League was in fact sending an observer because of Nehru's expressed support for Palestine. Meanwhile, the same paper reported that Syria, Lebanon, and Palestine were refusing to attend on account of the Hebrew University's invitation.[19] This reasoning was also repeated by the Egyptian delegate Mustafa Momin in a press conference he gave while he was India.[20] In these last two accounts, the Muslim League's boycott was not part of the delegations' calculus at all. Indeed, no history of the conference has mentioned the question of Palestine in determining the slim Arab presence, despite the significance Palestine took on in the course of the proceedings.

Nehru and the Indian Council of World Affairs (ICWA) sent invitations to all the Arab states and had a deep interest in Middle Eastern affairs. Throughout the period before and in the years following the conference, *India Quarterly*, the ICWA's flagship journal, published articles on Arab politics. Often the pieces were by prominent Arab intellectuals, like the Palestinian economist Burhan Dajani and the Lebanese historian Edward Atiyah.[21] Despite the Muslim League's boycott and the persistent claims that the Arabs followed suit, there is ample evidence that more Arabs were expected to show up, in particular a delegation from Damascus's Arab Academy. Repeatedly, in the archival record, the conference's preliminary program, and the press, the Syrian poet and diplomat Khalil Mardem Bey is mentioned as being a planned part of the conference. While he did not in fact attend in the end, at least one press report—relying no doubt on the previously circulated program rather than reality—mentions the presence of a delegation from the Arab Academy at the conference.[22] The possibility therefore remains that Mardem Bey's absence was not due to any political calculation, but rather logistical circumstances. A number of delegations were unable to attend or arrived tardily because of challenges with transportation or border regimes. Moreover, besides bureaucratic methods of delay, the British actively sought to dissuade some delegates from traveling to Delhi.[23] As near to the conference date as early March 1947, Mardem Bey was named in the ICWA's materials as one of the few attendees who was producing a special memorandum for the proceedings.[24] In fact, it was described as "among the most interesting papers submitted to the conference."[25] Mardem's "Indian Element in Arab Culture" was later published as an article in the Arab Academy's official journal. "When the Arab hears the name India," Mardem Bey begins his piece, "he thinks of wisdom, craftsmanship, and virtue."[26] He argues that Arabs have such a high opinion of India that they name their daughters "Hind," before giving a fairly bookish account of the Indian impact on Arab literature, music, medicine, and math. The usual touchstones are covered: chess (*shataranj*), Ibn al-Nadim's *Fihrist*, Kalila wa Dimna, al-Biruni, and so on. Contemporary political affairs are not raised. The impression, however, is a sense of admiration and solidarity.

Idris's memoirs, based on her daily diaries but written in the 1970s, shed further light on Indian efforts to court Arab participants in the face of the Muslim League's pronouncements. She recounts, for example, that the well-known Indian historian I. H. Qureshi of Delhi University was dispatched to the Arab states in order to make the case for the conference. Idris also reveals further details about how the Arabs negotiated the boycott call. For example, Azzam was made an unofficial observer rather than a delegate for diplomatic reasons, according to Idris. Egypt, she wrote, was a young nation seeking allies on the international scene. Sending Azzam as an observer was a compromise; neither the Muslims nor India could feel snubbed.[27] During the summer after the conference and in the months that followed, Azzam published his experiences in *al-Risala*, the widely read Egyptian weekly he had long been associated with. Azzam was cognizant of the conference's political volatility, the circumstances of its organization, and the call for a boycott. He wrote that India was eager to bring representatives from Muslim countries given the boycott, and to that end a private plane was dispatched to bring the sultan of Indonesia to the conference.[28] Azzam echoed Idris when he related that the Islamic countries that decided to attend the conference did so after much consideration. They reasoned in the end that Indian Muslims could only benefit from the world's Muslims witnessing their situation. Moreover, Azzam wrote, they decided that the conference was not simply the product of the congress and was intended to be nonpolitical, which was the official line of the ICWA.

In India, Azzam noticed that most of Delhi's Islamic institutions were involved in the conference, although the masses, in his estimation, were sympathetic to the Muslim League and its boycott. The Islamic delegations were invited to a party hosted by Abul Kalam Azad and were apprised of the Muslim contribution to India's freedom struggle. Azzam was nevertheless upset about the circumstances and keen to meet with Jinnah in order to express his feelings and learn firsthand about the league's quarrel with the congress. When he and Taqi al-Din al-Sulh went to do just that one morning, Jinnah immediately asked them if they had read the League's English-language paper, *Dawn*, as they began to apologize. Jinnah "then picked up a copy of the paper and read something about the participation of Islamic countries in the conference and Indian Muslims appreciation and hope that their presence at the conference is positive."[29] Jinnah added that that would be the end of the discussion.

The local press was indeed another arena of Asian relations during the conference. Outside the walls of the Delhi Fort, the Asian delegates were involved in a battle of ideas. A new fragile inter-Asian intellectual and diplomatic culture was being born out of decolonization. India, not yet quite independent, was facing an internal battle. *Dawn* reported daily on supposed Muslim discontent with the conference. Once it quoted a prominent if unnamed Muslim delegate as having realized that his attendance was "a mistake."[30] On another occasion the paper declared simply: "Foreign Muslim Visitors to be Politically Doped."[31] Idris recounts an incident wherein Mostafa Momin, the Egyptian delegate from the Muslim Brotherhood, earned the ire not just of the congress's leadership, but of his fellow Egyptians as well. Walking into the central meeting place one day, Idris was asked by a clearly upset Jawaharlal Nehru if she had seen the day's papers. She had not, so he informed her that the delegate from the Muslim Brotherhood had told the press that he was the head of the Egyptian delegation. Momin had also told the *Times of India* that "Indian Muslims boycotted the conference because they found that it touched on their religious sensibilities."[32] Idris immediately shared the news with the rest of the delegation. Azzam, especially, was outraged. The group drew up a letter stating that Momin's comments were inaccurate and were his alone. All the members, including a reluctant Momin, signed the letter, which was subsequently sent to the press. A diplomatic crisis was seemingly averted.

These events surrounding the conference make it clear that a narrative asserting that there was a general Arab boycott on the basis of Islamic solidarity cannot be easily accepted. However, it is impossible to deny that the Muslim League's call and the politics of the congress—and, of course, an impending partition—hung like a dark cloud over the conference. No doubt Islam and Muslim sentiments impacted the politics of some of the participants. In his meeting with Jinnah, Azzam repeatedly referred to the "Islamic countries." And, he and Mostafa Momin joined two delegates from Indonesia on a trip to Aligarh Muslim University, a hundred miles south of Delhi, in the final days of the conference. Their speeches there revealed the extent to which Islam drove Azzam and Momin's passions. "I go to a Muslim country in the world anywhere I do not feel like a stranger," Azzam said. "I wish and pray to God that this University may attain a unique and signal position in the Muslim world. I cannot help meeting each and every Muslim as one of my own blood."[33] Momin struck a more militant tone: "If you can collect the rays of Islam emanating from Morocco, Egypt, Pakistan, Iraq and Indonesia in the focus of the Quran and the Kalema you can smash not only foreign exploitation but the heathen culture from the Muslim countries all over the world." The Madras-based *Deccan Times* reported that Momin stressed to his Aligarh audience the need to establish "one Muslim Land, united and strong from the Atlantic to the Pacific."[34]

"Islamic country" and "Muslim land" are inadequate phrases. Polemical, perhaps aspirational, they offer very little in terms of explanation. Saudi Arabia, for example, was the very first country—Islamic, Arab, or otherwise—to reject the ICWA's invitation to participate in the Delhi conference, although no reason was given.[35] Yemen also refused the invitation but expressed its regrets. And although no Iraqis were officially in attendance, no fewer than six individuals and organizations sent messages of support, including the foreign minister and the prominent Iraqi intellectual Majid Khadduri, then a professor at Baghdad's Law College.[36] Turkey, on the other hand, sent a single observer, for which the India Office offered this reasoning: "True to Ataturk's policy, the whole trend of which was to identify modern Turkey with the West instead of the East, the Turkish Government only sent an observer to the Asian Relation Conference at Delhi, while expressing good wishes for the success of the meeting."[37] Iran, Indonesia, and Afghanistan, all Muslim or Islamic countries in some sense, were enthusiastic participants in the conference.

Palestine Is Asian

What is perhaps most striking about how the Arab participants in the conference have been written off or their presence overshadowed by the real and imagined specter of Pan-Islam is the impact they had on the event's actual proceedings. In the opening sessions of the conference, each delegation was asked to introduce themselves. Mostafa Momin declared that "liberty has dawned and the world is destined to see another renaissance in Asia."[38] Karima al-Said highlighted the persistence of the British occupation of Egypt, despite nominal independence. When Taqi al-Din al-Sulh took the microphone, he struck a historical note. He delineated, in the briefest terms, the colonial geography that bound South and West Asia: "[The countries of the Arab League] run between the East and the West and have always been known as the door to India. Most of the troubles we suffered from came to us because of this position, and we now share with you your freedom, as your freedom is necessary for our freedom."[39] Sulh ended by noting that "in the heart of these countries is Palestine," which was being taken advantage of by a "special minority under the defence of British bayonets." "We object to that," he continued, "and we hope that you will stand by the side of right with us."[40] His comments took this particular tenor because of who had preceded him at the podium that day: Hugo Bergman, the head of the Jewish Delegation from Palestine.

Some ten participants strong, the Hebrew University contingent outnumbered the Arab presence at the conference. Ironically perhaps, given the events that would follow, the Egyptian delegation and the Jewish delegation from Palestine arrived on the same flight. According to Idris, they both got on board a plane in Lydd, the Egyptians having just arrived there from Cairo. They flew together, to Dhahran and then Karachi, before disembarking finally in Bombay. It was only then that the Egyptians at last realized who they had been traveling with, as the Hebrew University delegation had sat together the entire time and spoke among themselves.[41] The logistics of the whole affair reflected the conference's political contentiousness. Idris relates that the British in Egypt had made visas and flights difficult to acquire, constantly delaying information and permissions on clearly false pretenses.[42] The British no doubt had their reasons, as Chatham House's confidential report on the conference stated that "the Egyptian delegates made more venomous attacks on Britain than anyone attending the conference."[43]

The Jewish delegation's remarks were provocative. Their main speaker was Hugo Bergman, a philosopher at Hebrew University. "Those are the greetings of the representatives of an old religion and an old Asian people which was driven from its Asian motherland 1800 years ago," Bergman introduced himself. He went on to elaborate the superiority of Asian values of religious tolerance to European intolerance, while praising Europe's "logical reasoning [and] methodical thinking." "It is our hope," he continued, "that Palestine, notwithstanding present difficulties, will not go the European way of 'solving' so to speak, problems by dispossessing populations."[44] The Arab delegates were incensed at the Jewish delegation's summoning of Asian feeling. Before Bergman was even finished speaking, Idris dashed off a note and had it sent up to Nehru. She demanded the Arabs have an opportunity to respond.[45]

Nehru repeated his wish that the conference steer clear of controversial matters; "nevertheless," he went on "if this conference enters into these questions, we will get involved in them."[46] He invited Said to speak. "I would like to place before you the views of the Arab women," Said began her retort. "We strongly object to any settlement in Palestine except for the Arabs," she continued: "The gentleman himself said that the Jews have been in Europe for the last eighteen centuries. I tell you that the Arabs have been in Palestine for the last fourteen centuries. . . . We have had no trouble with the

Jews at all. They have been welcome; they have been our friends; they have settled very happily among us; but we do not want British rule to be replaced by that of European Zionists. We object to them as foreigners. The Arabs must live in Palestine. Palestine cannot belong any more to its original inhabitants."[47]

Nehru refused Bergman's request to speak after Said finished, leading Bergman and the rest of the delegation to storm out of the meeting hall. Idris recalls that an Indian delegate followed them out and was able to cajole them back. Upon his return, Bergman shook the hand of Taqi al-Din al-Sulh, the Arab League's representative. Idris remarks that Bergman's handshake was clearly a performance, one, however, that had no effect on the Asians assembled.[48] In any case, Chatham House reported that the Jewish Delegation "received a rather cool reception."[49] Jansen wrote that the event "must have been one of the last occasions on which Zionist and Arab leaders experienced that minimal degree of physical contact."[50] Nehru, however, had the last word that day, announcing at the end of the plenary session that "the people of India ... have always said that Palestine is essentially an Arab country and no decision can be made without the consent of the Arabs."[51] He was echoing—almost to the word—remarks he had made scarcely a week before in the pages of the *Bombay Sentinel*.[52] In both cases, he attributed support for Palestine not to himself, but to the Indian people more generally. A typical move, perhaps, of the patriarchal and pedagogical mode of nationalism that Nehru was known for, but significant nevertheless, for the Muslim League actively sought to couch the Palestine question in communal terms.

The confrontation between the Arab delegates and the Jewish delegation was a rare sour moment in a conference better characterized by carefully choreographed consensus. It was, however, predictable, even by the organizers themselves, who had planned for a celebration of Asian unity. In one of the Indian Council of World Affairs's booklets for the meeting, "Racial Problems," the author, one T. K. Venkatram offered a particularly pessimistic assessment of Palestine's colonization: "Palestine presents a peculiar problem. It presents an ominous resemblance to [the] Indian problem in that the two elements of the population who have got to live in the country show a complete lack of any spirit of accommodation and refuse to agree about the form of the future constitution. It is difficult to say whether the Inter-Asian Conference could offer a just solution harmonising the interest of the Arabs or the Jews, or whether the Mandatory power will accept any proposal emanating from the Conference."[53]

While the booklet's characterization of the situation is not wholly accurate—Palestinians had been working for two decades to accommodate the British-backed colonization of their land—the author's comparative gesture is one that would be raised repeatedly by Indians and Arabs in their meetings together and writing about each other. In his own postscript to the conference, Kalidas Nag, a Pan-Asianist intellectual from Bengal and one of the chief theorists of the "Greater India" idea, made the comparison in surgical terms. He wrote in *New Asia*: "As in the case of India, some expert political surgeons have prescribed the remedy of cutting-up the country into two! The patients, of course, have no right of appeal or of protest; and so they must submit to lie on the operation table, with or without anesthesia. Thus within a couple of months from the termination of the first Asian Relations Conference, major operation[s] are being performed on the body-politic of the many oriental nations still under Western masters and caretakers."[54]

Nag's assessment is significant, as he knew Hugo Bergman personally, having visited Jerusalem and admired the academic work of the Hebrew University, especially the Indology of Immanual Olsavaanger. "It was, therefore, a matter of real joy to me," Nag wrote, "when I had the privilege of welcoming in Delhi the Jewish delegation."[55] Nevertheless, despite his sympathies with Bergman and the "Wandering Jews" in general, Nag's comments are supportive of the Arab position. He again compares Palestine to India when he calls on the Indian press to pay greater attention to the situation: "The whole country of Palestine is convulsed today, like India, with problems of partition or chaos."[56] Nag's book was published on August 15, the very day the partition of South Asia commenced.

. . .

Even among the Arab delegates and observers, the confrontation with the Jewish delegation had elicited some anxiety. Hawa' Idris writes that in the wake of Karima al-Said's speech, the ever-diplomatic Abd al-Wahhab al-Azzam admonished her for causing such a political stir. He told her that she had embarrassed Nehru and caused a rift between India and Egypt. Idris, however, was unfazed by Azzam's condescension; she told him: "If we did not defend Palestine, then the assembled would think that the Arabs have given up on Palestine.... I understand you [Azzam] are tied to the government and politics and cannot say certain things, but I am not, and the group that sent me here expects me to relay these facts."[57] A perturbed Azzam did not respond. In his own account of the conference, however, he reflected on the episode somewhat differently, unabashedly praising the activism of the delegation: "We worked to ensure that the conference delegates were aware that the Jewish delegation did not represent Palestine."[58]

As with the question of India's Muslims, the debate over Palestine continued in the Indian press after the conference had concluded. Azzam recounts that the Jewish delegation, in the wake of Karima al-Said's rebuke at the conference, published their case in a series of articles in India's English-language papers. Along with Taqi al-Din al-Sulh, Azzam wrote a response to the articles, rebutting them point by point. Among the claims criticized, Azzam recounts, was that the Jewish settlers had done much to develop the country, bringing industry and factories to Palestine. Azzam makes clear that they had indeed established some industries, but only for themselves, not for the Arab inhabitants. The article ends by rejecting the assertion on the part of the delegation that they simply seek peace. "We know what peace is," the Arabs responded, "an end to Jewish immigration and coexistence among those Jews already in Palestine and the Arabs together, democratically, as is now the global norm. Will the Jews accept this peace?"[59]

Although one contemporary press report speculated that "the incident would be forgotten," the events in Delhi had lasting implications.[60] As P. R. Kumaraswamy wrote in *India's Israel Policy*, "the New Delhi meeting was the first and last occasion when a delegation from the yishuv/Israel was invited to such a political gathering."[61] In 1947, an independent India voted against the partition of Palestine at the United Nations. A year later, it also voted against Israel's admission to the international body because, in the words of its ambassador at the time, India "could not recognize a state which had been achieved through the use of force and not through negotiations."[62] In 1955, when Israel was desperate to attend Bandung, it was blocked. Israel, at least for the time being, was excluded from Asia.

Palestine Is Feminist

Palestine, in part because of Nehru and Gandhi's loud and sensitive statements against its colonization, was a major concern of Indo-Arab collaboration, both before and after the Delhi conference.[63] Nowhere is this better illustrated than in the Arab women's movement's unique relationship with India and perennial commitment to the Palestinian cause. Karima al-Said and Hawa' Idris's involvements in the Delhi conference are a clue to this long entanglement. Women's conferences were held throughout the first half of the twentieth century across Asia, serving as less remarked upon preludes to the Asian Relations Conference.[64] In 1945, two years before her sister Karima set off for Delhi, Amina al-Said herself traveled to India. That year, the All India Women's Conference was holding its annual session in Hyderabad (Sind). Amina was one of the few international delegates, along with the four from Syria and Lebanon, invited to join the proceedings. Amina al-Said's presence was significant. As in Delhi in 1947, the question of Palestine—and the pressing question of partition generally—was not ignored.

Despite the ostensibly Indian focus of the event, matters of international politics were raised from the outset. A fervent, even exasperated, anti-colonialism can be felt throughout the proceedings, which were taking place shortly after the end of the Second World War. In her presidential address, the Indian intellectual and activist Hansa Mehta greeted her Western visitors: "I would like to tell them that we are not happy over what is happening in the East and the Far East."[65] She railed against the persistence of empire and the trials against the Indian National Army by the British. Nestled among the litany of domestic social and political demands raised by the conference, from housing, to food, to civil liberties, were two resolutions that spoke to a larger geography. At one edge of Asia, Indonesia, in the wake of the world war, was having its national aspirations crushed with the help of Indian colonial troops. At the other edge, on the Mediterranean shore, was Palestine.

In her speech, Said relayed the Egyptian Feminist Union's (EFU's) intersecting projects: "the cause of women and the cause of Palestine."[66] Her invocation is unsurprising, as the struggle for Palestine and the proliferation of the Arab women's movement had long been entangled. Indeed, the historian Margot Badran contends that the "pan-Arab feminist movement had roots in the Palestinian national struggle."[67] In 1936, in the midst of the rebellion in Palestine, the Arab Women's Committee there contacted Huda Shaarawi. In the face of repression on the part of a brutal British counterinsurgency that imprisoned or sent into exile their leaders, the committee called on Shaarawi for help. The EFU swiftly brought together an Eastern Women's Conference on that matter, and Shaarawi took the Palestinians' demands—chief among them the end of Jewish immigration to Palestine—to the world stage. Western audiences were not forthcoming with support. However sympathetic they may have been to Shaarawi and Arab women in the past, and even though she was a global celebrity, and her sisters were in need of "saving," the question of Palestine was not welcomed at international fora located in the West. Remarking on the 1939 International Women's Congress in Copenhagen, Saiza Nabrawi, a prominent member of the EFU, had this to say: "The congress, far from representing global views of women, was too often the echo of the political or racial preoccupations of the so-called democratic states and Zionist groups."[68] Indeed, since the early 1920s, when Shaarawi began to raise her concerns over the persistence of Britain's occupation of Egypt and the Zionist colonization of Palestine at international women's meetings, she faced resistance from Western activists. Indeed, the attacks on her were predictable and familiar to anyone acquainted with the colonial lexicon. In 1935, for example, the prominent British suffragist Margery Corbett Ashby wrote that Shaarawi was "terrifically nationalist and tyrannical."[69]

In the East, however, Palestine found ample support. In *Mushahadat fi al-Hind*, Said's account of her trip to India published a few months after the conference, she recalls that she had not been aware of the conference's significance until she arrived in Karachi and realized the coverage the event was receiving. Reading the program, she was impressed by Indian women's courage in raising urgent political questions. Emboldened, she resolved to focus her remarks at the conference on Palestine.[70] In her speech to the assembled, Said analogized the situation in Palestine to that of women's rights: "Palestine too, is a case of confiscated right which should be restored at once."[71] And in her closing remarks, Said anticipated the Asian Relations Conference when she said, "I appeal to all the people of India to stand beside the Palestinians and to defend them against their usurpers.... I also deliver to you their great hope of you and us working together in an Oriental Federation that would work for the great cause all over the East."[72] In her travelogue, Said notes that support for Palestine was not initially forthcoming. The communal political situation in the country had, from her vantage point, relegated Palestine to a Muslim issue. The conference, however, was mostly Hindus, as most Muslims boycotted the organization based on its closeness with the Indian National Congress. Hindus in India, Said argued, would not support causes seen as Muslim and vice versa. Whether Said's reading of the conference is accurate or not is unclear, as the Indian National Congress had been supportive of the Arab cause in Palestine since at least 1936.[73] Nevertheless, it is likely that a determined Said did in fact bring up the Arab viewpoint repeatedly in formal and informal gatherings at the conference as she claims, for her impact was clearly felt. Based on the proceedings, no other delegate received the kind of salutations that she did. The proceedings relate that Said's "striking and passionate patriotism evoked warm sympathy from the large assemblage."[74] Said wrote that her strategy first and foremost was making clear to the Hindu attendees that Palestine was not a Muslim question in the least. "I explained to the Hindu women," she recounts, "that the Palestine problem is a political problem not a religious one, and that anyone interested in justice must support it, anyone interested in the freedom of small countries."[75] Striking and passionate her explanations must have been, for Indian speeches in support for Palestine were enthusiastic.

On the third day of the conference, Kamaladevi Chattopadhyay, an outspoken internationalist and member of the Congress's socialist wing who would later visit the Middle East in 1949, introduced the resolution on Palestine.[76] It announced that "this Conference stands for peace and is against the imposition by force of the will of the strong nations on the weak," and demanded that the Balfour Declaration be immediately rescinded.[77] After the resolution was put forward, Chattopadhyay added: "Americans and Britishers want that [sic] Palestine should be split up into two divisions—one Jewish land and the other Arab land. We know in India what sort of harmful policy it is.... The very difficulties that are facing Palestine are facing India also."[78] The speeches in support of the resolution continued along these lines, comparing the Indian and Arab conditions. "It is because of our personal experience," Rameshwari Nehru said, "that our sympathy is so deep and we are so ready to raise our voice in their favour."[79] The resolution was passed unanimously.

As postcolonial nation-states instituted new boundaries on and scripts for international collaboration and state feminisms abandoned particular goals in order to celebrate others, certain struggles, like those of sexual, religious, or ethnic minorities, were deferred for the good of the nation.[80] The candor of the feminists present in Hyderabad in 1945, or even in Delhi in 1947, could not be easily replicated. A hunger strike at Cairo's Indian Embassy in 1957 reveals the antagonisms obscured by both nationalism and internationalism in the process of decolonization. Doria Shafik, a prominent feminist activist and journalist who had earned her doctorate from the Sorbonne in 1940 and founded the popular women's magazine *Bint al-Nil*, was the protagonist. Following the international reception she received from her first hunger strike against the formation of an all-male constitutional committee by Egypt's revolutionary government in March 1954, she embarked on a world tour. In December of that year she arrived in India, where she was met by Jawaharlal Nehru.[81] Shafik was enthralled with the Indian freedom struggle. It was Gandhi's hunger strike that inspired hers. She wrote in her memoirs how she felt upon arriving in India, "the land of Gandhi!

My master! Satyagraha, power of truth, non-violence! I approached this land with the respect one feels only toward sacred places."[82] On February 6, 1957, Shafik entered the Indian embassy with a copy of the Quran, a biography of Gandhi, and a volume of the French surrealist poet Pierre Reverdy.[83] Ensconced in the premises of what she called "a neutral country," Shafik issued a declaration announcing that she would "hunger unto death" for her "external and internal freedom." "As an Egyptian and as an Arab," she wrote in the declaration circulated to the local and international press, "I demand that the international authorities compel the Israeli forces to withdraw immediately from Egyptian lands and reach a just and final solution to the problem of the Arab refugees. Second I demand that the Egyptian authorities give back total freedom to Egyptians, whether male or female."[84] Again, Arab feminist commitment to Palestine, beyond the bloviating of the Arab states' leaders, is laid bare. Shafik places the question of Palestine before that of her own freedom in Egypt. However, as with her previous hunger strike, responses were not all enthusiastic. Shafik's biographer Cynthia Nelson details how some Egyptian feminists opposed her actions and publicly criticized her, for reasons of unity and sobriety.[85] Under threat of arrest, Nehru convinced Nasser to allow Shafik to return without consequences back to her home. Feminism was eclipsed by the demands of other solidarities, not for the first or last time.

After Asia

Between July 28 and September 8, 1947, no installments of al-Azzam's Asian Relations Conference reports were published in *al-Risala*. This despite the fact they were previously published on a weekly basis. Between the late July dispatch and that of early September was a date marked in blood and borders, August 15. In the post-partition installment, Azzam abandons the conference's intrigues and turns to the history of Delhi, a city long familiar to him through Persian literature. After describing the city's latitudinal and longitudinal coordinates, its climate in relation to Cairo, and its place in the geography of South Asia, Azzam notes the strangeness of Delhi's present political boundaries: its separation from Punjab by the new state of Pakistan. Delhi's place in the history of Islamic culture, Azzam argues, cannot be overstated. He notes, perhaps ironically, that a number of important cities in the history of Islam in South Asia are not located in Pakistan, including Lucknow, Agra, and Ahmedabad.[86]

Before leaving India, Azzam went to Lahore to deliver a message at the grave of Muhammad Iqbal, the man whom he had spent years translating into Arabic and introducing to Arab audiences. At Lahore's Forman Christian College, Azzam lectured on Egyptian-Indian relations. Along with Ali Ashghar Hekmat from the Iranian delegation, he also visited Iqbal's home and spent hours speaking with his son Javed. Finally they both visited Iqbal's tomb on the grounds of the seventeenth-century Badshahi Mosque. "Iqbal poet of Islam ... poet of the East ... poet of life ... of self!" Azzam exclaimed in a reverent speech.[87] He then placed flowers and a marble plaque, which he had had inscribed in Delhi with a poem for his beloved Iqbal:

An Arab brings flowers to your garden, where he is proud and honored to be
These words contain every meaning from the lands of Islam
For these words are in the language of the Qur'an, they contain the scent of revelation and impossibility
Accept from me these words despite my low stature
for they are along the lines of armakan al-Hijaz.[88]

The final line, with the Persian word *armaghan* rendered into Arabic, references Iqbal's final book of poetry, *Armaghan-i-Hijaz* (The gift from Hijaz), published in 1938. The gift of course was Islam.

Here it contains a double meaning, for Azzam's familial roots were in the Hijaz as well. The indelibly Islamic is also therefore deeply personal for Azzam. In the years to follow he would have further opportunities to reflect on his Iqbal, for he was appointed the Egyptian ambassador to Pakistan in 1950. In 1954 Azzam published a full-length biography and study of Iqbal in Cairo, with an introduction by Taha Hussein. That same year, he took his considerable talents to the Hijaz itself, becoming the Egyptian ambassador there. In 1957 he founded and headed Riyadh University, later King Saud University, the first such institution in that kingdom. Azzam's movement away from Egypt and India and toward Saudi Arabia and Pakistan reflects one route of Indo-Arab collaboration, resting on Islam's ample foundations.

Azzam's movement speaks to a more general shift away from Asia and toward Islamic political geography over the course of the Cold War. Two conferences from the 1960s mark this profound transformation. The first is basically forgotten, so much so that one recent academic article bafflingly contends that the event did not even take place.[89] The African-Asian Islamic Conference convened in Bandung in 1965, a decade after the African Asian Conference of 1955 and only about a year before Sukarno would be deposed in a series of the political events that culminated in the US-backed murder of some one million Indonesians, mostly communists and other progressives. This meeting represents, in the Indonesian case, perhaps one of final opportunities in which Islam was summoned in a progressive, internationalist idiom. Islam being, as the drafters of the conference's final declaration put it, "the religion of peace and progress," the attendees made the following recommendations: "The African-Asian Islamic Conference condemns imperialism, colonialism and neo-colonialism in all its forms and manifestations, political, military, economic, cultural and moral, because colonialism creates dissensions among mankind and has robbed many Muslim peoples of their natural rights." They also declared themselves, in the manner of the Non-Aligned Movement in general, in opposition to nuclear weapons. They called too for economic cooperation, in much the same manner as the meetings on economics convened at Delhi in 1947, including the development of a common market against the "economic bloc established by the colonialist and neo-colonialist forces." Other resolutions of the declaration called for the establishment of an institute for Islamic research and "as enjoined by Islam" considered it necessary to improve the standard of living of the Muslim workers and peasants.[90]

The language is not entirely novel; to some extent it simply adds *Islam* and *Islamic* to those statements that had been produced time and again in the meetings that followed the first conference at Bandung, only this time the Quran and Sunna are cited as fundamental sources of inspiration. Comparing Sukarno's opening speech from 1955 to his 1965 speech, however, reveals the challenges that lay beneath the rhetoric of anti-imperialism. Sukarno's revolutionary exuberance had turned defensive, for good reason, as the events of 1966 attest all too well. Most of Sukarno's extemporaneous, English remarks focus not so much on the Afro-Asian and the international, but on the Indonesian and the national. Sukarno repeatedly mentions the complexity of the Indonesian revolution, given the size and diversity of the archipelago nation. Only in the end do the affairs of the other thirty-some countries assembled enter into his remarks: "All of you, my dear Brothers and Sisters, we all have come here, what for? We have come here of course to make Islam in our countries prosper, to make Islam in our countries blossom, to make our countries a fertile country for Islam."[91] Sukarno injects Islam into the Bandung spirit, as it was known: "Freedom, free air for Islam cannot be given by imperialism. We cannot beg the imperialists: 'Please give us free air for our Islam, please make our country free for Islam'. We cannot beg, we cannot ask, we can only rely on our own strength and struggle."[92] Afro-Asia, it still seemed in that final hour, could be made in the image of Islam. Turbaned ulema marching down Bandung's streets below banners proclaiming "We Destroy Capitalism and Build Up Socialism" is an image strikingly different from the forms of Islamic cooperation that were to come.

Only a few years later, at the opposite end of the Islamic world on Morocco's Atlantic coast, a meeting in Rabat heralded Asia's political retreat. In response to the dramatic attempt by an Australian man to burn down the Al-Aqsa Mosque in Jerusalem a month earlier, a meeting of Islamic nations was convened in Morocco at the end of September 1969. The diplomatic history of this event is interesting in and of itself. The Indian delegation, including the prominent Islamicist Abdul Aleem, were excluded from the meeting.[93] Despite the fact they had been unanimously invited to attend, some delegates were locked out of the meeting hall.[94] But the content of the Organization of the Islamic Conference's (OIC's) declaration at that first meeting and the group's subsequent charter are even more revealing. Just four years after the Islamic Bandung, the language of Islam on the international stage had been transformed. Given the impetus of the event, it is not surprising that its primary concern was the question of Palestine in general and of Jerusalem in particular, which the declaration stated should be returned to its pre-1967 status. The OIC's principal appeal in its declaration, however, is not to the colonized, or even the Muslims in whose name the organization sought to speak, but rather the governments of France, the Soviet Union, the United Kingdom, and the United States, "the great powers which have a special responsibility to maintain international peace."[95] This is quite a remarkable departure, and a familiar one today. Alongside "great powers" the declaration mentions that amorphous "international community." Places like Africa and Asia—visions like Afro-Asia—and phrases like colonialism and imperialism are missing entirely from the 1969 declaration and the OIC's charter of 1972. While Sukarno's 1966 remarks departed rhetorically from his speech in 1955, his targets remained the same. The OIC, however, removed the target altogether, preferring to beg, as Sukarno warned was impossible.

At the end of his *The Politics of Pan-Islam*, the Israeli political scientist Jacob Landau reflected on the creation of the OIC: "The Anti-Israel stand and the desire to regain Palestine and Jerusalem for Islam were, indeed, the only constant factors agreed upon in the organization ... to paraphrase Voltaire, had Israel not existed someone would have to invent it—to cement the bonds of Islamic solidarity."[96] Of course, Palestine was a constant presence in the meetings of Muslims, as indeed it was at every conference of the Non-Aligned and the Afro-Asian countries (formations with a considerable number of Muslims therein), not because of some essential attachment, but because Palestine represented a fundamental aberration in the history of twentieth-century decolonization. If one looks at the proceedings of such conferences, the names of various nations involved in struggles for freedom come and go, as their political decolonization is gained, while the demand for Palestine remains. Landau's remarks represent a profound misreading of this history of solidarity. Palestine's transformation into an "Islamic" cause—championed by the pliant regimes of the Baghdad Pact and those monarchs patronized by the late British Empire—was a response to efforts to reorder the world initiated in the crucible of revolutions for national liberation and consecrated in meetings like Delhi's in 1947. The anti-colonial struggle of the Palestinians was conceived as such, unevenly to be sure, because it was structurally and historically linked to colonialism and anti-colonialism elsewhere.

4   *Nonalignment*

At the first Seminar on India and the Arab World in April 1965, the Palestinian historian Ahmad Mustafa Abu Hakima recalled: "When I was in the U.K. unfolding the papers of the East India Company at the India Office Library, London, my Indian friends and research scholars working on various subjects there were not astonished to see an Arab research student working on papers considered their personal historical property; but the English put questions such as: Have you come to write your History in London from English records? What relations could be revealed from Indian English sources? Of course, I did not blame them because Indo-Arab relations were not seen in the light this meeting sees them."[1] It was in the very moment of building the modern Indo-Arab world at the middle of the twentieth century that the first histories of such entanglements were narrated. To do so, however, the archive needed to be approached obliquely. Abu Hakima, whose research in the India Office records would yield a number of volumes on the modern history of Kuwait and Eastern Arabia, was then a professor of Arab history at the University of Jordan. He was one of some fifteen Arab participants in the conference hailing from Lebanon, Syria, Egypt, Algeria, Sudan, Tunisia, and the Arab embassies of Delhi. The meeting took place at the headquarters of the ICCR. Abu Hakima's comments on the archive of Indo-Arab relations speak to the general tenor of much of the conference, whose Indian and Arab participants repeatedly lamented the disappearance of their entanglements from the historical record. The intellectuals who labored in the wake of that profound geographical transformation adopted among their tasks the project of rewriting their past, in defiance of colonial historiography and its archival logic.

In the preface to the published proceedings of the conference, the 1947 Asian Relations Conference and the Asian History Congress of 1961 were named as forerunners to the seminar. The conference consisted of six sessions total, and each was followed by long discussions. Many of the participants, like Abu Hakima, shared personal anecdotes, some going as far back as their childhoods, to emphasize the depth of the relationship between Indian and Arab cultures. This conference represented a rich and important moment of Indians and Arabs thinking together. The ICCR was a regular and important site of these encounters. Its founder was independent India's first minister of education, the great anti-colonial writer and thinker Abul Kalam Azad, who was himself born in Mecca to an Arab mother and Indian father. In 1950, the same year the ICCR was established, they began publishing an Arabic language journal, *Thaqafat al-Hind*, which is still published to this day. Although the council always set its sights on world outreach, the Middle East dominated its efforts from the start. "In order to make a beginning and also to ensure that the initial efforts were not dissipated," Azad reflected in a speech shortly before his death, "we decided that we would divide the work of the council into different regions. We started with the division for Middle East, Turkey, and Egypt."[2] Azad reflected on the communal violence of the 1947 partition and its effects on world perceptions of India, especially among Arabs and Muslims. He elaborated: "I have to say with regret that the newly created State of Pakistan gave only one side of the story and started a propaganda campaign against

India. One result of this was that an impression was created that India was partitioned on a communal basis and India now meant a solely Hindu country. They came to believe that even if a few Muslims remained in India, they had no religious or civic freedom."[3] To prove his point, Azad recounted the story of India's first ambassador to Egypt, the Bengali Muslim Syed Husain. Upon his arrival in Cairo, Husain announced that he was the Indian ambassador, but the Egyptians insisted he was the Pakistani ambassador, given that he was a Muslim, a fact that was subsequently relayed widely in the press until corrected the next day with the Indian embassy's intervention.[4] "I am however glad to inform you that soon after the establishment of the Indian Council for Cultural Relations, the situation dramatically changed," Azad claimed, "the articles published in this journal had an electric effect on the people of the Muslim world."[5]

Although West and South Asia have for centuries been linked by networks of trade, knowledge, and kinship—the anti-colonial links of the first half of the twentieth century would be fresh in the memories of those living at the dawn of its second half—Arab and South Asian perceptions of each other remained piecemeal and pockmarked. "At the time," K. M. Panikkar recalled, "India and Egypt were not as friendly as today."[6] Panikkar arrived in Cairo in 1952. It would take a few crucial years of Egyptian, Indian, and global transformation for India's stature in Arab minds to transform apace. Only after the 1956 invasion of Egypt by Israel, Britain, and France, when India vocally came to Egypt's defense, did Arab ideas of India decisively advance. In a short but perceptive article, Mona Abaza registered this shift in the work of the travel writer Hussein Fawzi, who wrote his travel books under the moniker Sindibad. Abaza noted that Fawzi's 1938 travelogue to India was replete with stereotypes about Indians and Orientalist imagery. Some forty years later, when Fawzi returned to India and penned a new travelogue, such attitudes had disappeared and been replaced by effusive statements of fraternal feeling, appreciation, and awe. Fawzi in fact apologized for his previous, youthful digressions.[7] The transformation of Arab attitudes about India was made under the moon of nonalignment. New sites of Indian and Arab interaction would be inexorably tied to older histories of connection. They also relied crucially on the efforts of people imagining a radically different world than the imperial wreckage they had been reluctantly bequeathed.

Arabs, Afro-Asia, and Nonalignment

It is not uncommon to find references to Arabs as progenitors of Afro-Asianism and as predisposed to nonalignment in both scholarly or journalistic accounts and some of their own self-representations. The first idea stems from the role of the Arab League in the development of the Arab Group at the first sessions of the United Nations, where the question of Palestine's partition was an important site of contention. Even at the very first meeting of the United Nations in San Francisco in 1945—when European imperialism in Asia had not yet begun its retreat—Arab states constituted five of the seven Asian countries in attendance. The Arab-Asian Group was initiated shortly thereafter in the midst of efforts at the UN to stop war in Korea. The word *nonalignment* emerged from this war.[8] Individuals wove their own stories of Afro-Asia's rise. In tracing the roots of the 1955 Bandung conference in his memoirs, the Iraqi politician Muhammad Fadl Al-Jamali recounts the scene in a cafe in Queens, New York, at a lunch arranged by India's first ambassador to the United States, Asaf Ali: "At that luncheon the foundation stone of the Asian African group was laid, and contact between the Asian and African members became a regular practice in dealing with any problem brought before the United Nations that affected the Asian and African members."[9]

Studies have also shown that Arab nonalignment has its beginnings in the pre–Cold War era.[10] Certainly by 1946 some kind of neutralism, in this case a refusal to align with one or another major power, flourished. In a speech at the American University of Cairo on January 4, 1946, Abd Al-Rahman Azzam, first secretary of the Arab League, made his stance clear: "If we are presented with a choice between two evils—extremist capitalism or the escape into Communism—we have to say that our message endorses neither the one nor the other. Whilst the former ensures the happiness of one class, the second comes along to chop off its head, but in time will engender the opposite of what is sought. We refuse to accept either Anglo-American capitalism or Russian communism."[11] Given this early legacy, it is surprising then that the vitality of Arab thought was sidestepped in the decision to take Nasser as the prime representative of Arab neutralism.[12]

Consider, for example, Mehdi Ben Barka, chief theorist of the tricontinental, who was disappeared before he could arrive at the 1966 conference in Havana.[13] Or take the Algerian philosopher Malek Bennabi, whose reflections on Bandung, *L'Afro-Asiatisme*, written in Cairo in 1956, are perhaps the most well-known Arab pronouncements on the subject besides Nasser's. Bennabi's key insight was that the anti-colonialism raised by the meetings of Africans and Asians was not in and of itself a sufficient program for the future: "Anti-colonialism is only a reaction which will disappear along with the colonialism which gave it birth." "Moreover," he concluded, "Afro-Asian culture cannot find inspiration in a simple anti-colonialism destined itself to disappear."[14] Reference to nonalignment and India's example (personified by Gandhi and Nehru) has been a key part of the Arab nationalist repertoire. Recall, for example, that Kamal Jumblatt was famously an Indophile, devoting considerable time and energy to both the study of yoga and the elaboration of Arab neutrality. For Arab intellectuals in the twentieth century, India represented both an exemplary anti-colonial space and a romantic, Oriental ideal.

An indispensable guide to the study of nonalignment worldwide remains the Palestinian philosopher Fayez Sayegh's sophisticated typology of neutralism and its associated tendencies. First published in 1964, Sayegh's essay identifies a point that other Arab thinkers would regularly raise themselves in their turns to nonalignment:

> In the case of the neutralist countries of Asia, Africa, and the Arab World, the adoption of neutralism associated, or immediately followed, emancipation from Western domination, colonial or otherwise. Opposition to their pursuit of neutralist policies, like the suppression of their struggle for national liberation, invariably came from the West. It was not the Soviet Union, but some Western powers, that exercised hegemony over the lands of Asia and Africa until very recently; and it was the Western bloc, not the Eastern bloc, that sought to obstruct or punish the espousal of neutralism by Afro-Asian countries after their independence. These facts must be borne in mind when one seeks to identify the causes, or to interpret the meaning and import of the anti-Western feelings which have manifested themselves with greater or lesser intensity in various regions of Asia and Africa."[15]

Nonalignment, Sayegh makes clear, represented an anti-imperialist position. Indeed, it represented an internationalist front against imperialism. While it cannot be denied that neutralism and nonalignment—but not Afro-Asianism—often manifested themselves in anti-communist guise, whether regarding the Soviet Union or local communist parties, nonalignment and Afro-Asianism emerged fundamentally from particular conditions of global inequality. In fact, Samir Amin insisted that historians look beyond photogenic leaders to the Third World's communist parties themselves, which recognized that imperialism was central to the immiseration of African and Asian toilers. In a later essay, Amin raised this point elegantly:

"This history should be written as it will help people to understand that Bandung did not originate in the heads of the nationalist leaders (Nehru and Sukarno particularly, rather less, Nasser) as is implied by contemporary writers. It was a product of a radical leftwing critique which was at that time conducted within the communist parties."[16] Even noncommunist anti-imperialists, like K. M. Panikkar, recognized the seismic shift that communism engendered and the possibilities it revealed for Asians. "The proletarian state is ... one of the major characteristics of the 20th century, in Asia especially its influence is great," Panikkar announced at the inauguration of the Indian School of International Studies in October 1955. "It is not the influence of communism," he continued, "for the Asian states, which admire the achievements of the Soviet Union, make a clear distinction between the political structure of the Communist state, and its social, economic and scientific programme. This is the reason for the other characteristic of the 20th century—Asian 'neutralism' in the rivalry between the two worlds."[17] In their efforts toward decolonization, the Arab states hardly represented the left wing of a global project. Edward Said indicted Arab leaders of all stripes for their attachment to retrograde or foreign ideas, insufficiently linked to the social and cultural realities of the contemporary situation, in his 1979 book *The Question of Palestine*. "In this way," he wrote, "the Arab Middle East remained a middle place, at a kind of equidistance from the overall bourgeois stability of the Atlantic world and the cataclysmic revolutions of the postwar Third World."[18] However flawed Arab engagements with nonalignment may have been, the idea represented one important entry into the arena of international thought and politics that was otherwise dominated by US and European power. Palestine's dismemberment, authorized as it was by both the United States and the USSR, served as a perennial reminder that Arab states could not rely upon the "superpowers" for dignity or defense. India, confidently sovereign and historically linked to its West Asian neighbors, offered an example of what a postcolonial nation-state could achieve, both within its borders (development) and beyond (solidarity and friendship). Nonalignment then allowed Arab intellectuals to imagine a fundamentally different future.

Enter Clovis Maksoud

In Arabic, Clovis Maksoud was the most articulate theorist of positive neutrality, nonalignment, and the third force. He also developed the deepest ties with nonaligned intellectuals in India. Maksoud identified the beginnings of nonalignment in the Arab world with Lebanon's Progressive Socialist Party (PSP), with which he was closely affiliated. Kamal Jumblatt, one of the party's founders, shared this assessment, stating in an interview that "it is well-known that the party was the first to state such ideas."[19] Jumblatt went on to cite articles he had published in the Beirut journal *Les Cahiers de l'Est* as evidence of this fact. Maksoud himself published a series of articles in the Beirut weekly *al-Anba'*, such as "What Is the Third Force" (Ma hiya al-quwwa al-thalitha?) in 1951. Born to Lebanese parents in the United States in 1926, Maksoud was a teenager when he moved to Beirut, where he was inducted into the doctrine of Arab nationalism. Between 1944 and 1947 he studied at the American University of Beirut. By the time he returned to the United States to study law at George Washington University in 1948—the year, as he notes in his memoirs, of the *nakba*—Maksoud was already a firm believer in the necessity of Arab unity. His career, however, would demonstrate clearly his attachment to global thinking and his capacious understanding of Arab nationalism, even when he resorted to romantic idioms.

When he arrived at Oxford in 1954 to study with the Fabian socialist G. D. H. Cole, Maksoud was already entrenched in Arab political struggles and committed to elaborating a theory of nonalignment worldwide. He was contributing regularly to the Arab press and had traveled to Yugoslavia and met Tito. It is no surprise then that he was drawn into the extracurricular activities of the day. Maksoud cut his teeth at the dais of the Oxford Union and Hyde Park's infamous Speakers' Corner in London, sharpening the public voice for which he would become best known. At Oxford, Maksoud sat among what Jamaican Stuart Hall described as the independent Left, neither part of the Communist Party nor one of the Labour Party's budding MPs. The group convened in debate at the Socialist Club and, in Hall's words, "attracted more than its fair share of exiles and migrants, which reinforced its cosmopolitanism."[20] Hall recalls Maksoud's presence alongside himself, the Canadian Charles Taylor, the Trinidadian Doddridge Alleyne, and the Sudanese Sadiq al-Mahdi. Elsewhere on campus, Maksoud was the chairman of the Asia-African Socialist Group and the president of the Arab Student Union, and Mahdi served as its secretary.[21] Other Arab students in Maksoud's circle included the Palestinian historian Walid al-Khalidi, the Sudanese writer and diplomat Jamal Muhammad Ahmad, and the Egyptian Magdi Wahba.[22] In these years, Maksoud would also encounter the pro-Israel Left in Great Britain and the rest of Europe, noting painfully their lack of solidarity.[23] Like the anti-colonial Africans and Asians who had connected and commiserated in the imperial capitals of London, Paris, and Berlin a generation earlier, Maksoud's English sojourn was a key part of his intellectual development and an important site for the elaboration of his nonaligned socialist politics. For a 1954 issue of the Oxford Labour Club's journal, Maksoud penned the article "Socialism in the Arab World," pronouncing, in its first line, that "the socialists are the strongest revolutionary force in the Arab World."[24] The short article focuses principally on elucidating a socialist critique of Zionism and Israel, which "acts as an agent of war and imperialism." Israel, Maksoud argues, is a unique problem that faces Arab socialists. As far as the "Arab nation" is concerned, Maksoud makes clear that the only path to radical social transformation is nonalignment. "The true interest of the Arabs in international affairs," he writes, "lies in pursuing a vigorous and positive neutralism."

Beyond world socialism and Arab nationalism, India—as a successful anti-colonial and national project—represented a third well from which Maksoud would draw in the development of his thought. Maksoud's engagement with India began at George Washington, where he was inspired by reading the works of Nehru. Then, at Oxford, he commiserated with Indian students during the heady days of the 1955 Bandung conference. He first traveled to India in 1958 to join Delhi's Indian School of International Studies, where he served as a visiting professor for four months. On that trip Maksoud began his conversations with the socialist intellectual and theorist of the "Third World Force" in India, Ram Manohar Lohia, who had years earlier collaborated with Jumblatt to produce a joint statement with the Indian Socialist Party and the PSP.[25] It was upon his return to Lebanon from those months in Delhi that Maksoud founded the Third Force Association with Ali Bazzi, a Lebanese parliamentarian. Maksoud discloses the quotidian but profound challenges to the cultivation of popular support for nonalignment when he shares an anecdote about Bazzi, who, while in South Lebanon, encountered some peasants who asked him forthrightly: "The [US] Point Four [program] gives us aid, so why doesn't the Third Force?"[26] Despite these challenges, during much of the 1950s and 1960s, ideas of nonalignment and positive neutrality had a major impact on Arab political and intellectual currents, especially in Iraq, Syria, Lebanon, and Egypt. During that time Maksoud continued to write about nonalignment. In September 1960 Maksoud was asked to become the Arab League's first permanent representative to India.[27] He eagerly accepted the offer, arriving in Delhi in February 1961.

India became an essential part of Maksoud's theory of nonalignment. He referred directly to his Indian experiences in his 1960 treatise, *Ma'na al-Hiyad al-Ijabi* (The meaning of positive neutrality).[28]

And he argued, for example, that nonalignment was a far greater challenge for the Arab states than it was for India. Oil reserves and proximity to the USSR led the Middle East to constantly face assaults on its sovereignty, as US intervention in the 1950s made clear. Arabs had to commit to nonalignment precisely because of these challenging conditions. The Indians, Maksoud argued, must convince the Arabs of this fact. Disarmament was also a fundamental part of his nonaligned thought. It was a goal, he wrote, that was "morally sound, pragmatically useful, humanly desirable, practicably realizable, and existentially necessary... and urgent!"[29] Indeed, Maksoud's nonalignment was ever urgent. In 1966 he said that nonalignment's primary objective was "the mobilisation of forces to extricate Palestine and Vietnam from 'crisis areas.'"[30] In the introduction to *Ma'na al-Hiyad al-Ijabi*, he wrote, "Positive neutralism will no longer be necessary once peaceful coexistence is achieved."[31] Internationalism in general was foundational for Maksoud. Arab states could only be understood—then changed—if their international conditions were attended to. The nakba and the political travails of postcolonial Syria, Egypt, and Iraq, for example, revealed the extent to which political decolonization at the national level remained an insufficient political program. "Liberation," Maksoud wrote, "no longer means demanding legal sovereignty in a specific Arab state. Liberation has become the insistence to take public international positions with complete freedom."[32] Liberation of this type, Maksoud would later contend, did not simply liberate the Arabs and Indians, for example, but liberated the West itself from its superiority complex.[33]

In India, Maksoud was able to see nonalignment in action. He witnessed the war with China, wherein Egypt sought unsuccessfully to negotiate a peace settlement. "That was a great, enriching experience," Maksoud later recalled, "the first test of non-alignment in resolving a conflict and with all the ramifications that it had on the non-aligned movement."[34] Maksoud described the three principal challenges of his time in Delhi. First and foremost was to strengthen Arab ties with India and urge Arabs to adopt Indian principles of politics. Second and third were to advise Nasser and other Arab leaders on the conflicts between China and India and between Pakistan and India (in the latter case, over Kashmir). Despite this intense ambit, Maksoud always cultivated an independent political position. He was, for example, outspoken in his support of Bangladeshi independence during the war of 1971, in which all Arab states came to Pakistan's aid, supporting it in the press or in the halls of the United Nations. Bangladeshi economist and freedom fighter Rehman Sobhan recalls being introduced to Maksoud in Delhi in the midst of the Bangladeshi struggle. "Clovis," Rehman writes, "a socialist by persuasion, was thought to be amenable to indoctrination about the emergence of an independent Bangladesh as part of the anti-imperialist struggle."[35] Rehman nevertheless concluded that Maksoud was not in a position to influence Arab leaders. Indeed, in diplomatic terms, Maksoud's influence was minor, as Arab leaders refused to budge in their opposition to Bangladesh given their long allegiance to Pakistan, which had cultivated substantial support from Arab states on Islamic terms.[36] Demoralized and dejected by this state of affairs, Bangladeshis resolved to close their information center in Beirut a year after their independence. Maksoud gave a forceful speech, lambasting Arabs who had "subordinated their principles to the exigences of reactionary notions of foreign policy."[37] While Maksoud was speaking out against Arab governments and in support of Bangladesh, the Indian government was secretly procuring arms from Israel to support its efforts in aiding Bangla independence from Pakistan.[38] Bangladesh therefore reveals one of the great ironies of this age of intense violence. It is an exemplary flashpoint—like Jordan's Black September in the 1970s or Indira Gandhi's Emergency in 1975—in the global transformations that threatened the Third World's rise.

In the 1970s, nonalignment as an ideal began to collapse. The rise of authoritarianism across the purportedly postcolonial world was coupled with the decline of nonaligned politics. Right-wing revanchism, popular separatism, imperial militarism, and structural adjustment transformed the conditions under which movements for Afro-Asian collaboration and national liberation (like that of the Palestine Liberation Organization) operated. Under duress, nonalignment began to traffic in name only. Indeed, nonalignment's political viability was always less powerful than its force as an idea. Even in the late 1950s, efforts were afoot to temper its radical implications. Regarding the Egyptian situation, Anouar Abdel-Malek wrote that "positive neutralism began to seem too explosive for its initiators."[39] The tragedy of this political history then reinforces the need to be attentive to ideas and activities of particular intellectuals and institutions. These are often missing from standard diplomatic accounts, generically attached as they are to the exigencies of war in its many means.

Nonaligned Print

In his nearly six years in Delhi, Maksoud laid the foundations of a remarkably rich center of Indo-Arab cultural contact. Beyond the intrigues surrounding its formation and an arid literature on "regionalism," the Arab League, Maksoud's platform for spreading his nonaligned gospel, has received scant historical attention, especially its international and cultural activities. The league's mission in New Delhi was the first established outside of Europe or the Americas.[40] And in 1965 India was the first nation to recognize the league with diplomatic status.[41] While there, Maksoud did not confine himself to governmental matters in Delhi. He traveled across the subcontinent giving speeches and regularly published articles in *Seminar* and other prominent and progressive Indian journals.[42] He was in frequent contact with left-wing writers like Mulk Raj Anand and Sajjad Zaheer. And, his home became a well-known international meeting place.[43] Maksoud, as one Indian observer put it, "gave a new impetus to the Indo-Arab political and cultural relations. Through seminars and speeches he provided the Indian people with a first hand knowledge of the socio-political problems of the Arab world."[44] Maksoud was not universally well received, however. An article in the right-wing Indian magazine *Swarajya* described Maksoud as a "chimerical entity" and criticized the Indian government for its support of the Arab League in New Delhi and its exclusion of Israel and the Jewish Agency.[45]

The Arab League's Delhi office oversaw an incredible array of publishing projects. *Al-'Arab* was the principal magazine of the mission, renamed the *New Arab* in 1974. Published monthly in full color, the richly illustrated journal was no mere gazette transcribing trade deals and reproducing photos of official functions. *Al-'Arab* traced the development of the Indo-Arab relationship, including the presence of Arab students in Indian universities and the spread of local Indo-Arab societies across the country. Much of the journal's space, however, was consumed by discussions of Arab literature, culture, and history. Prominent Arab artists and writers were among the contributors. In one issue, a translation into English from Mu'in Bseiso's play *Thawrat al-Zanj* was printed alongside Kamal Boullata's manifesto "A Revolutionary Arab Art."[46] Another issue featured "Indians in West Asia," by Maqbul Ahmad, a historian and the director for West Asia Studies at Aligarh; an interview with Yasser Arafat; an article on the Baghdadi painter Naziha Harithi; and a short introduction to Ibn Rushd.[47] The Delhi office also published books. Some were strictly political, like the straightforward *Palestine: A Symposium*, an edited collection featuring some seventeen contributors—Indian, Arab, and otherwise—in addition to maps, images, and documents.[48] Others continued along the lines of the magazine, such as a collection of Mahmoud Darwish's poetry.

In this regard, Maksoud had an important counterpart in Egypt, the aforementioned scholar-diplomat K. M. Panikkar. While Panikkar was uniquely sympathetic—among Nehruvians—to the Zionist cause in the years before partition, he played an important role in Indo-Arab relations during his brief stint as the Indian ambassador to Egypt and Lebanon in the period right before and after the 1952 Egyptian Revolution.[49] While it is impossible to account for his rich life here, including the contents of his influential history *Asia and Western Dominance*, suffice it to say that during his West Asian career, Panikkar oversaw with prominence and verve an important cultural enterprise, the Arabic magazine *Sawt al-Sharq* and the Indian Embassy's cultural center. A testament to the importance of the Arab world to India's representatives was that *Sawt al-Sharq* was one of only two magazines "produced for external publicity," the other being the English-language *March of India*. Despite Panikkar's documented tryst with Zionism (largely in private correspondence), he was open to the Palestinian cause in his autobiography, first published shortly after he left Egypt. Therein he recounts his meeting with the controversial, and pro-Pakistan, Amin al-Husseini, the one-time mufti of Jerusalem, who happened to be the uncle of Panikkar's secretary, "a Palestinian youth named Sayed."[50] Panikkar arranged to meet with al-Husseini, and al-Husseini visited him in turn. "Evidently," Panikkar wrote, "no one had thought of meeting the Mufti till then! Our embassy officials had adopted a negative attitude by regarding the friends of Pakistan as the enemies of India!"[51]

Like Abul Kalam Azad's designs for *Thaqafat al-Hind*, *Sawt al-Sharq* was to serve the same purpose of countering Pakistan's influence on the Arab public, only in a less academic register. For its inaugural issue Nehru submitted a note of greeting, and Panikkar himself contributed an article on the history of Indian and Egyptian relations, from antiquity to the nationalist collaborations of the 1930s and 1940s. Ahmed Qasim Gouda, himself a veteran of those collaborations—he published a book-length account of his travels in India in 1949—was tapped to serve as the magazine's editor. "If this magazine," Gouda wrote in his first editor's note, "is able to contribute with a modest effort to strengthening the cooperation of countries in the Arab-Asian bloc, as a means of achieving the global cooperation we desire, then it will have fulfilled its mission."[52] The magazine featured interviews with Doria Shafik, essays on Indian freedom fighters by Amina al-Said, denunciations of atomic weapons by Abbas al-Aqqad, paeans to Egyptian and Indian cinema, and a guide on how to wrap a sari. Indo-Arab cultural events and visits by Indian dignitaries were also closely covered. The correspondence pages of *Sawt al-Sharq* and Maksoud's *Al-'Arab* testify to a wide and engaged readership. They represented a popular nonalignment that was sustained not simply by the charisma of national fathers but by the continuous efforts of some—like Maksoud and Panikkar—to imagine new institutions and write new histories.

History after Colonialism

"Perhaps," Nehru speculated at the inauguration of the Asian Relations Conferences in 1947, "one of the notable consequences of the European domination of Asia has been the isolation of the countries of Asia from one another."[53] As I noted at the outset, this trope of separation was increasingly summoned by Indian and Arab intellectuals in the heady decades of decolonization. At the Seminar on India and the Arab World at the ICCR in 1965, Syria's ambassador to India, the well-known poet Omar Abou Risha, made the point powerfully. "Colonialism," he proclaimed, "with the forces of evil at its disposal, separated India from the Arab World and created between them a wide gap; which, after a long and hard struggle for freedom, the Arabs and the Indians are trying to bridge. The renewal of these old contacts, these golden links, is in itself a creation of new history."⁵⁴ This was indeed the project of those assembled and one that consumed many Arab and Indian intellectuals. Humayun Kabir, close confident of Abul Kalam Azad and director of the ICCR at the time of the seminar, made a similar point a year after Abou Risha: "It was one of the paradoxes of this period that contact between Asian and African neighbors could take place only through a European intermediary! This state of affairs was, however, unnatural and could not endure."⁵⁵ With anti-colonialism, Kabir concluded, contacts resumed. For Abou Risha, India was nourishing. He referred to Nehru as his "spiritual leader."⁵⁶ His poetry is rife with references to Indian temples and landscapes.⁵⁷ And fellow Syrian poet Badi' Haqqi recalls Abou Risha encouraging him to translate Tagore's *Gitanjali*.⁵⁸ Abou Risha was no doubt keen on creating a new history.

The most outspoken Arab participant at the conference, however, was Maksoud himself. While the past was the topic of much of the seminar, Maksoud was keen on talking about the future. At the outset, he questioned the very terms of the seminar. "Arab world," he said, should not be used. The phrase, he argued, "is used in westernized textbooks and journalistic literature . . . [and] is a dilution of the general objective of Arab nationals."⁵⁹ The phrase "Arab nation" was preferred (Maksoud often made this point in his writing). Beyond his lexical quibble, Maksoud had larger aims. Acknowledging that until the nineteenth century at least, Islam had been a major point of connection between the peoples of West and South Asia, he argued that new forms of unification must be raised. Three things in particular, Maksoud argued, should bring Indians and Arabs together anew: socialism, secularism, and nonalignment. Islam was not going to be enough.⁶⁰ Although Maksoud would regularly make paeans to the Islamic past, the future was his more urgent concern. In a speech at Aligarh Muslim University in 1966, Maksoud declared that the university "represents to us a projection of the greatest revolutionary development that the Arabs have had, the growth and development of Islam. Islam is a revolution against all forms of obscurantism, social obsolescence and economic exploitation." Nevertheless, he would again insist that "our classical relations might not be enough to sustain our future relations... the future not only in terms of India-Arab relations but in terms of Afro-Asian problems of development."[61] Maksoud was keen to develop the terms of a new Indo-Arab political future, drawn substantially from his own experience in India and the nonaligned theory he espoused.

At the end of the seminar at the ICCR, after the resolutions promising intellectual and institutional cooperation were passed, Maksoud had one last word: "We are beginning to know each other through each other; we are beginning to realize that the nature of the relationships between the Arab countries and India is of such a manner that we have to constantly make known our achievements and failures to each other, and in this process of self-analysis to unfold ourselves to each other and the world."[62] He had described the Arab League's mission in Delhi in similar terms in *The Arab Image*: "We must begin to know each other through each other and not through others."[63] Maksoud's sentiment is significant. Knowledge was fundamental to his political theory. In the context of impoverished representations and scarce efforts at Indo-Arab study, Maksoud demanded forms of knowledge attuned to a future-oriented political project. Elsewhere in *The Arab Image* he insisted that Arabs and Indians are not, in fact two nations. "Somehow or the other," he wrote, "they blend and the blending itself is stimulating, interesting, sometimes irritating, but in general a very powerful impetus for the minds and hearts of both Indians and the Arabs."[64] He certainly wrote with romance here, but he was also speaking against a chauvinism that would in the end prove to be nationalism's most lasting rhetorical legacy. Attending to other appeals for national belonging, which transcend state, linguistic, or racial bounds, reveals one of the possibilities raised by decolonization.

Nonalignment, for Maksoud, was never simply a diplomatic agenda or political project, but rather a matter of profound epistemological concern. In an essay on Mohandas Gandhi, Maksoud was explicit: "Non-alignment prepares the ground for ultimate unity through co-discovery. In a world where many powers are in an emotionally intransigent posture, non-alignment has insisted on pointing out the threads of unity in mankind's destiny."[65] The link with India was of course fundamental for Maksoud. "Non-alignment," he wrote, "has rendered India and the Arab countries able to prevent this collapse of nationalism. Perhaps this partnership in making nationalism a humanist undertaking is the very essence of Indian-Arab friendship."[66] Maksoud saw internationalism as indispensable to the very project of the Arab nation that he so relentlessly championed. If the nation was going to remain a meaningful vehicle for human emancipation, as its theorists claimed, its furies would need to be contained by collaboration, or as Maksoud called it, "co-discovery."

In this regard, the geographic dimension was as key as the historical one. One could refer, for example, to the work of Boutros Boutros-Ghali, the prolific Paris-trained Egyptian theorist who would of course go on to have a controversial career in international affairs after joining Anwar Sadat's cabinet (and later at the UN). Boutros-Ghali was particularly interested in thinking about the Indian Ocean (as was Panikkar). In an article for *al-Siyasa al-Dawliya*, the journal he edited and the principal site of his academic interventions, Boutros-Ghali considered politics and strategy in the Indian Ocean.[67] This article is important, as it reveals the horizons of Arab political thought, which is often represented as ineluctably insular. Boutros-Ghali offers a riposte to the imperial description of the ocean as a "British Lake." "The Indian Ocean," he writes "is an Afro-Asian sea or a Third World Sea."[68] If one seeks to study Afro-Asian solidarity, Boutros-Ghali contends, it is of foremost importance to study the Indian Ocean. And if the Atlantic Ocean was the key site for the elaboration of Western ideology, Boutros-Ghali continues, the Indian Ocean is the key to Afro-Asianism.[69] Boutros-Ghali outlines the contours of "neo-imperialism" on the ocean: rather than formal colonies, he contends, the ocean is populated by air bases and navy commandos.[70] In an article for *al-Ahram al-Iqtisadi*, ten years after his first, Boutros-Ghali reiterated the importance of the Indian Ocean on the eve of the Suez Canal's reopening. "These Afro-Asians want to keep the ocean out of the Cold War, because they consider it an Afro-Asian ocean, a Third World ocean," he wrote.[71] Spatial idioms were tied inexorably to political projects.

Today, the *Third World* and *Afro-Asia* have all but disappeared in scholarship and politics. The *global South* has decisively displaced other idioms. It is easy to see the phrase as so broad as to be useless, or worse, depoliticizing.[72] And certainly in the hollowed-out university of today, where the time and resources required for serious area study have evaporated, recourse to the global can always seem suspect. But global South also contains radical possibilities. In the fall of 1991, for example, a year after resigning his post as the Arab League's ambassador to the United Nations in the midst of the first Gulf War, Maksoud founded the Center for the Study of the Global South at the American University in Washington, D.C.[73] It was the first center of its kind. The center was dedicated to "examining critical issues related to the role of the South in a changing international equation," and its first annual conference was titled "Environmental Challenges and the Global South."[74] In a 1993 essay, Maksoud—ever with his eyes on the future—laid bare the situation without nostalgia: "The terms 'non-alignment' and 'Third World' are no longer germane to the discourse in the new global equation."[75] At the end of the essay, however, he returned to a turn of phrase from his Indian career. "Ultimately," Maksoud wrote, "if co-existence was the optimum objective during the Cold War, co-discovery between

North and South should become the inspiring incentive for the genuinely new international relations."[76] In the late 1970s and 1980s, when Maksoud lived in the United Sates, he poured his energies into defending Arab nationalism as he shuttled between Washington, D.C., and New York City. He was tasked with convincing an American public that was increasingly supportive of a belligerent Israel to empathize with an Arab world devasted by imperialism and gripped by authoritarianism. Maksoud rode the wave of nonalignment until it crashed, and when the swell of Arab unity came crashing down with it, he remained nevertheless committed to—at least—imagining a future far greater.

History's Challenge

Nonalignment, as one of decolonization's forms of knowledge, represented a profound challenge to the methods and mechanisms of study in the West. When, for example, nearly a hundred delegates convened in Delhi for the first Asian History Congress in December 1961, it was not without its external critics. "Some of the participants," one prominent US observer of the meeting remarked, "seemed inclined to belabor Western scholars for alleged or real misinterpretations and distortions of Asian history and institutions. And a few seemed to be more interested in criticizing Western historical writing on Asia than in writing sound history themselves."[77] Norman Palmer, the writer of this report, was not a disinterested party. A professor of political science at the University of Pennsylvania and an adviser to the US government, Palmer was a foundational figure in the development of South Asian studies in the United States, alongside his Penn colleague, the Sanskritist W. Norman Brown. Palmer went on to lament the lack of US representation at the event, which was attended by historians from the Philippines, Iran, Lebanon, Afghanistan, and Indonesia, among other countries. The United

States, for Palmer, was the center, and "the rapidly developing US interest in Asian affairs," was his primary concern. That he was a visitor to a Delhi convulsing in nonaligned feeling seems only to have distressed him. One is reminded of Richard Wright's comment regarding American observers of the first Asian-African Conference: "They had no philosophy of history with which to understand Bandung."[78]

Among the delegates at the Asian History Congress there was considerable debate and disagreement, on matters specialized and small, and on those larger questions that have long plagued the philosophy of history. In fact, Maksoud and Panikkar debated the place of politics and ideology in the writing of history during the concluding session of the congress. Maksoud, for his part, would argue that history writing must not pretend that "objectivity" is opposed to "commitment" (the great maxim of Maksoud's generation of Arab leftists, *iltizam*). History, Maksoud argued, must consciously serve any ideology, lest it mask its ideological aims. "This kind of objectivity... is rather dangerous," Maksoud said. He may have been recalling Frantz Fanon's famous line from *The Wretched of the Earth*: "For the native, objectivity is always directed against him." "If we adopt the classical conception of objectivity," Maksoud concluded, "as being only [the] exclusive writing of foot-notes, we will lose the purpose of historicism and the role of history in shaping modern ideas."[79] Panikkar, who chaired the concluding session, responded to Maksoud by drawing a distinction between history and the interpretation of history. He agreed with Maksoud in general, but argued that interpreters of history, like Maksoud himself, need not be professional researchers producing "raw material."[80] "The interpreters are not necessarily historians and all historian are not interpreters," Panikkar emphasized. He hoped that a second congress—which, alas, never materialized—"would have much clearer ideas as to how to proceed in our interpretation of history, not from a purely nationalistic point of view but for a very permanent value of Asia."[81] At bottom, Panikkar and Maksoud agreed on the political significance of historical writing. Panikkar himself was particularly concerned with how institutions of historical study operated, the limits of their geographical assumptions, and the political implications of specific patterns of study. In his address to the Indian History Congress in 1955, Panikkar argued that "the history of India, unless it is related to the developments in Central Asia, and in South East Asia, would lose its full significance."[82] He deplored the neglect of Asian history in Indian universities and lamented Indian dependence on European historians. Under the moon of nonalignment, history writing and historical research were tasked with undermining Eurocentrism—the North Atlantic's narrative of itself. This was not conceived of as simply a methodological matter. It was both fundamentally political and inextricably linked to the material development of institutes and archives. "Historical underdevelopment," Walter Rodney once put it, "is also reflected in the material base for historical reconstruction."[83] One simply could not write the history of Afro-Asia without Afro-Asian archives.

The production of new histories and the elaboration of a new geography, therefore, were conscious elements of nonaligned thought, however obscured they might be by the trials of Cold War diplomacy. Long before the institutions and idioms of global historical study were fashioned in the West, the majority of the world wrote its history as a matter of political necessity. In the end, history's political project and history as the practice of construction and collection—or reconstruction out of imperial narratives and the recollection of looted local materials—were the foundations of nonalignment's vision for the future. A world unmoored from great power politics and Western imperialism necessitated a world history independent of Western historiography and its attendant hostility to the non-West.

5   *Area*

On February 2, 1945, M. L. Roy Choudhury, a Bengali historian teaching for the year at Cairo University, met with the Palestinian physician and ethnographer Tawfiq Canaan at his home in Jerusalem. Canaan, just released from imprisonment for his nationalist activities in British Mandate Palestine, inquired about the status and whereabouts of India's anti-colonial leaders, like Jawharlal Nehru, who was himself in and out of prison. Canaan also asked Choudhury about how the war was affecting the economic life of British India. Choudhury proceeded to vividly narrate the famine he had witnessed in his native Bengal in 1943, in which millions perished. Choudhury recounts that Canaan was "spellbound" as he listened: "The blood practically disappeared from his face."[1] Canaan suddenly went to the other side of the room and began to weep as he sat at his piano. "The doctor," Choudhury wrote of his Palestinian host, "played a tune—mournful and pensive; it was raining terribly outside; and there was dead silence inside; we could feel the breath of each other present. The cloud was in sympathy with the tragic scene I had described." When his song was done, Canaan came to Choudhury and told him, "tell your countrymen that there are men in the world who feel for you, weep for you." Choudhury recounts this story in the introduction to a rich collection of essays on contemporary

Egypt, which he edited and published with the University of Calcutta Press in 1946. "As I write these lines," he ended his introduction to the volume, "[Canaan's] vision reappears before me, an emblem of international friendliness. That is what induces me to present this book to the reading public."

Choudhury taught at Calcutta University and was the head of its Department of Islamic History and Culture, one of the oldest such departments in South Asia. And Calcutta University itself was an important institution of higher learning on the world scale, not simply in India or Asia. "By 1918," Partha Chatterjee wrote, "Calcutta University, with twenty seven thousand students, was the largest university in the world, and the proportion of literate people taking full-time university courses was the same as in the United Kingdom."[2] Choudhury, then, was part of a global undertaking, certainly as much as any Orientalist in Oxford or Paris. Choudhury's diaries of his Egyptian sojourn were first published in the Bengali monthly *Bharat Varsha*. The pharaonic past was the object of a substantial romance on the part of Choudhary's generation of Bengal *bhadralok*, who traveled—in their heads—to ancient Egypt in an effort to map out a scientific concept of race.[3] Choudhury's Egypt was real and his engagement mediated by his own substantial investment in Arabic and Islam and Egyptian interest in British India's twilight. Indeed, Cairo at the time was thoroughly imperial, teeming with Indian military personnel conscripted into the Allied war effort in North Africa.

In his diaries Choudhury notes that Canaan invited him to his home upon learning via the local newspaper that he was visiting the country. Choudhury writes, with some exaggeration, that "Canaan's place in Palestine is almost the same as that of Gandhi in our country."[4] Canaan gifted Choudhury three English books about Palestine, including Wadiʽ al-Bustani's on the British Mandate. Besides Palestine, Choudhury visited Lebanon, Syria, and the Arabian Peninsula during his stay in Egypt. Reporting on Choudhury's activities, the *Calcutta Review* noted that he was "accorded a very hospitable reception by intellectual circles in Cairo."[5] Choudhury recounts at length the many meetings and requests he made to secure contributions to the wide-ranging volume, at Al-Azhar, in Port Said, among the Egyptian Feminist's Union. Nehru's preface to Roy Choudhury's book repeats the now familiar idioms of Indo-Arab cooperation: "It is inevitable that in the future that is taking shape, Egypt and India will have much to say to one another." Musatfa Nahas would similarly write a preface. A brief message from Huda Shaarawi opens the book. International conditions—friendships, alliances, solidarities—dominate.

But the vagaries of national life enveloped Choudhury's scholarship as well. Shortly after arriving back in Bengal from his stay in Egypt in 1946, Calcutta was engulfed in violence. Despite staging encounter after encounter of Egyptian communal harmony for the Bengali press, Choudhury was settling back into his academic duties and serving as the superintendent of a graduate student hostel when the deadly riots of the Muslim League's Direct Action Day tore through the city and beyond. For four days Choudhury stayed in the apartment with dozens of students and hardly any provisions as a mob surrounded the hostel. An attempt to escape led to the deaths of four students and severe injuries to at least two more. But the violence that would culminate in the great partition of 1947 was only just accelerating. In October 1946, Choudhury's older brother, a lawyer and leader in the Hindu Mahasabha in Noakhali, was killed along with twenty-nine other men visiting his home, while the women and children took shelter on the roof. "The next morning," Choudhury's daughter recalls, "some innocent tailors and labourers who lived in the neighbourhood, whose only fault was that they were Muslim, were dragged in front of our house and brutally slaughtered before my own eyes."[6]

A few years later, after Bengal was split between two new countries, Choudhury would dedicate his book *The State and Religion in Mughal India* to "the sacred memory of my brother Late Rajendra Lal Roy Choudhury and Twenty-two other members of my family who lost their lives in the communal fury and religious frenzy of October, 1946 at Noakhali, in East Pakistan." It is ironic, but not unique, that for Choudhury, who devoted considerable energy to thinking about Islam's place in India, and India's place in the world, communal violence would characterize his life. It is telling, then, that Choudhury's intercommunal efforts were not universally admired. The Hyderabadi journal *Islamic Culture* registered that his 1940 book on Akbar's Din-i-Ilahi was the "subject of strong comments and criticism by some scholars and newspapers of Calcutta." In an article for the Calcutta newspaper *Star of India* a writer from Azamgarh's Shibli Academy claimed that Choudhury had made claims that were "false and spurious," and therefore the book was "only a texture of distorted facts and perverted truths." Praise for the book by Sachchidananda Sinha and Radha Kumur Mokerjee, also quoted by *Islamic Culture*, did not, therefore, "seem to be deserved or justified."[7] Such criticisms do not seem to have deterred Choudhury's project of Islamic study. In 1951 he published an Arabic translation of the Gita in Calcutta, completed with the assistance of Al-Azhar's Muhammad Habib Ahmad, who had earlier been a part of the Azharite mission to India.[8] Choudhury's constitution was undoubtedly nourished by his study of Mughal history and his vision of the subcontinent's future drawn from its past. In his book on the Mughal state he would conclude that "on the whole, the rights and privileges of the conquered, including even those which were directly against the tenets of Islam, were tolerated by the Mughals not always merely as policy, but as the result of a synthesis."[9]

Beyond the activities of individual scholars, the first efforts to institutionalize Islamic studies in India were produced in the service of national unity, communal understanding, and the elaboration of this often-repeated history of synthesis. In 1927 Rabindranath Tagore secured from the Nizam of Hyderabad, a major patron of Islamic institutions worldwide, 100,000 rupees to establish a chair of Islamic studies at Visva-Bharati, the university Tagore had built in Santiniketan.[10] While successive vice chancellors at Calcutta University advocated for increased attention to Islamic history and culture, and the establishment of a department was first suggested in the 1920s, it was only in 1940 that the Department of Islamic History and Culture, which Choudhury was a part of, was founded. In his convocation address that year, Vice Chancellor Azizul Haque celebrated what he hoped would be the scholarly significance of the department in years to come. He also drew attention to the dire social and political situation that the department must serve. "Living in the world today," Haque told the graduating students assembled for the occasion, "when mistrust, misunderstanding and doubt dominate all aspects of human relationship, I look forward to the growth of a generation under the fostering care of this University who by their studies of the culture of Ancient India and of Islam will succeed in ushering an era of mutual understanding and amity."[11] Retrospective estimations of the department similarly drew upon this language. After partition there remained a desire to frame the department in these liberal terms. Calcutta University's official study of its postgraduate departments announced that there was a "special objective behind the establishment of the Department." There was a hope, among faculty members and administrators at least, that a department of Islamic studies "might contribute in a handsome manner to the growth of inter-communal toleration and understanding." "The last few years of Indian history have, however, been abnormal in more than one sense," the university remarked in 1949, "and during the hectic days through which people have passed it was not possible for the Department to exert its liberalising influence as much as in other circumstance it might. But as the last embers of communal conflagration are dying out, we may certainly look forward now to the Department being one of the outstanding liberalising forces in the country."[12] However well intentioned, such statements were produced in the face of overwhelmingly grim conditions. Only a paltry number of Muslim students remained on the university's rolls, and Choudhury's senior Muslim colleague in the department, A. B. M. Habibullah, had decamped for Dacca in 1947.[13]

Partition, in its violence and disappointment, was of course also the occasion of independence. And these national initiatives came to be supplanted more directly by an international view. In an address broadcast on All-India Radio for Middle Eastern audiences, Vice Chancellor P. N. Banerjee recounted the history of Islamic studies at Calcutta University and its place among the university's distinguished other disciplines. Describing a Sanskritic language and literature as one stream of Indian civilization and an Islamic stream as the other, Banerjee concluded that his university "will live for the ideal that the two streams of civilization may flow side by side so that their cultures mingle in the eternal ocean of humanity."[14] But this veritable ocean of humanity in the years after 1947 became profoundly demarcated by political struggles over India's place in Islam, Asia, and the world, as the previous chapters have demonstrated. Among other necessary accoutrements of this arrangement, the new states of India and Pakistan needed those institutions of knowledge production deemed necessary for participation in an international system.

Between Empire and the Area

The trials of national life, including the exigencies of state and university budgets, the zeal of anti-imperialism, the furies of communalism, and the anxieties of sovereignty, determined much of the scope and a syntax of area studies in independent India. But no account of the Third World's social science can ignore the global and imperial conditions that first nurtured the epistemology and infrastructure of area studies programs in the North Atlantic, including Orientalism, the United Nations Educational, Scientific and Cultural Organization (UNESCO), the Ford Foundation, and the Central Intelligence Agency (CIA). The beginnings and elaboration of imperial knowledge are so well-known that their rehearsal is not necessary here. Suffice it to say that the world as we know it is the product of the grand accumulation of knowledge that accompanied the grand accumulation of land by the European empires from the fifteenth century onward. World politics and international social science determined the course of knowledge's decolonization.

The period between the world wars, and especially the demands of the second war, transformed the conditions of what would come to be called *area studies*. By the middle of the twentieth century the contours of this knowledge were being increasingly determined by a new language of social science tied inexorably to the formalization of imperialism under the guise of global economic governance, united nationhood, and development. So-called classical knowledge—the search for origins, the construction of a deep human past—was superseded by a new focus on understanding the present. When the past was studied it was for the purposes of telling the future. "Stasis was assumed, and history, including the effects of colonial processes, was erased," Bernard Cohn wrote of this era of American social scientific inquiry.[15] This ontological shift was accompanied by a geographical one. During the Second World War, the US view began to stretch far beyond its continental empire and Pacific colonies. A properly imperial view of the globe was cultivated through the establishment of specialized wartime agencies and efforts. The Army Specialized Training Program enlisted specialists in East Asian and European affairs to train officers. The wartime recruitment of such experts was frenzied, archaeologists were brought on to teach geography, "men were brought back from retirement," and refugees were hurried off ships and into classrooms. Universities building their area programs "were forced into competition with each other and persistently scanned the passenger lists of the [diplomatic ship MS] *Gripsholm* for possible academics returning from Japan and China."[16] The war exposed the gaps in American knowledge and the limits of the British imperial way of study, attached as it was to traditions of philology, theology, and philosophy. The study of modern languages and collaboration across the new social scientific disciplines was taken as the new program. "Modernization theory"—later epitomized in Walt Rostow's *The Stages of Economic Growth: A Non-Communist Manifesto* (1960)—became gospel. The Soviet Union became the necessary foil for a world-spanning project of knowledge accumulation. A postwar report commissioned by the American Council on Education referred to "the shadow belt of languages and cultures that stretches from the Arctic Circle to the Equator and separated the Western world from the Slovnic [sic] culture area and the Middle East."[17] To the study of the languages of Central, Eastern, and Southeastern Europe, the report suggests adding "Turkish ... and also Arabic, the lingua franca from Gibraltar to the Persian Gulf, to complete the shadow belt." The shadow, of course, refers to the USSR.

After the war, American anti-communism, the proliferation of atomic technology, and the space race were the conditions of this knowledge's effervescence. Key veterans of the wartime knowledge effort, like Mortimer Graves, who would become head of the ACLS in 1953, led the way in expanding the scope and defining the structure of area knowledge in American universities. In collaboration with the Social Science Research Council (SSRC), area knowledge was organized, consolidated, and distributed through committees, conferences, publications, and fellowships.[18] By the end of the 1950s, federal patronage was significantly expanding. Sputnik's arrival in Earth's orbit was the impetus for the passage of a sweeping piece of legislation to support the sciences in the United States less than a year later, the National Defense Education Act. Title VI of the act provided for the establishment of centers for area study at specific research universities across the country, with funding for language learning and programming. The United States emerged at the forefront of social scientific developments, especially when it came to area knowledge. In the United Kingdom, the University Grants Committee's 1961 Report of the Sub-Committee on Oriental, Slavonic, East European and African Studies—better known as the Hayter Report—would look to the United States as an example for how to rescue its own imperial knowledge centers from their terminal state. Across Western Europe and nearly everywhere else—except the Soviet Union and its satellites—the American style of area study was being readily adopted.

This knowledge did not travel on its own. The backing for this imperial venture was supplemented by the emergence of a new regime of financing. It is impossible to account for the twentieth century, and the outsized influence of the United States in world affairs after the Second World War, without attention to the role of philanthropy, principally the foundations established by the Ford, Rockefeller, and Carnegie families. "Like all great fortunes," Zachary Lockman put it in his history of Middle East studies, "those that funded the new foundations were stained by blood."[19] The social programs initiated by these foundations, from the inner cities of the United States to the rural villages of India, were paternalistic and authoritarian, if not genocidal. In his indispensable 1983 book, *The Ideology of Philanthropy*, Edward H. Berman delineated the implications of these foundations dictating solutions to poverty, hunger, and war worldwide. "The poor, dispossessed, and minority groups in whose names many of their programs are launched," Berman wrote, "infrequently participate in the decisions to initiate these projects."[20] Moreover, the staff and trustees of these foundations and the government, elite universities, and groups like the Congress of Cultural Freedom (CCF), shared both personnel and ideas. As Inderjeet Parmar put it: "The relationship between the CIA, CCF, and numerous other opponents of communism and anti-Americanism was close, enduring, and smooth."[21] The development of Afro-Asian social science and imperialist area study was similarly interlinked. Not without conflict, Third World intellectuals regularly sought knowledge and patronage from Western universities and institutions. The outcome of these collaborations, however, was uneven.

The long march toward decolonization and the meteoric rise of area studies were synchronous. With the emergence of independent national and international locations of intellectual production, established sites of imperial study themselves became potent arenas of struggle. Existing arrangements were challenged even while they were patronized. Area study was but the newest imperial view of a world already contending with scholarship on Asia and Africa: the Orient, the East, and the South. As the formalization of area studies in North America began to displace the Old World's imperial disciplines and scholarly formations, so too did the Third World's reserve army of intellectuals demand a new relationship to imperialist knowledge making. It is prudent, then, to consider the confrontations staged under international auspices, to examine the demands and concessions made to colonial forms of knowledge amid efforts for decolonization.

From December 11 to 18, 1962, hundreds of scholars converged on the University of Ghana in Accra for the First International Congress of Africanists. Scarcely a year later, on January 4, 1964, the 26th International Congress of Orientalists convened in New Delhi, the first time that scholarly body—initiated in Paris in 1873—had met in Asia. For the Africanists assembled, the prospect of doing African studies in Africa was paramount. "It is therefore proper and fitting," Kwame Nkrumah announced at the opening of the Accra meeting, "that a

Congress of Africanists should take place in Africa."[22] Nkrumah's address was a blistering critique of colonial knowledge, and he demanded that new knowledge of Africa serve African political projects, "for the progress of the African." "While some of us are engaged with the political unification of Africa," he concluded, "Africanists everywhere must also help in building the spiritual and cultural foundations for the unity of our continent."[23] In New Delhi, the spirit of the congress was somewhat different. Humayun Kabir, a prominent Indian intellectual and bureaucrat, presided over the events. Unlike Nkrumah, who offered a succinct history of Africanist participation in the immiseration of Africans, Kabir's opening speech bordered on the sycophantic. "The fact that the Congress has never before met outside the European Continent is a tribute to the many savants and scholars of Europe who have pursued with single-minded devotion their studies in various aspects of the life of non-European peoples."[24] Even Nehru, who offered his own remarks during the opening session, did not raise the same criticisms of Western knowledge that he had done on other occasions.

It must be noted, however, that Kabir's claim that this was the first meeting of the Orientalists "outside the European Continent" is not true. The 22nd Congress (1951) was held in Istanbul and presided over by Zeki Velidi Togan. The meeting was held at Istanbul University, on the "European" side of the city, so in this case Kabir's claim may be said to still hold. And the conveners of the Istanbul conference did not lay claim to Asia, although there was the usual talk of a bridge between continents. But it was in fact the 14th Congress, held in Algiers in 1905, that was the first outside of Europe. That congress was an opportunity to showcase the jewel of France's Oriental empire to Europe's scholar-combatants. In a sense, the 1905 meeting belongs to a wholly different era, when European imperialism was still waxing steadily across the globe. But attention to the event reveals how the debate over colonial knowledge that raged at the acme of the anti-colonial struggle was intimately related to that struggle's very beginnings. In his report on the congress the French Orientalist Édouard Montet praised the French colonial government in Algeria for its role in organizing the meeting. Montet wrote that the then governor-general, Charles Jonnart, "belongs to this little group of colonial administrators who understand the great importance of scientific studies in the field of colonization and who help the role of science and the activity of scholars by the great authority they exercise."[25] Despite this praise for the meetings' organization, Montet was keen to make clear that the Orientalists should not meet in such an Oriental, African, place again. "I do not think," he wrote, "that after the experience obtained at Algiers, it would be proposed to assemble, in a hurry, another Congress of Orientalists in the Musulman Orient."[26] The reason for this, according to Montet, was "the notable participation in it of the Musulman element, and the attitude taken by believers in Islam." Montet went on to recount three incidents. One of them, a dispute between the German Orientalist Karl Vollers and the Egyptian radical intellectual Abd al-Aziz Jawish, centered on the Quran and its interpretation. Purportedly Jawish, "the eloquent and impassioned interpreter," responded to Vollers's presentation by "claiming for Musulmans only the sole study of the sacred book." This incident, Montet concluded, "shows the unfathomable abyss (not too strong a word to use) which separates the Musulman from the European mind."[27] A British observer for the *Athenaeum* confirms the account, although in less apoplectic terms: "No jihad was preached, however, although an attempt on the part of Dr. Vollers to demonstrate to the presence of vulgarism in the Koran was met with lively protests."[28]

One needs to look no further than Jawish's own work for elaboration. The incident became an infamous, indeed key, part of Jawish's biography. An heir to the intellectual tradition of Jamal al-din al-Afghani, Jawish was an Egyptian nationalist writer and adept anti-imperialist strategist. In addition to his schooling in Egypt, Jawish was immersed in English Orientalism, having studied pedagogy in London and taught Arabic at Oxford and Cambridge. His intervention in the discussion was published in Cairo the same year as *al-Islam din al-Fitra* (Islam, religion of instinct) by his comrade, the journalist Ahmad Hilmi. In his introduction to Jawish's text, Hilmi noted that anyone who "tasted the eloquence and power of its argument" was "astonished," hence the need to reprint it.[29] Jawish's text served as a testament to his countrymen and to anti-imperial Pan-Islamists worldwide that the confrontation with Europe—and the defense of Islam against Orientalists—was as much a struggle on the ground as it was in the mind. "If Egypt had indeed been colonised by representation," the historian Hussein Omar wrote of Jawish's treatise, "then its decolonisation had to undo the relationship between the words and things upon which its colonisation was premised." Jawish, therefore, Omar continued, "was not engaging in a facile apologetic, but rather asserting that Muslims held the universal capacities for self-rule that his colonial oppressors persistently denied him."[30] It is difficult to say that Kabir was ignorant of Algiers; it is, after all listed in the proceedings of the Delhi conference and those of previous congresses of Orientalists. More tellingly, however, Algiers's disappearance speaks to what is being proffered in Kabir's account. Kabir may very well not have known what transpired at Algiers, what it represented to the French Empire and to a group of Egyptian radicals. But it is precisely the narrative that Kabir relates, of rapprochement between Orientalists and Orientals and of a hidden history of Oriental suzerainty vis-à-vis Orientalist knowledge, that is significant. Kabir's, in the end, is a story of cooperation rather than confrontation. It is precisely this tension, between those making knowledge in the center and those on the periphery, that is repeated again and again in the production of area knowledge in the Third World. Kabir, as an important bureaucrat in the educational ministry and director of the ICCR, would have a direct impact on the course of area knowledge in India after 1947. But his was not the only path.

Both the Africanists Congress of 1962 and the Orientalist Congress of 1964 had their prelude in the 1960 Congress of Orientalists in Moscow, a major event for the Soviet Union and the largest congress to date. In "Orientalism in Crisis," Anouar Abdel-Malek distinguished what he saw as the burgeoning efforts to renew Orientalism's categories, methods, and institutions for an era of neo-imperialism in United States and Europe, with area studies then being developed in the Soviet Union.[31] The demands of Bandung transformed the course of Orientalism in the USSR. The 1956 Communist Party Congress revitalized the Soviet Union's institutions for Oriental studies and imbued them with the express purpose of serving the anti-colonial efforts of the oppressed peoples of the East.[32] The decision to separate the—generally very small—"Africa Section" of the Congress in future meetings was also made at Moscow. The Africanists Congress sat right at the heart of the Cold War's multiple paths toward the decolonization of knowledge. Melville Herskovits, doyen of (white) African studies in the United States, and I. I. Potekhin, the Soviet Union's premiere Africanist, were the chief progenitors of the Accra meeting, which was funded, most significantly, by UNESCO and the Ford Foundation.

Accra, then, was another stage upon which the intellectual history of decolonization was performed. "Everyone behaved very well, I thought," Basil Davidson wrote in his report from the congress, "although the delegations from France and the United States sometimes gave the impression of being much too large and too vocal for a gathering that was intended to emphasize African participation."[33] Indeed, foreign, especially American, control of the congress was a major concern among the Africans there. Americans, for their part, were on the defensive. In his address to the congress on the development of African studies, Herskovits referred to the establishment of the African Studies Association a few years earlier, in 1957.[34] Nkrumah's condemnation of the field speaks to a set of contradictions that would come to explode in the next decade, culminating in the confrontation between whites and Africans at the 1969 African Studies Association meeting in Montreal. Regarding the African studies of the West, of which Herskovits was a chief representative, Nkrumah was unsparing: "Even the most flattering of these writings fell short of objectivity and truth." "This explains, I believe," he concluded, "the popularity and success of anthropology as the main segment of African Studies."[35] While Potekhin was predictably vocal in his celebration of national, anti-imperialist revolution in Africa and the "duty of scientists" to serve the peoples of Africa in their struggle, Herskovits, an anthropologist, appears to respond directly to Nkrumah in his remarks.[36] "The reason anthropology dominated Africanist studies was because it brought to the African field the techniques of cross-cultural research." The international idiom of crossing cultures, rather confronting empire, was hegemonic in American "area study" and was then exported with gusto. Back in Delhi, Kabir would conclude a session called "Role of Oriental Studies in the Humanities" with his own modest proposal. "Perhaps," he speculated, "a special discipline of Occidentology should therefore be developed to balance the field of studies that is broadly described as Orientology."[37] The conflict between a form of study attached unabashedly to anti-imperialism and one premised fundamentally on imperialist institutions if not imperialist attitudes is readily seen from the imperial view. At the national level, however, the question of imperialism and anti-imperialism recedes from view, not because it disappears, but because different relationships emerge as significant and with them different histories. As I turn to the articulation of "West Asian studies" in India below, the nation and its affairs come again into view. There, the principles of Third

World social science and its conditions become exposed plainly. Even "independent" institutions were not independent. Their constitution was the product of a complex array of funds and political forces. Moreover, the challenge of making something new and different with area knowledge was ever elusive. As Issa Shivji put it, "Africans in Africa study Africa in centers of African studies in the image of centers in the North."[38] But the study of other areas from the areas themselves demands that we look beyond the question of decolonization and national self-definition to consider how "the other," as it were, can be approached in a nonimperial way, even as the demands and promises of empire are ever present.

Aligarh's Institute for Islamic Studies and "Muslim India"

Aligarh Muslim University (AMU) was founded as Muhammadan Anglo-Oriental College in 1875 by Sir Sayyid Ahmad Khan, a patrician reformer and one of Muslim India's most important nineteenth-century intellectuals. The university Khan called "the Oxford of the East" was the culmination of his intellectual project of modernist reformation and efforts at incorporating a purportedly backward Muslim population into the ranks of the British imperial administration. By the first half of the twentieth century, Aligarh had established itself as one of the most important institutions of higher learning on the subcontinent and was officially designated as a "central university" serving the whole of British India. Its prominence as a school and significance for India's Muslim intelligentsia made it an important center for Islamic and West Asian studies in the second half of the twentieth century. Even before 1947, Aligarh was designated as an important site for such studies to be developed. In a note he appended to the 1939 report of the All-India Muslim Educational Conference, the prominent lawyer and educator Azizul Huque argued that Aligarh "needs a full-fledged department of Islamic History and Culture."[39]

Partition devastated AMU. As a major center of support for the Muslim League—described once by Muhammad Ali Jinnah as the "arsenal of Muslim India"—a significant proportion of its faculty and students decamped for Pakistan in 1947 and the years that followed. India's first education minister, Abul Kalam Azad, called on Zakir Husain, a founder of Aligarh's nationalist rival Jamia Millia Islamia in the 1920s, to become vice-chancellor and rebuild the university. Husain was also a member of the Radhakrishnan Commission, established by Azad to examine university education in 1948, which recommended in its final report that "Aligarh University should be encouraged to develop a strong centre for Islamic studies."[40] Thus, the establishment of the Institute for Islamic Studies at AMU in 1954 was initiated at the federal level, involving some of India's most prominent Muslim intellectuals.

An August 1952 letter to Jawaharlal Nehru from Asaf Ali Asghar Fyzee, scholar of Islamic law and then India's ambassador to Egypt, ignited the discussion that culminated in the institute's funding. Fyzee's principal concern, as related to the prime minister and the Ministry of External Affairs, of which Nehru was also the head, was the importance of teaching modern Arabic in India: "The essential importance of Modern Arabic is neither religious nor even cultural, but as I have demonstrated above, it is important for trade and commerce, social life and diplomacy, it being the language of eighty million people." Fyzee argued that Arabs had great admiration for India and that the Middle East was of paramount political importance for Indian affairs. "Thus," because of French colonialism in Maghreb, oil in Iran, and the tense political circumstances of the Suez Canal, Israel, and Kashmir, Fyzee concluded, "in the whole of this belt, elements of instability are present and a solution is not easy to find."[41] The teaching of modern Arabic should be facilitated in order to produce a corps of diplomatic officers capable of speaking, reading, and writing Arabic. In the hierarchy of foreign languages to be encouraged by the Indian government, Arabic, Fyzee surmised, was of equal importance to Russian and Chinese.

Fyzee's report was forwarded by the Ministry of External Affairs to Azad's Ministry of Education, where Humayun Kabir looked favorably upon the scheme. Zakir Husain, then the new vice-chancellor at AMU met with Azad shortly thereafter. In 1949 Husain had proposed to establish a chair each in Arabic, Persian, and Turkish at AMU, but the proposal was dropped in 1951 due to lack of funds. With Fyzee's letter, Husain's efforts were rekindled. He wrote to Azad expanding on his previous plan: "We feel," he wrote, "that the establishment of an Institute of Islamic Studies at this University will serve a very useful purpose."[42] The institute was to serve three primary roles: the study of Islamic culture and civilization; the study of contemporary West Asia and North Africa; and the study of Turkish, Persian, and Arabic. To accomplish these tasks, the institute would publish "books, monographs, and papers" and hold "seminars, symposia, and conferences," in addition to teaching modern languages. While Husain was explicit in stating that he did not minimize the importance of studying ancient history and classical languages, he distinguished his scheme from already existing sites of Islamic knowledge in India: "A number of Indian Universities have, no doubt, established departments of Arabic and Persian but the courses of studies pursued in them are, generally, confined to classical literature. There are a number of Muslim educational institutions like Darul-Ulum, Deoband and Darul Ulum Nadwat-ul-Ulema which devote themselves to theological studies and teach Arabic and Persian merely as aids to such studies. Thus the facilities for modern studies relating to the above mentioned countries are scarcely available."

Husain was also deeply aware of the political importance of his project. In a revised version of the scheme he sent a month later to S. S. Bhatnagar, the chemist, known for his work in developing India's national research laboratories, he placed the question of international politics at the very top. "With the advent of freedom," Husain wrote, "the question of India's international relationships has assumed paramount importance." The specter of Pakistani and Muslim solidarity was predictably present. The countries of the "Near East," Husain continued, "are, not infrequently, being subjected to interested propaganda palpably hostile to Indian interests; closer relations with them on the cultural and intellectual plans [sic] can be of great use to our country."[43]

Husain's plan was to cost the government 35,000 rupees (20,000 for books manuscripts, furniture, fans and fittings, and records for language instructions) and 60,000 per year (45,000 for three professors and allowances for fellows). The 1949 proposal to simply appoint three professors in modern West Asian languages was to cost 45,000 rupees, so the institute scheme was, as the Ministry of External Affairs noted, "more ambitious, but at the same time more expensive."[44] But political questions were becoming more urgent, and the need for proper training was worth the cost. Less than a month later R. K. Nehru wrote to Kabir inquiring about the status of Fyzee's proposal: "This ministry is naturally anxious to see the study of Asian languages promoted, in view of our increasingly close political and other contacts with our Asian neighbours."[45] But the prospect of establishing an institute was seen as "not essential" by the Ministry of External Affairs.[46] Nevertheless, the Ministry of Education endorsed the proposal. "An Institute of Islamic Studies," Kabir wrote, "would be a very valuable acquisition, as there is no such institution in the country." And after some cost cutting at the Ministry of Finance—the request for four fellows was turned into three—the government of India accepted AMU's proposal.

By September Husain was growing frustrated with the delay and wrote a long letter to Azad, noting that his budget for the institute was already modest, and further efforts to limit the scope of the scheme would only lessen its impact: "Trying to do the work piecemeal will,

I am afraid, defeat the objective we have in view. I feel convinced that when established this Institute will justify itself not only by its academic achievement, but also by helping effectively in establishing closer relations and better understanding with some of our very important Asian and African neighbors."[47] The institute was established in 1955. In December and January 1954/1955 Husain traveled to Lebanon, Syria, Egypt, Turkey, and Iran to seek out recruits and build academic connections with the region. He took with him Abdul Aleem, whom he tapped to become the institute's first director.

Aleem represents an important bridge between the anti-colonial struggle and the development of political and academic institutions in independent India. Born in 1907 in the town of Ghazipur in today's Uttar Pradesh, Aleem was involved in the Khalifat and noncooperation movements in his youth. "His beard," the poet Ale Ahmad Suroor emphasized, "was a little longer than Mualana Azad's and a little shorter than Zakir Sahib's."[48] A student of Arabic and Persian all his life, in 1926 Aleem received his BA from Jamia Millia University. He then traveled to the University of Berlin, where he received his PhD in Islamic studies in 1931, with a dissertation on i'jaz or inimitability of the Quran. In Germany he became associated with the Indian anti-imperialists who were organizing there in exile. Aleem also became closely acquainted with Marxism. Upon his return to India, he taught briefly at Aligarh, before moving to a more permanent position at Lucknow's distinguished department of Arabic. There, Aleem became attached to the still nascent progressive writer's movement. Though not an avid writer of poetry or fiction like many of the more well-known writers associated with the group, including Faiz Ahmed Faiz and Sajjad Zaheer, Aleem was a key and indeed foundational member of the Progressive Writers Association (PWA or Anjuman Taraqqi Pasand Mussanafin-e-Hind), writing its first constitution and later serving as its secretary. Aleem's small house in Lucknow became the hub for the PWA's activities beginning in the late 1930s and early 1940s. Zaheer wrote in his memoirs that Aleem "was matchless in the brevity and clarity of expression in his language."[49] One fellow traveler of the progressive writers observed that Aleem was "an excellent organizer, and in my view, the PWA's most effective propagandist."[50] Another wrote that Aleem was "the group's major theoretician."[51]

At the height of the struggle against British rule in India, Aleem was in and out of British prisons, and he could be found everywhere from anti-fascist meetings in Delhi to conferences of independent Muslims. Aleem would also publish and speak widely about West Asian affairs in the Urdu press, including the journal *Hindustan*, which he edited. Purportedly, Aleem never called himself a Marxist. Instead, he referred to himself as "the knowledge bearer of historical materialism." "Even Marx," he would say, "did not refer to himself as a Marxist."[52] In 1954 Aleem published an essay, "Marxism and Literature," laying out a defense—through Marx, Lenin, and Gorky—of literary aesthetics and social realism, which he emphasized, did not need to be dreary or dull.[53] His work, however, was not limited to expounding upon "the means of mental production," as Marx himself famously put it. The Communist Party of which Aleem was a part required its members to be part of a labor union, so he was a longtime member of the Railway Workers Union and participated in its organizing activities.[54] When Aleem arrived in Aligarh in 1950 he openly supported and worked with Communist Party candidates running in the Aligarh district in the first general elections. Riaz-ur-Rehman Sherwani, an Aligarh Arabic professor, recalls that Aleem subsequently became discreet about his political commitments, under pressure from the administration of the university.[55]

Aleem's strong presence indicates a certain distance between the demands of the ulema—or increasingly, the demands of a disaffected Muslim minority—and the intellectual activities and political aims of the institute. In the first issue of the Institute's English-language bulletin (an Urdu edition would follow a few years later), Aleem reflected on the purpose of the institution of which he was the head. His was a nationalist internationalism, which insisted on the West Asian horizons of India's political project. He wrote that the institute was established "to promote the study of Islamic culture and civilisation as well as to contribute to the understanding of political, economic, social and cultural trends in the Arab world, Iran and Turkey. Such a study is important for us in India by reason of the close associations which have existed between our respective countries since the ancient past as well as for our national needs."[56] In the early years, Aleem shepherded a serious, important, if fairly conventional program of scholarly production. Attached to formidable traditions of Arabic philology and German historicism, the first publications in the institute's series were an edition of the tenth-century jurist al-Khattabi's *Al-Bayan fi i'jaz al-Qur'an* prepared by Aleem himself and Maqbul Ahmad's edition of al-Idrisi's eleventh-century description of the Indian Ocean.

The activities of the Institute were very much in line with the work of like-minded centers around the world, including its namesake at McGill. Nevertheless, from the outset the strictly "Islamic" character of the institute was a subject of significant debate and consternation. Part of this had to do with the arrival, after the exodus occasioned by Partition, of a large number of left-wing faculty members at what was historically a fairly conservative institution. Aleem's daughter recalls him being smeared as an atheist and "infidel communist."[57] Nevertheless, the Islamicity of the Institute was also raised in official, secular quarters. With regard to Zakir Husain's initial proposals for the Institute for Islamic Studies, B. N. Nanda from the Ministry of Education expressed considerable skepticism about the scheme. Despite Husain's explicit distancing of the project from India's well-known centers of Muslim theology, Nanda wondered if in the end the Institute might in fact come to be the same type of thing. "We have to guard against this," he wrote. "It would perhaps be inconsistent with our Constitution to promote studies in or relating to any particular religion as such."[58] Nanda's interpretation coincided with the approach of the Indian state to Islamic institutions in general. This can be seen most dramatically in the once-princely State of Hyderabad, where "nationalization" was violently enacted. The Nizam's institutions—represented as indelibly Islamic—were defunded, dismantled, and finally neglected by the civilian government appointed by New Delhi after the infamous "police action" that deposed the Nizam and killed tens of thousands. The hegemonic interpretation of secularism that animated the activities of the central government dictated strict limits upon or the total elimination of funding. This despite the fact, as Kavita Datla powerfully narrated, that the builders of institutions like Hyderabad's Osmania University worked assiduously to produce work that was self-consciously modern, national, and even secular.[59] Democracy and secularism, however, were interpreted by some of India's influential bureaucrats in largely majoritarian terms, "insisting," as one historian put it, "that the government ought to act in the interests of an imagined Hindu majority."[60] Kabir, in any case, did not take kindly to Nanda's suggestions: "While it is necessary to offer any comments on the views expressed by some officers of the E. A. Ministry on the educational and general aspects of the scheme, I might perhaps point out that one of the specific functions of this University, under the Act, is 'to promote Oriental and Islamic studies' (which, incidentally, is something quite different from Muslim theology)."[61]

While the status of Indian Muslims was hotly contested, sometimes very violently, the status of Islamic or West Asian studies was of minor national concern when compared to other disciplines and scholarly fields. Across Indian universities, the study of Mughal India—which AMU was a leading center of thanks to the efforts of historians like Irfan Habib and Narul Islam—was a major field with wide appeal, as the annual proceedings of the Indian History Congress and the publications of the Indian Council of Historical Research amply attest. By contrast, the study of Arabic, Islamic, and West Asian history was comparatively insignificant on the intellectual scene. The major sites of study and research in India largely neglected the field. The long-standing sections on Islamic culture and "Arabic and Persian" were by far the smallest at the biennial All India Oriental Conference, which had been convened since 1918 by Pune's Bhandarkar Oriental Research Institute. Emphasis at those meetings was laid largely on Sanskritic knowledge. To illustrate the difference, one need only survey the comparative lengths of the different sections. For example, in the proceedings for the 1961 conference, the address for the Vedic section constitutes some twenty pages; the classical Sanskrit section occupies more than sixty; and Islamic culture, a paltry two and a half, much of it devoted to vague statements of Islam's "composite" nature and the unity of the world. The Institute of Islamic Studies would establish a counterpart conference, the All-Indian Islamic Studies Conference, in 1958.

In the first two meetings of the conference held at Aligarh, Aleem struck an optimistic chord in his remarks advocating for greater cooperation between those studying Islamic and West Asian topics in India. He celebrated the historical impact of Indian Islam on the world and the role of India in future international relations.[62] By 1964, at the Conference in Hyderabad, Aleem's survey of the field was more reserved. He criticized the narrow sense of Islam as simply a religion, a "traditional concept which persists in many circles in our country."[63] Aleem's vision of Islamic studies for the future necessitated collaboration with other disciplines and area studies along with the intensive study of the relevant Asian and African languages. Aleem was also acutely aware of the social aspects and political implications of Islamic studies in India. "It is a pity," he said, "that in this country non-Muslim scholars have not yet engaged themselves seriously in Islamic studies. There is hardly any non-Muslim Indian scholar who possesses adequate knowledge of Arabic for utilising original Islamic source material."[64] Islamic and West Asian studies, then, meant to serve the Indian nation as a whole, was institutionally and demographically an Indian Muslim undertaking. K. M. Panikkar, whom Zakir Husain described as "his first teacher," lamented this communal divide over India's history, but in the opposite direction.[65] Reflecting on his short time as a history professor at Aligarh in the nineteen-teens, Panikkar wrote: "No one in Aligarh had the least interest in the long pre-Islamic history of India. It struck me as strange that while a great number of Hindu scholars had written on Indo-Muslim history, and the classic biography of Aurangzeb is by a Hindu writer, not a single Muslim scholar had contributed anything on any period of pre-Islamic history."[66] The problem of history and who wrote it seemed to stem from a larger, still unresolved social condition.

Back at Aligarh, these conflicts came to a head in 1965, when newly appointed vice-chancellor Ali Yavar Jung was almost killed by protesting students. "The students marched with a coffin to the office where the Vice-Chancellor was holding a meeting of the court," M. C. Chagla, then minister of education, claimed in his autobiography.[67] Jung, formerly India's ambassador to Egypt and elsewhere, was taken by some corners of the university community to be another interloping secularist; more pressing than his reputation, however, were his actions. Jung's predecessor had raised the quota of internal students entering AMU from 50 to 75 percent. These internal students were overwhelmingly Muslim, so the change was meant to increase the proportion of Muslim students at the university. The change, therefore, was certainly reasonable at the political level and had indeed been endorsed in principle by the central government. For some perspective, while some 40 percent of AMU's students and staff were non-Muslim, at its counterpart at the other end of Uttar Pradesh, Benares Hindu University (BHU), "a mere 1 percent of students and staff were non-Muslim."[68] Jung reversed the change, returning the quota to 50 percent. Aligarh exploded, police were brought onto campus, and the university was closed in an effort to halt the insurgency. The events of 1965, coming on the heels of Nehru's death, stretched far beyond AMU. As Laurence Gautier has demonstrated, they catapulted the activities of the university into national, popular politics, mobilizing Muslims who were exasperated by nearly two decades of Congress rule to make new demands as a minority.[69]

AMU's West Asian studies scholars were of course caught up in this tumult. As Aleem's experience attests, these conflicts long predated Jung. Maqbul Ahmad, Aleem's younger colleague who taught at AMU from 1950 onward, was disturbed by accusations that were made by conservatives at Aligarh and beyond. "Rumors" Ahmad wrote in his memoirs, "started in some circles that these progressive people did not deserve to teach Islamic studies, it was also discussed in Urdu newspapers."[70] The Jung incident, in Ahmad's estimation, "was a watermark in the life of Aligarh. . . . [S]ince then the political climate has deteriorated . . . and reactionary factions have dominated."[71] "No one in Aligarh could believe that even Maqbul Ahmad could perform Hajj," Ahmad recounted: "A friend said that it is really surprising, until yesterday there were riots against you and today you are a Hajji."[72]

Such conflicts plagued Aligarh from its inception, when Sayyid Ahmad Khan's ideas about religious practice were seen as bordering on apostasy to the ulema, who perceived him as a layman or worse. According to David Lelyveld, "Criticism of Sayyid Ahmad's personal religious views threatened, in fact, to undermine his whole educational movement."[73] For an outside observer, the challenges faced by India's Arabists were clear. On his first visit to Aligarh, the Palestinian historian Nicola Ziadeh noted that while European Orientalists approached their subjects dispassionately, "Indian researchers, who were Muslims, spoke from a special position. They are a minority in a strange atmosphere." Ziadeh continued, "While it is true that everyone is an Indian citizen and the state does differentiate between this and that citizen, it nevertheless seemed to me, based on my conversations with colleagues, that the lessons of Islam and its civilization is one of the shields that the minority resorts to to defend itself, whether this situation is justified or not."[74]

Ziadeh's skepticism of Indian democracy did not temper his anxiety over his Indian Muslim colleagues' approach. His speculation about whether their defensiveness, their use of scholarship as a "shield," is "justified" as instructive. What claims on history and the future of India did India's West Asian studies scholars make? What pasts did they claim, and which did they disavow? Which India, or idea of India as it were, did they serve?

I turn to these questions in the remainder of this chapter, but first one last word on the problem of the nation and its limits is in order. India, especially "Muslim India," was and remains a contested field of thought and site of sovereignty. The aforementioned 1961 Oriental Conference took place in Srinagar, Kashmir, and must be seen as part of a concentrated effort, institutional, infrastructural, and educational, to normalize Kashmir's place in the Indian polity, a colonizing project, as Hafsa Kanjwal has argued.[75] Attendees, including Panikkar, who played a key role in the reorganization of India's states in the 1950s and would briefly serve as the vice-chancellor of Kashmir University, would use the occasion to assert that Kashmir was and must remain part of India. And he was not alone; nearly every section head would adopt some refrain. As India's role in the world is queried later, it would be prudent to remember India's so-called frontiers, its edges, and indeed, its colonies.

The Indo-Arab Past (and Future)

It is ironic that Aligarh's Arabists were attacked so vociferously for being un-Islamic. For it was precisely their attachments to the Islamic past that they regularly professed, rehearsed, and even reenacted, that distinguished them from their counterparts in the North Atlantic. Attention to the Indo-Arab past was a major preoccupation; even when their work broached other topics, contemporary Indo-Arab relations framed their work. Maqbul Ahmad's efforts were perhaps the most prominent in this regard. He joined Aligarh in 1951 as a senior lecturer of Arabic and was promoted to reader in 1954; in that role he played a key part in the development of the Institute for Islamic Studies that was founded the same year. Born in 1921, Ahmad studied Urdu and Persian with his mother at home and may have studied Arabic at the madrasa of Taj ul Masjid in Bhopal. Ahmad went on to study at Ismail Yusuf College in Bombay, graduating in 1942 at the top of his class. At this time, Ahmad himself claimed, he was beginning to "step out of tradition and enter modernity."[76] In 1944 he earned his MA in Urdu and Arabic from Bombay University and was awarded a scholarship to Oxford.

Ahmad went to work with the prominent Orientalist Hamilton Gibb. Gibb immediately put Ahmad to work translating Masudi's Muruj al Dahab, which Ahmad completed a year later and for which he was awarded a B.Litt. He then began a doctorate on al-Idrisi. In England, Ahmad became acquainted with Krishna Menon and participated in the political activities of the India League, traveling around Great Britain in that capacity. Ahmad later traveled widely across West Asia, especially from the 1960s onward. In 1963–64 he did so at the behest of Clovis Maksoud's Arab League office in Delhi, traveling to and lecturing in Egypt, Lebanon, Syria, and Iraq.[77] But his most significant travels were more directly tied to his imagination as a scholar. "In 1974," Ahmad writes, "I went to Fustat in Egypt to search for the grave of al-Masudi.... [I]n 1973 I'd gone to Ghazni in search of al-Biruni's tomb."[78] By his own admission, however, Ahmad's most interesting fieldwork took place at sea. In 1963, when departing Baghdad, he traded his airline ticket for ship passage and took the train to Basra's port. "There was a certain preponderance in my subconscious mind that one would get to see the places mentioned by al-Masudi from the ship."[79] Early in the morning on May 3, 1963, Ahmad boarded the MS *Santhia*. Ahmad described it as his most adventurous and interesting sea voyage. The seascape that Ahmad observed, however, was significantly different from al-Masudi's, characterized principally by oil refineries and naval installations.[80] The Indian Ocean, long characterized by trade and translation, was now heavily militarized and encircled by the machinery of extraction. But Ahmad's enthusiasm for al-Masudi went far beyond his efforts to embody him at sea. In January 1959 he convened a conference in honor of Al-Masudi's millinery at Aligarh. Among those invited was Nicola Ziadeh, who represented one of the strongest links between this coterie of Indian scholars and developments to the west.

Ziadah taught at the American University of Beirut, which was undertaking its own profound efforts to transform the study of West Asia—the Arab world, for the denizens of Beirut—after empire.[81] As a visiting professor at Harvard, Ziadeh encountered Professor Henry Kissinger, who would ask him for suggestions about whom to invite to his prestigious International Seminar. In 1958 Kissinger asked Ziadeh to be a guest, but Ziadeh refused, telling him he needed to attend to urgent matters back home. In his memoirs, Ziadeh recounts that upon his return to Lebanon from the United States, he received a letter of invitation from Aligarh Muslim University to participate in a conference for Al-Masudi's millinery. Ziadeh recalls that his wife Margaret asked him if he would accept the invitation, having just refused Harvard's, to which he replied: "Margaret, this is something new—to India."[82] He arrived in Delhi in December 1958. Ziadeh was not shy about his enthusiasm for Aligarh. In his remarks at the conference itself, he said, "To-day our Kaʻba is Aligarh University. This University is not unknown to us. We have read the works of its professors and we have known a great deal about them. But to know of a place is one thing and to be in it and meet the people who inhabit it is another. We have come together to this Kaʻba of learning to place al-Masudi on his pedestal so that his knowledge may be better appreciated. We are grateful for the people of Aligarh for the choice of the saint and the Kaʻba of the day."[83]

That Al-Masudi was the source of this collaboration is not surprising, but speaks to how past Indo-Arab engagements catalyzed and inspired new ones. Al-Masudi is well known for spending some two years in India in the tenth century and writing about the geography of the Indian coast. In a letter to Abdul Aleem, Abul Kalam Azad, who died a few months before the conference convened, recommended that the organizers "emphasize wherever necessary that the Millennium of Al-Masudi at the University is being commemorate because of the services of this great writer and world tourist in making India more acquainted to the Middle Eastern counties by means of his writings about the social, political and religious conditions and about India's geography."[84]

The collapse of past, present, and future was emblematic of these intellectual collaborations. In his 1969 book, *Indo-Arab Relations*, published by the ICCR, Ahmad noted his debt to earlier efforts like Tara Chand's *Influence of Islam on Indian Culture* and Sulieman al-Nadwi's *'Arab-o-Hind ke Taʻluqqat*.[85] Ahmad's book focuses almost exclusively on the premodern. "As for the modern period," he wrote in its epilogue, "the available data and material pertaining to the last one and half centuries is so vast and varied that it requires a special study, and for this reason it has largely been excluded from the scope of the present volume."[86] Nevertheless, Ziadeh's Arabic translation of the book, published in Beirut in 1974, is illustrated with images speaking directly to the present political situation, which is entirely absent from the content of the book itself. The cover page has photographs of Nehru meeting (separately) with Nasser, King Hussein of Jordan, and King Faisal of Saudi Arabia. Other pages in the book are devoted to similar photographs. Content notwithstanding, Ahmad's book was not shy about its uses in the present, of which Ziadeh's translation is a clear instantiation. Beyond its stated intellectual contribution, Ahmad admitted larger aims: "It is hoped that a study of the past history of Indo-Arab relations as attempted in the present work, will help the peoples of India and the Arab world to understand each other better, and to cement more firmly the good and cordial relations that exist between the two peoples today."[87] Despite the perennial recourse to past events and emblems, the future was the principal focus of an Indian state keen to lead Asia and the nonaligned. But the future also animated the activities of individual scholars, passionately invested in their research and motivated personally and politically to collaborate with their neighbors to the west.

Area studies in India did of course serve a direct political function for the state. New Delhi, the capital, was the center of this effort. And the Indian Council of World Affairs, erstwhile organizer of the 1947 Asian Relations Conference, was a key site in this regard. After significant gestation, the ICWA founded the Indian School of International Studies in 1955 (later folded into the new Jawaharlal Nehru University [JNU], to considerable controversy).[88] The Rockefeller and Ford Foundations played an important role in the school's establishment, including extensive funding for its library and other funds for fellowships for staff.[89] These developments should not be seen as belated, but concomitant to developments elsewhere. The Massachusetts Institute of Technology's CIA-funded Center for International Studies was founded only a few years earlier, in 1951.

Aligarh's philologists and historians nourished the growth of the school. Aleem played an essential role in the institution, serving on its board and giving regular lectures.[90] In 1954, Aleem hired a young scholar by the name of Mohmmed Shafi Agwani, better suited for the social scientific age. Agwani came from a different class than Aleem's *zamindari* background and was of a different generation. Born in 1928 in Udaipur, Agwani described his experiences as a youth witnessing the freedom movement as formative. His father read nationalist Urdu papers from across India, and a photograph of Gandhi addressing a meeting of the Indian National Congress hung prominently in his childhood home. Agwani studied at the University of Rajasthan, receiving an MA in political science there in 1952. While there he was involved in the All India Student Federation, a group affiliated with the Communist Party. After getting his MA, Agwani was awarded a scholarship to study at the Institute for Social Studies at the Hague, which had just been founded. Its students at the time were mostly from the colonies and were there to be trained in economics, sociology, international relations, and public administration, in the disciplines of what was being called "development." In Agwani's day, the largest group of students hailed from India like himself. Upon completion of an international relations MPhil, which he wrote on the Arab League, Agwani earned his doctoral dissertation at the University of Utrecht under the supervision of the Dutch professor of contemporary history C. D. J. Brandt, on the topic of US-Arab relations from 1945 to 1952.[91]

Agwani arrived at the Indian School of International Studies in 1957, two years after its founding. "My task at the school," Agwani wrote, "was essentially twofold: to help prepare the ground for study and research on contemporary West Asia and North Africa; and to teach a composite pre-doctoral course on the history, politics, and social, economic and religious background of the region."[92] In 1958 the ISIS funded Agwani to visit Egypt and Libya, where in addition to his own research he wrote a note on the archives and libraries about their relevance to researchers studying the modern Arab world.[93] The school became a key site for the export and articulation of area knowledge in the defense infrastructure of the Indian state. Agwani notes that faculty members were regularly asked to lecture at the nearby Ministry of External Affairs and at the colleges of the Defense Department. "Similarly," Agwani wrote, "my association with the National Defence Colleges began since its inception in 1960 and continued for over thirty years."[94]

What was the purpose of this knowledge making? Albert Hourani, the doyen of Arab studies in the Anglophone world who had helped advise Agwani during the course of his dissertation research, provided the foreword to Agwani's study when it was published as a book by Aligarh in 1955. "The Republic of India," Hourani writes, "having secured and consolidated its own freedom, now acquires an increasing influence in the outside world. Whether or not Indians want it, they may find their influence growing in the Arab world, and their security bound up with it."[95] Hourani's words here echo those of Valentine Chirol, the British imperial strategist, who in 1902 defined the Middle East as "those regions of Asia which extend to the borders of India or command the approaches to India, and which are consequently bound up with the problems of Indian political as well as military defence."[96] Ironically, Hourani shares Chirol's logic of boundary and security, despite approaching the space from the other side. Hourani concludes his foreword by writing that Agwani's book "will have special value if it helps his fellow-countrymen to understand the situation of their Middle West."[97] Hourani's conscious inversion of the standard imperial area—and yet the maintenance of the regional demarcation—speaks to the contradictions at the heart of area studies practiced from areas themselves. Agwani himself would disrupt the very genealogy of area study during a seminar on West Asia at Aligarh in January 1978, announcing: "The concept of area studies is often mistakenly regarded as an American invention."[98] In truth, he argues, one need only reference the eleventh-century Central Asian polymath Al-Biruni, known for his great *Tarkih al-Hind*. "I do not know of a more scientific definition of area studies than the one given by al-Biruni,"[99] Agwani concludes, drawing, as was common among his colleagues, upon those past representatives of an Indo-Arab intellectual tradition. Al-Biruni's aims, Agwani summarizes, "was to afford the necessary information and training" to discuss with Indians the basis of their civilization.[100] Even for Agwani, who would become India's most prominent West Asianist, training dozens of students during his long and controversial career at JNU, the idioms of friendship, understanding, and solidarity were paramount in his conceptualization of West Asian studies.

The historical framework, political commitments, and social worlds of India's Arabists often stood in sharp distinction to the area studies that were then ascendant in the West and with which the ostensibly non-West had to incessantly contend. Nurtured by the nineteenth century's colonial categories and consecrated in the Cold War's institutionalization of empire, the area studies practiced in US universities and exported elsewhere valorized nations, races, and regions in the service of ongoing projects of extraction and exploitation, from Egypt to India to Vietnam. While West Asian studies in India was not innocuous, or even methodologically distinct from the international social science that reigned, its aims were not—and could not necessarily be—domination and destruction. The areas' areas, so to speak, could never be so divided and disrupted as those areas conceived from afar and with condescension. Even in the midst of regular, national turmoil over knowledge and its institutions, Indian intellectuals still adopted an internationalist, anti-imperialist posture toward the Arab world. Just as it is now commonplace to recognize the imperial dimensions of Western social science, even and especially when it is framed as apolitical, so too must we attend closely to the scholarly activities of Asians and Africans, whose ideas we may yet have an opportunity to salvage in our own efforts.

Epilogue

Let us turn again to the question of Palestine. In a context of decolonization and anti-imperialism, it is no surprise that at a time when Western intellectuals—except for a few—were constantly producing work in defense of Israel and Zionism, the situation in South Asia was markedly different. In an essay from around 1971 on Asia and Palestine, printed both as a pamphlet by the Arab League's New Delhi office and as a chapter in Ibrahim Abu-Lughod's influential volume *The Transformation of Palestine*, M. S. Agwani traced Asian diplomatic relations with Israel and Palestine and explained the political and philosophical reasons Asians have opposed Israeli colonialism and supported Palestinian anti-colonialism. Agwani rebuts declarations that Asians' opposition to Israel is a product of their ignorance of Jewish history, as some had asserted. "Asia," he wrote, "has viewed the Zionist claim with suspicion and disapprobation. An explanation for this must be sought in the incompatibility between the anti-colonial upsurge in Asia and the methods and goals of the Zionist movement."[1] Agwani rehearses the details of British imperial support for the Zionist project in Palestine before describing the entanglements of Indian anti-colonialism with the Arabs and Afro-Asian opposition to Israel at the United Nations.

Agwani concludes that "the Zionist belief in the uniqueness of the Jewish race and its 'historic mission'; the ideological amalgam of race, religion, and politics; and above all, the Israeli model of a garrison state ... have little practical relevance to the pressing needs of the Asian nations for development and peace."[2] The idioms of non-alignment, "development and peace," are summoned against the racism and militarism of an Israel still serving imperial power. The Asian perspective, as it were, pulls Israel into the context of Asian history in order to declare it alien to Asian space and time. The irony, of course, is that this is in a sense the mirror opposite of the reigning American view, of ubiquitous defensiveness with regard to Israeli actions coupled with a mythology of historical and geographical justification. The circumvention of an Afro-Asian United Nation's decolonizing agenda in the 1960s by alternative mechanisms of international governance controlled by American capital, namely the World Bank and the International Monetary Fund, and the US militarization of the world, meant that no Asian power was equipped to confront Israel effectively on the diplomatic score or in the battlefield. But in arenas of knowledge, the Asian view and the American view could sometimes clash. As a visitor to the United States in 1968–69, Agwani was party to such a confrontation. In his memoirs, Agwani recounts a seminar with J. C. Hurewitz, one time Office of Strategic Services Near East specialist and longtime director of Columbia's Middle East Institute:

> The discussion was on a field work report by a student who had spent several months collecting data about the modalities and consequences of establishing Jewish settlements by Israeli authorities in the occupied West Bank. At some point in the discussion I observed that a distinction must be made between Israeli security and its obligations under international law to protect Palestinians civil rights. This visibly annoyed J. C. Hurewitz who, was in the chair. He got up

and pacing up and down the seminar room tried to trash my comment as unacademic.[3]

Minor as it may seem, the scene Agwani paints speaks to precisely the assumption this book has sought to contest: knowledge in the Third World—attuned as it is to various projects, call them nonalignment, anti-imperialism, or decolonization—is denigrated on that basis. It is seen as not particularly significant, not serious, not scholarship. By virtue of its location, its language, or its attitude, Afro-Asian thought is condemned to be irrelevant, derivative, or degenerate. One could turn to the example of David Gordon's deeply condescending book *Self-Determination and History in the Third World*, published the same year as Agwani's essay, to witness his criticism of a Palestinian physicist at the American University of Beirut (AUB), Antoine Zahlan, who has dared to "turn himself into something of a sociologist-historian" and "thus becomes something of an ally of Constantine Zurayk ... a lifelong intellectual leader of the Arab cause."[4] According to Gordon, Zahlan became an "ally" of Zurayk, a prominent Syrian historian best known for his 1948 book *Maʿna al-Nakba* (*The Meaning of Disaster*), when he wrote an article from the Asian perspective on the history of American support for Israel. Gordon would go on to argue that Zurayk and Nabih Amin Faris, a Palestinian historian at AUB, sacrificed their professionalism in serving a struggle for self-determination, a fact Gordon determined to be "sad but understandable."[5]

Gordon was a colleague of all these Arab men whom he held in contempt. He taught at AUB from 1949 to 1954, went to Princeton for a PhD in history, and returned to teach from 1958 to 1975. His was a thoroughly imperial career, straddling precisely that period in West Asia when American institutions became increasingly contested, much to his chagrin. Gordon was born in Istanbul in 1926, where his father worked for the American Express Company. Before teaching at AUB—once known as the Syrian Protestant

College—Gordon taught at Istanbul's Robert College, founded by the same group of American missionaries. When he departed Lebanon at the outbreak of the Civil War there in 1975, Gordon had had enough of the "radicalism" and "Third Worldism" on campus and outside its gates. "I found it increasingly difficult to make personal contact with students, especially the activists," Gordon wrote after his departure. "Arabists," he continued, "now openly resented me and my colleagues as American.... Often in the heat of student activism one was denounced as an agent of the CIA."[6] Gordon was unable to recognize the distance between his own scholarly practice and desires and those of his colleagues and students. Gordon's resentment that he might be viewed in the same way he viewed Third World intellectuals, as unfortunately saddled with the burden of politics, tarring their scholarship and stunting their ambitions, was beyond the pale.

This book has sought to relay the challenge of confronting imperial knowledge, its mores, and its institutions for the Third World's intellectuals. That rapprochement or reconciliation might elevate one in the eyes of a better resourced, well-connected, erudite, imminent, Western scholar is not lost on anyone, then as now. Agwani's retrospective narration of his altercation with Hurewitz redeems the American: "A colleague later told me that he and some other faculty members had earlier called on the director expressing strong disapproval of Hurewitz's conduct. The same evening Hurewitz met me in the faculty club to convey profound regrets. Thereafter, our relations became as smooth and cordial as before the unpleasant event."[7] Agwani turns a structural conflict into a personal disagreement, easily healed. In explaining away Hurewtiz's violent reaction to the mere mention of Palestinian rights, Agwani elevates himself to Hurewtiz's level, so to speak. It is for the same reason, perhaps, that Agwani wrote a rave review of Gordon's *Self-Determination and History in the Third World*. Psychoanalysis isn't even necessary to explain such cases; we can simply map them upon the unequal geography of knowledge that encircles our world.

Let me end then where I started, with the problem of decolonization today. In the absence of a genuine effort to undermine the material basis of American imperialism and its adjuncts worldwide, there is enthusiasm now for the decolonization of knowledge or curricula, and for the restitution of stolen artifacts from museums, the destruction of imperial statues, and the renaming of streets and institutions. These are all projects with their origins in the anti-colonial struggles of the twentieth century, when across Afro-Asia statues were felled, even blown up; spaces and streets were renamed; and demands were made for the loot carried off in the preceding centuries to be returned. It is for this reason that I have sought to bring attention to the work of intellectuals who labored in the heyday of decolonization to get a sense of their imperfect efforts, before embarking upon our own.

We may, for example, take notice of the genealogy of "settler colonialism" as a way of understanding the colonization of Palestine, and much else. Settler colonialism has become something of a keyword as of late, much to the chagrin of settler colonists. "Israel," Fred Moten observes, "is called almost everything but the settler colony that it is in official media and intellectual culture."[8] The study of Palestine in terms of settler colonialism, we may emphasize, has long been a concerted, transnational effort. The work of the Palestine Liberation Organization's Research Center in the 1960s demonstrates this clearly. Fayez Sayegh's *Zionist Colonialism in Palestine*, published in English in 1965, is exemplary in this regard. We must also mention the work of the Israeli revolutionary socialist organization, Matzpen, which clearly critiqued the settler colonial nature of Israeli society and Zionist ideology in its work during the 1960s and 1970s in Israel and in European exile. By the mid-1970s, understanding Israel in relation to settler colonialism elsewhere was well established; we may briefly mention Ibrahim Abu-Lughod and Baha Abu-Laban's volume *Settler Regimes in Africa and the Arab World : The Illusion of Endurance*, published by the Association of Arab American University Graduates in 1974; Richard Steven's *The Settler-Colonial Phenomenon in Africa and the Middle East: The Passing of an Era?*, published by Khartoum University in 1976; and Jamil Hilal's "Imperialism and Settler Colonialism in West Asia: Israel and the Arab Palestinian Struggle," *Utafiti* 1 (1976), the journal of the Faculty of Arts and Social Science, University of Dar es Salaam. This geography of scholarly interaction demonstrates the extent to which, on the one hand, the Palestinian struggle has always been understood by the global majority, the global South, the Third World, as part and parcel of their efforts. And also, relatedly, to counter again the hegemonic view in the West that the struggle in Palestine is somehow transhistorical, or even outside of history, beyond the grasp of materialist thinking, or the categories we can demonstrably understand: settler and native, colonizer and colonized, and so on.

But "method" does precede the history of knowledge I have related thus far: the historical riposte to racist history, the honest attachment to political and social ends rather than their obfuscation, and the establishment of independent institutions. Method alone, I think, is not enough. We have witnessed decolonization's transformation into diversity in the twenty-first century university and decoloniality's deployment for chauvinist ends, most spectacularly perhaps in the Hindu supremacist rhetoric of contemporary India. In the end, there is no decolonization of the curriculum, no decolonization of the mind, without attachments to popular efforts for decolonization. Across the Third World, before structural adjustment, before the triumph of neocolonialism, before the ruling classes of the Third World abandoned ideas entirely for Swiss bank accounts or American armaments, many wrote, published, taught, and thought under the moons of anti-imperialism and nonalignment. I have tried to account for this intellectual history so that we may draw lessons from its insights and understand too its profound limits. In examining major and minor events, forgotten thinkers with their out-of-print texts and defunct institutions, attending to their language, locution, and points of emphasis, I have tried to narrate how we arrived at global articulations for and against Muslim unity, Pan-Asianism, or nonalignment.

I also hope I have instilled some caution over any celebration of the global. The challenge of solidarity is just that. A working toward, a struggle with, an attempt. The illegibility of caste to an Arab 'alim, the primacy of race under modern imperial rule, the invisibility of sects to the majority, the erasure of capitalism's unevenness in the pursuit of an umma, patriarchy's persistence, nationalism's contradictions, internationalism's denials—all of this, I think, must force us to pause before the global's shimmering mystique on our melting earth. Not every linkage or connection is the occasion for friendship, solidarity, or genuine exchange. Indeed, more often, the annihilation of space by time, as Marx put it, is the occasion for exploitation. But the thought of our anti-imperialist past cannot be the subject of nostalgia or be mummified by the university; it must be a source for our thinking today.

Genocide in Gaza revealed anew, as I completed this book, the sheer extent to which the project of liberation remains unfinished. Even if this is not a book about Palestinian history, Palestine, from the outset, has powered this account. The colonization of Palestine and the dispossession of the Palestinian people—and they are not alone—will always suspend any triumphalist accounts of decolonization. That Israel can destroy Gaza's universities in a matter of months and leave dozens of university professors dead in its wake testifies again, as if it needs to be said, that intellectuals in the colonized world do not labor under conditions of their own choosing. That Israel proudly defies the majority of nations in its destruction of the Palestinians is only evidence that the geographical hierarchy of peoples instituted in the nineteenth century remains solidly in place. Against novelty, then, scholarly practice and intellectual culture in North America and Europe needs to practice some humility, not just in the face of the past I have sought to account for in this book, but in honor of our comrades and colleagues—living and recently deceased—who resist actually existing colonialism today.

Notes

Introduction: Decolonization and Its Forms of Knowledge

1. Historians as different as Rebecca Karl and Ashin Das Gupta would agree on this score. Karl, for example, writes of China's "forced entry" into a capitalist world system. "The fellowship upon the ocean was broken" is how Ashin Das Gupta describes Europe's arrival in the Indian Ocean. Karl, *Staging the World: Chinese Nationalism at the Turn of the Twentieth Century* (Durham, NC: Duke University Press, 2002), 12; Ashin Das Gupta, "India and the Indian Ocean in the Eighteenth Century," in *The World of the Indian Ocean Merchant, 1500-1800: Collected Essays of Ashin Das Gupta* (New Delhi: Oxford University Press, 2001), 219. We may even quote Du Bois, who wrote in 1946: "For a thousand years Asia and Africa strove together, renewing their spirits and mutually fertilizing their cultures from time to time.... But at last Europe encompassed them both." W. E. B. Du Bois, *The World and Africa: An Inquiry into the Part Which Africa has Played in World History* (New York: International Publishers, 1946), 200.

2. These succinct categories are borrowed from George Padmore, *The Life and Struggles of Negro Toilers* (London: Red International of Labour of Unions Magazine for the International Trade Union Committee of Negro Workers, 1931).

3. Edward Said, "The Intellectual Origins of Imperialism and Zionism," *Gazelle Review* 2 (1977), 50.

4. Victor Kiernan, *The Lords of Human Kind* (Boston: Little, Brown, 1969), 319.

5. I have previously sought to consider the usefulness of this spatial orientation for the writing of modern history. Esmat Elhalaby, *Arab Archives and Asian Histories*, World Humanities Report (CHCI, 2023).

6. Until the last decade of the twentieth century, the partition of South Asia did not receive sustained historical treatment. Scholars, as Daisy Rockwell argued in a trenchant essay, generally ceded the work of narrating the traumatic events to literature. Lapata [Daisy Rockwell], "Particularities of Partition Literature I," *Chapati Mystery*, February 19, 2010, https://www.chapatimystery.com/archives/particularities_of_partition_literature_i.html. Works such as Joya Chatterji, *Bengal Divided: Hindu Communalism and Partition, 1932-1947* (Cambridge: Cambridge University Press, 1994); Urvashi Butalia, *The Other Side of Silence: Voices from the Partition of India* (New Delhi: Penguin Books, 1998); and Gyanendra Pandey, *Remembering Partition: Violence, Nationalism and History in India* (Cambridge: Cambridge University Press, 2001) moved the historiography decisively forward. In addition to ever more granular and ambitious studies of the event of partition and its representations drawing upon archives from across the subcontinent and beyond, a growing body of work has sought to think comparatively and transnationally, with uneven results. See Joe Cleary, *Literature, Partition and the Nation-State Culture and Conflict in Ireland, Israel and Palestine* (Cambridge: Cambridge University Press, 2001); Jonathan Greenberg, "Generations of Memory: Remembering Partition in India/Pakistan and Israel/Palestine," *Comparative Studies of South Asia, Africa and the Middle East* 25, no. 1 (2005): 89–110; Arie Dubnov and Laura Robson, *Partitions: A Transnational History of Twentieth-Century Territorial Separatism* (Stanford, CA: Stanford University Press, 2019); and Victor Kattan and Amit Rajan, *The Breakup of India and Palestine: The Causes and Legacies of Partition* (Manchester: Manchester University Press, 2023).

7. Eduardo Mondlane, *The Struggle for Mozambique* (London: Penguin, 1970), 58.

8. Hollis R. Lynch, *Edward Wilmot Blyden: Pan-Negro Patriot, 1832–1912* (Oxford: Oxford University Press, 1967), 151. Like many intellectuals attached to the millennial zeal of the late nineteenth-century missionary enterprise, Blyden (who died in 1912) traveled to Palestine and expressed interest in Zionism. For a discussion of Blyden's Orientalism in relation to Palestine, see Alex Lubin, "Locating Palestine in Pre-1948 Black Internationalism," *Souls: A Critical Journal of Black Politics, Culture, and Society* 9, no. 2 (2007): 95–108.

9. Yvonne Quiles, "Hand and Hand: Cairo Plays Host to the First Afro-Asian Women's Conference," *Women of the Whole World* 4 (April 1961), 8.

10. Sigfried Kracuer, *History, the Last Things before the Last* (New York: Oxford University Press, 1969), 88–89. I should note that while Kracuer was a trenchant critic of fascism, he wrote deeply Orientalist reports on the contemporary Middle East while working for projects attached to the US government. Osamah Khalil,

America's Dream Palace: Middle East Expertise and the Rise of the National Security State (Cambridge, MA: Harvard University Press, 2016), 189–90.

11. See, for example, the discussions of Qutb and related thinkers in the following works of critical theory: Retort, *Afflicted Powers: Capital and Spectacle in a New Age of War* (London: Verso, 2005); Susan Buck-Morss, *Thinking Past Terror: Islamism and Critical Theory on the Left* (London: Verso, 2006); and Anne Norton, *On the Muslim Question* (Princeton, NJ: Princeton University Press, 2013). In his influential essay on "delinking," Walter Mignolo argued, speciously, that "de-coloniality was clearly formulated, in the sixties and seventies, by radical Arabo-Islamic thinkers (Sayyid Qutb, Ali Shariati, Ayatollah Komeini)." Mignolo, "Delinking: The Rhetoric of Modernity, the Logic of Coloniality and the Grammar of De-Coloniality," *Cultural Studies* 21, no. 2 (2007): 457. For an important study of Qutb attuned to his place in the Arab literary-intellectual scene, see Giedre Šabaseviciute, *Sayyid Qutb: An Intellectual Biography* (Syracuse: Syracuse University Press, 2021). For an important essay that links Qutb's work to the challenges of accounting for twentieth-century Arab intellectual history in general, see Omnia El Shakry, "'History without Documents': The Vexed Archives of Decolonization in the Middle East," *American Historical Review* 120, no. 3 (2015): 920–34.

12. Foreword to *Social Justice in Islam*, by Sayed Kotb, tran. John B. Hardie (Washington, DC: American Council of Learned Societies, 1953).

13. Zachary Lockman, *Field Notes: The Making of Middle East Studies in the United States* (Stanford, CA: Stanford University Press, 2016), 90.

14. Talal Asad, response in "Indigenous Anthropology in Non-Western Countries: A Further Elaboration," *Current Anthropology* 21, no. 5 (1980), 662.

15. Immanuel Wallerstein, *The Modern-World System I: Capitalist Agriculture and the Origins of the European World-Economy in the Sixteenth Century* (New York: Academic Press, 1974), 4. Thanks to Ahmad Shokr for alerting me to this passage.

16. "Dr. H.F. al-Hamdani," *Al-Urwa* 2, no. 1, January 1948, xi.

17. Farhad Daftary, *Historical Dictionary of the Ismailis* (Lanham, MD: Scarecrow Press, 2012), 64–65.

18. Some biographical details on al-Yafi are drawn from a brief account written by Syrian Social Nationalist Party secretary Labib Nassif, "Al-Consil al-Fakhri fi al-Hind wa shah al-Intikhabat fi Trabulus al-rafiq Tariq Ghalib Abu-Nasr al-Yafi," *Shabakat al-Maʿlumat al-Suriyya al-Qawmiyya al-Ijtmaʿiyya*, https://www.ssnp.info/?article=18902. Al-Yafi appears to have been a prominent member of the party.

19. "Notes and News," *Al-Urwa* 1, no. 1, July 1947, 7.
20. "Notes and News," *Al-Urwa* 1, no. 1, July 1947, 1.
21. "Notes and News," *Al-Urwa* 1, no. 1, July 1947, 2–3.
22. Only one book, a translation into English of the tenth-century grammarian Ibn Duraid's *al-Maqsurah*, was ever published in the series. Ibn Duraid [pseud. of Muhammad ibn al-Hasan], *Al-maqsurah*, trans. Muhammad Ibrahim Dar (Bombay: Indo-Arab Cultural Society, 1947).
23. *Al-Urwa* 1, no. 1, July 1947, iii. The page lists those offices and bookshops where the Al-Urwa can be found.
24. "Century Old Ties Must Be Revived: Mr. Nehru on Task before Indo-Arab Society," *Times of India*, October 8, 1954, 3; and "Indo-Arab Goodwill," *Times of India*, October 8, 1954, 6.
25. *India and the Arab World: A Symposium* (Bombay: Indo-Arab Society, 1955), 28.
26. "Arab-Indian Friendship Association," *Times of India*, June 5, 1960, 9.
27. For a general, *longue durée* overview of economic links across the Indian Ocean, see K. N. Chaudhuri's classic text, *Trade and Civilisation in the Indian Ocean: An Economic History from the Rise of Islam to 1750* (Cambridge: Cambridge University Press, 1985). On the genealogical links between the region of Hadramawt on the Arabian Peninsula and points farther afield, see Engseng Ho, *The Graves of Tarim: Genealogy and Mobility across the Indian Ocean* (Berkeley: University of California Press, 2006). For an important recent study of how social, religious, and economic links shape life between West and South Asia's peripheries, see Fahad Bishara, *A Sea of Debt: Law and Economic Life in the Western Indian Ocean, 1780–1950* (Cambridge University Press, 2017). For recent histories of the Gulf attuned to those Indian Ocean links transformed by the British Empire, see Abdel Razzaq Takriti, *Monsoon Revolution: Republicans, Sultans, and Empires in Oman, 1965–1976* (Oxford: Oxford University Press, 2013); Johan Mathew, *Margins of the Market Trafficking and Capitalism across the Arabian Sea* (Oakland: University of California Press, 2016); Rosie Bsheer, *Archive Wars: The Politics of History in Saudi Arabia* (Stanford, CA: Stanford University Press, 2020); Omar Hesham AlSehabi, "Policing Labour in Empire: The Modern Origins of the Kafala Sponsorship System in the Gulf Arab States," *British Journal of Middle Eastern Studies* 48, no. 2 (2021): 291–310; and Laleh Khalili, *Sinews of War and Trade: Shipping and Capitalism in the Arabian Peninsula* (London: Verso, 2021). The historical study of slavery and its afterlives across East Africa, West Asia, and the Indian Ocean has produced a particularly rich body of work that moves across region,

race, and religion; see, for example Abdul Sheriff, *Slaves, Spices and Ivory in Zanzibar: Integration of an East African Commercial Empire into the World Economy, 1770-1873* (London: James Currey, 1987); Ahmad Alawad Sikainga, *Slaves into Workers Emancipation and Labor in Colonial Sudan* (Austin: University of Texas Press, 1996); Matthew S. Hooper, *Slaves of One Master Globalization and Slavery in Arabia in the Age of Empire* (New Haven, CT: Yale University Press, 2015); and Beeta Baghoolizadeh, *The Color Black: Enslavement and Erasure in Iran* (Durham, NC: Duke University Press, 2024). For histories of anti-colonialism between West and South Asia to which this study seeks to contribute, see Noor-Aiman Khan, *Egyptian-Indian Nationalist Collaboration and the British Empire* (New York: Palgrave Macmillan, 2011); Amal Ghazal, *Islamic Reform and Arab Nationalism: Expanding the Crescent from the Mediterranean to the Indian Ocean 1880s-1930s* (London: Routledge, 2010); and Hala Halim, "'A Theatre—or, More Aptly, a Laboratory': India in the 1940s Egyptian Left as an Antecedent of Bandung Internationalism," *Comparative Literature Studies* 59, no. 1 (2022): 49–76. This study also contributes to important recent work that has sought to bring Urdu sources in conversation with Arabic and Persian sources in the study of West and South Asia; see the essays in Nile Green, ed., "Arabic as a South Asian Language," *International Journal of Middle East Studies* 55, no. 1 (2023): 106–70; John Willis, "Debating the Caliphate: Islam and Nation in the Work of Rashid Rida and Abul Kalam Azad," *International History Review* 32, no. 4 (2010): 711–32; and Alexander Jabbari, *The Making of Persianate Modernity: Language and Literary History between Iran and India* (Cambridge: Cambridge University Press, 2023). And although links between West Asia and Latin America do not reach back into antiquity, studies of Arab diasporas in the Americas from the nineteenth century onward and their social, political, and intellectual activity offer some background to the solidarities forged in the second half of the twentieth century. See, for example, Ilham Khuri-Makdisi, *The Eastern Mediterranean and the Making of Global Radicalism, 1860-1914* (Berkeley: University of California Press, 2010); and Nadim Bawalsa, *Transnational Palestine: Migration and the Right of Return before 1948* (Stanford, CA: Stanford University Press, 2022). For a study of Latin American solidarity with the Third World, including the national liberation struggles of Palestine and Algeria, see Jessica Sites Mor, *South-South Solidarity and the Latin American Left* (Madison: University of Wisconsin Press, 2022).

28. *Faiz A. Faiz: The Living Word* (Tunis: Lotus Books, 1987), 79.

29. Stuart Schaar, *Eqbal Ahmad: Critical Outsider in a Turbulent Age* (New York: Columbia University Press, 2015).

30. Eqbal Ahmad, "An Address in Gaza," in *The Selected Writings of Eqbal Ahmed*, ed. Carollee Bengelsoorf, Margaret Cerullo, and Yogesh Chandrani (New York: Columbia University Press, 2006), 377.

31. Edward Said, *Representations of the Intellectual* (New York: Vintage, 1996), 32.

32. Ahmad, "Address in Gaza," 378.

33. Michael Goebel, *Anti-Imperial Metropolis: Interwar Paris and the Seeds of Third World Nationalism* (Cambridge: Cambridge University Press, 2015), 144.

34. Benjamin Siegel, "The Kibbutz and the Ashram: Sarvodaya Agriculture, Israeli Aid, and the Global Imaginaries of Indian Development," *American Historical Review* 125, no. 4 (2020), 1187.

35. Siegel, "Kibbutz and the Ashram," 1183. For the classic study of the "conquest of land" and "conquest of labor" in the colonization of Palestine, see Gershon Shafir, *Land, Labor and the Origins of the Israeli-Palestinian Conflict, 1882-1914* (Cambridge: Cambridge University Press, 1989). See also Areej Sabbagh-Khoury, *Colonizing Palestine: The Zionist Left and the Making of the Palestinian Nakba* (Stanford, CA: Stanford University Press, 2023).

36. See, for example, Derek Penslar, "Zionism, Colonialism and Postcolonialism," *Journal of Israeli History* 20, nos. 2-3 (2001): 84-98; and Arie Dubnov, "Notes on the Zionist Passage to India, or: The Analogical Imagination and Its Boundaries," *Journal of Israeli History* 35, no. 2 (2016): 177-214. For a critique of this approach, see Esmat Elhalaby, "A Dying Postcolonialism," *Palestine Yearbook of International Law* 24 (2023): 155-64.

37. For a brief appraisal of the field, see Ilan Pappé, Tariq Dana, and Nadia Naser-Najjab, "Palestine Studies, Knowledge Production, and the Struggle for Decolonisation," *Middle East Critique* 33, no. 2 (2024): 173-93. See also Tarif Khalidi, "Palestinian Historiography: 1900-1948," *Journal of Palestine Studies* 10, no. 3 (1981): 59-76; Beshara Doumani, "Rediscovering Ottoman Palestine: Writing Palestinians into History," *Journal of Palestine Studies* 21, no. 2 (1992): 5-28; Omar Jabary Salamanca, Mezna Qato, Kareem Rabie, and Sobhi Samour, "Past Is Present: Settler Colonialism in Palestine," *Settler Colonial Studies* 2, no. 1 (2012): 1-8; Walid Khalidi, "Palestine and Palestine Studies: One Century after World War I and the Balfour Declaration," *Journal of Plaestine Studies* 44, no. 1 (2014): 137-47; and Hana Sleiman and Kaoukab Chebaro, "Narrating Palestine: The Palestinian Oral History Archive Project," *Journal of Palestine Studies* 47, no. 2 (2018): 63-76.

38. G. H. Jansen, *Zionism, Israel and Asian Nationalism* (Beirut: Institute of Palestine Studies, 1971); and Asʿad ʿAbd al-Rahman, *Al-Tasallul al-Israʾili fi Asya: al-Hind wa Israʾil* (Beirut: Markaz al-Dirasat, Munazimat al-Tahrir al-Falistini, 1967).

39. Nadia Yaqub, *Palestinian Cinema in the Days of Revolution* (Austin: University of Texas Press, 2018); Noura Erekat, *Justice for Some: Law and the Question of Palestine* (Stanford, CA: Stanford University Press, 2019); Michael R. Fischbach, *Black Power and Palestine: Transnational Countries of Color* (Stanford, CA: Stanford University Press, 2018); Hana Sleiman, "The Paper Trail of a Liberation Movement," *Arab Studies Journal* 24, no. 1 (2016): 42–67; Rana Barakat, "Lifta, the Nakba, and the Museumification of Palestine's History," *Native American and Indigenous Studies* 5, no. 2 (2018): 1–15; Abdel Razzaq Takriti, "The Kurd and the Wind: The Politics and Poetics of Palestinian-Kurdish Affiliation," in *The Political and Cultural History of Kurds*, ed. Amir Harrak (New York: Peter Lang, 2021): 2:19–78; Mezna Qato, "Forms of Retrieval: Social Scale, Citation, and the Archive on the Palestinian Left," *International Journal of Middle East Studies* 51, no. 2 (2019): 312–15; Sherene Seikaly, "The Matter of Time," *American Historical Review* 124, no. 5 (2019): 1681–88; Dana Sajdi, "The Pasha's New Clothes: The History Section (*tārīkh*)," in *The Library of Aḥad Pasha al-Jazzār: Book Culture in Late Ottoman Palestine*, ed. Said Aljoumani, Guy Burak, and Konrad Hirschler (Leiden: Brill 2025); Hilary Falb Kalisman, "'A World of Tomorrow': Diaspora Intellectuals and Liberal Thought in the 1950s," *Journal of Palestine Studies* 50, no. 2 (2021): 92–107; Nasser Abourahme, "Revolution After Revolution: The Commune as Line of Flight in Palestinian Anticolonialism," *Critical Times* 4, no. 3 (2022): 445–75; Sonja Mejcher-Atassi, *An Impossible Friendship: Group Portrait, Jerusalem before and after 1948* (New York: Columbia University Press, 2024); and Sorcha Thomson and Pelle Valentin Olsen, *Palestine in the World International Solidarity with the Palestinian Liberation Movement* (London: I. B. Tauris, 2023).

40. Ibrahim Abu-Lughod, "The Pitfalls of Palestiniology," *Arab Studies Quarterly* 3, no. 4 (1981): 405.

41. Edward Said, "Deir Yassin Recalled," in *The End of the Peace Process: Oslo and After* (New York: Pantheon, 2000), 159. First published in *Al-Ahram Weekly*, April 17–23, 1997.

42. June Jordan, *On Call: Political Essays* (Boston: South End Press, 1985).

43. Frantz Fanon, *The Wretched of the Earth*, trans. Constance Farrington (New York: Grove, 1963), 102.

44. As Nicholas Gulihot wrote: "All academics have participated in gatherings ... where budget constraints, political decisions, promotion opportunities, off-the cuff ideas, and institutional strategies are coated with the gloss of intellectual necessity and scientific progress. Yet academics write disciplinary history as if such meetings never take place or have any epistemic effect. The denizens of the cave seem indeed quite reluctant to talk about their natural habit, and

they much prefer to have others believe that they inhabit a region of pristine ideas and celestial doctrines." "One Discipline, Many Histories," in Gulihot, *The Invention of International Relations Theory: Realism, the Rockefeller Foundation, and the 1954 Conference on Theory* (New York: Columbia University Press, 2011), 16. See also Su Lin Lewis, "Conferencing: The Global South as Public and Counterpublic," *American Historical Review* 129, no. 2 (2024): 587–94. Histories of the Afro-Asian and nonaligned have long used conferences to organize their narratives and construct their arguments, including G. H. Jansen, *Afro-Asia and Non-Alignment* (London: Faber and Faber, 1966); A. W. Singham and Tran Van Dinh, *From Bandung to Colombo: Conferences of the Non-aligned Countries, 1955–75* (New York: Third Press Review, 1976); and Vijay Prashad, *The Darker Nations: A People's History of the Third World* (New York: The New Press, 2007). Attention to the Bandung Conference itself has reinvigorated the study of Afro-Asianism, Third Worldism, nonalignment, and their ideological and material limits. See the following important volumes: Christopher J. Lee, ed., *Making a World after Empire: The Bandung Moment and Its Political Afterlives* (Athens: Ohio University Press, 2010); Natasa Miskovic, Harald Fischer-Tiné, and Nada Boskovska, eds., *The Non-Aligned Movement and the Cold War: Delhi-Bandung-Belgrade* (London: Routledge, 2014); and Luis Eslava, Michael Fakhri, and Vasuki Nesiah, eds., *Bandung, Global History, and International Law: Critical Pasts and Pending Futures* (Cambridge: Cambridge University Press, 2017).

45. Maha Nassar, *Brothers Apart: Palestinian Citizens of Israel and the Arab World* (Stanford, CA: Stanford University Press, 2017); and Rossen Djagalov, *From Internationalism to Postcolonialism: Literature and Cinema between the Second and the Third Worlds* (Montreal: McGill-Queen's University Press, 2020). The links between Arab intellectuals and the Third World, as well as the Afro-Asian Writers' Association, have recently received sustained attention, especially by literary scholars. See, for example, Hala Halim, "*Lotus*, the Afro-Asian Nexus, and Global South Comparatism," *Comparative Studies of South Asia, Africa and the Middle East* 32, no. 3 (2012): 563–83; Olivia C. Harrison, *Transcolonial Maghreb: Imagining Palestine in the Era of Decolonization* (Stanford, CA: Stanford University Press, 2015); Eman Morsi, "Cuba in Arabic and the Limits of Third World Solidarity," *Global South* 13, no. 1 (2019): 145–77; Sophia Azeb, "Crossing the Saharan Boundary: Lotus and the Legibility of Africanness," *Research in African Literatures* 50, no. 3 (2019); 91–117; and Maru Pabón, "In Search of the 'Voice of the People': Mahmoud Darwish's Third-Worldist Genres," *Middle Eastern Literatures* 25, no. 2 (2022): 168–86. Scholars have also recently attended to South Asian writers' engagements with the Afro-Asian Writers' Association beyond

Faiz Ahmed Faiz's well-known prominence in the organization. See the following important contributions: Haider Shahbaz, "Fahmida Riaz's *Āwāz*: Translation and Solidarities in the Global South," in *Translation and Decolonisation: Interdisciplinary Approaches*, ed. Claire Chambers and Ipek Demir (New York: Routledge, 2024), 154–68; and Aditya Bahl, "Green, Red: From *Pragati* to *Jujhar* in the Cold War Punjab," in *The Oxford Companion to Modern Indian Literatures*, ed. Ulka Anjaria and Anjali Nerlekar (Oxford: Oxford University Press, 2024), 473–90.

46. Richard Wright to Roy Wilkens, March 22, 1956, Papers of the NAACP, Part 24: Special Subjects, 1956–1965, Series B: Foreign Affairs-Leagues and Organizations. Group III, Series A, Administrative File, General Office File, Library of Congress. See the essential work of Merve Fejzula, which has revealed the role of women like Christiane Yandé Diop and Dorothy Brooks, whose labors have been obscured in *Présence Africaine's* own publications as well as subsequent narrations of the conference. Fejzula, "Gendered Labour, Negritude and the Black Public Sphere," *Historical Research* 95, no. 269 (2022): 423–46.

47. Penny Von Eschen, *Satchmo Blows Up the World: Jazz Ambassadors Play the Cold War* (Cambridge, MA: Harvard University Press, 2004). The question of jazz was hardly the only point over which the question of communism and anticolonialism could be relayed. It is impossible to summarize the totality of the discussion here; see the discussion in Penny Von Eschen, *Race against Empire: Black Americans and Anticolonialism, 1937–1957* (Ithaca, NY: Cornell University Press, 1997), 174–75; and Bennetta Jules-Rosette, "Conjugating Cultural Relations: *Présence Africaine*," in *The Surreptitious Speech: Présence Africaine and the Politics of Otherness 1947–1987*, ed. V. Y. Mudimbe (Chicago: University of Chicago Press, 1992), 14–44.

48. Anouar Abdel-Malek, *Egypt: Military Society* (New York: Vintage, 1968), 218; and Richard Jacquemond, *Conscience of the Nation: Writers, State, and Society in Modern Egypt*, trans. David Tresilian (Cairo: American University in Cairo Press, 2008), 18–20.

49. Yusuf al-Seba'i, "Kalamat al-Muharrir: Suq al-abad . . . wa suq al-Zalat," *al-Risala al-Jadida* 1 (April 1, 1954): 3.

50. Allione Diop, "Opening Address to the First International Congress of Negro Writers and Artists," *Présence Africaine* 8, no. 10 (1956): 9.

51. "Discussion, 20th September 1956," *Présence Africaine* 8, no. 10 (1956): 222.

52. For biographical information on Abdel-Malek, see his own account of his life. Anouar Abdel-Malek, "'Ishtu Marhalat Siyaghat al-Khat al-am lil-Haraka

al-Wataniyya al-Misriyya," in *Al-Takwin: Hayat al-Mufakirin wal-Uduba' wal-fannanin bi Qalamihim* (Cairo: Dar al-Hilal, 1998), 275–309.

53. Abdel-Malek was not alone among Arab intellectuals in recognizing the Black Writers Conference as significant. The Lebanese communist magazine *al-Thaqafa al-Wataniyya*—which Abdel-Malek would sometimes write for—printed the conference's final declaration: "Bayan al-kuttab al-sud," *al-Thaqafa al-Wataniyya* 1 (January 1957): 65.

54. *Presence Africaine*'s published list of attendees includes two from "Soudan": "H. Ba" or Amadou Hampâté Bâ, who was actually from "Soudan Francais," as Mali was then still known, and one "Abdul Wahal," undoubtedly a distortion of the common Arabic name Abdul Wahab ('Abd al-Wahhab). The latter's biography is not included with those of the other delegates.

55. Seba'i, in *Mu'tamar al-udaba' al-'arab al-thani* (Damascus: Ittiḥad al-Udaba' al-'Arab, 1956), 31.

56. "Nada' al-Mu'tamar," in *Mu'tamar al-udaba' al-'arab al-thani*, 159. The conference took place in September, and the Seba'i proceedings were not published in full until December, but this call and selections from the proceedings were published in the October issue of the Beiruti magazine *al-Adab* 4, no. 10 (1956).

57. Quoted in Irwin Silber, ed., *Voices of National Liberation: The Revolutionary Ideology of the "Third World" as Expressed by Intellectuals and Artists at the Cultural Congress of Havana, January 1968* (New York: Central Book Company, 1970), 118. For a rich account that captures the quotidian aspects of the Cultural Congress and features James, see Andrew Salkey, *Havana Journal* (Harmondsworth: Penguin, 1971).

58. Amílcar Cabral, "The Weapon of Theory," in *Unity and Struggle: Speeches and Writings of Amilcar Cabral* (New York: Monthly Review Press, 1979), 121.

59. Ruth First, *The Barrel of a Gun: Political Power in Africa and the Coup d'etat in Africa* (London: Penguin, 1970), 49.

60. C. L. R. James, "The Destiny of the Negro: An Historical Overview," in *C.L.R. James on the "Negro Question"*, ed. Scott McLemee (Jackson: University of Mississippi, 1996), 90.

61. "Answer of Jamal al-Din to Renan," in *An Islamic Response to Imperialism: Political and Religious Writings of Sayyid Jamal ad-Din "al-Afghani"*, by Nikki Keddie (Berkeley: University of California Press, 1968), 181–87; Abdallah Laroui, *The Crisis of the Arab Intellectual: Traditionalism or Historicism?*, trans. Diarmid Cammell (Berkeley: University of California Press, 1976).

62. Walter Rodney, *The Russian Revolution: A View from the Third World* (London: Verso, 2018), 67.

63. Ussama Makdisi, *Age of Coexistence: The Ecumenical Frame and the Making of the Modern Arab World* (Oakland: University of California Press, 2019), 87.

64. *Asia-Africa Speaks from Bandung* (Jakarta: Ministry of Foreign Affairs Republic of Indonesia, 1955), 125.

65. *Afro-Asian People's Conference: Held at Cairo from 26 December 1957 to 1st January 1958; Inaugural Addresses, Resolutions, Closing Addresses* (Cairo: Permanent Secretariat of the Afro-Asian Peoples' Solidarity Organization, 1958), 63.

66. George Lamming, *The Pleasures of Exile* (Ann Arbor: University of Michigan Press, 1992), 155.

67. See, for example, the distinction made between the "terms of White social science" and the "terms of Black social science" in Abd-al Hakimu Ibn Alkalimat [Abdul Alkalimat], "Common Problems, Common Solutions: Toward a Pan-African Ideology," *Journal of Black Poetry* 1, no. 14 (1970-71): 23-30.

68. Satish Chandra, "A Note on the Decentering of History and Apprehension by All People of Their History," *Diogenes* 20, no. 77 (1972), 103.

69. Israelis were not excluded from all Asian and African bodies; perhaps most significantly, the Asian Socialist Conference convened from 1953 to 1965.

70. Uriel Heyd, "Congress ha-Mizrahanim be-New Delhi Dvari Havirim Shil Mishlahat ha-Universita ha-Ivrit la-Congress ba-Asifa she-Nirikha me-Taam ha-Hivra ha-Mizrahit ha-Yisrailit be-Yom 10.2.1964 be-Yerushalayim," *Hamizrah Hahedesh* 14, no. 1 (1964), 107. Much thanks to Aamer Ibraheem for helping me with the Hebrew.

71. Pessah Shinar, "ha-Kenes ha-Benliumi ha-Rishun shel ha-Afrikanistim be-Akra," *Hamizrah Hahedesh* 13, nos. 1-2 (1963), 50-51.

72. Amnon Kapeliuk, "Israel Orientalists in India," *New Outlook* 7, no. 3 (March-April 1964), 56.

73. Khalil Nakhleh and Elia Zureik, eds., *The Sociology of the Palestinians* (London: Croom Helm, 1980), 11-12. See also the discussion of Israeli social science in Elia Zureik, *The Palestinians in Israel: A Study in Internal Colonialism* (London: Routledge and Kegan Paul, 1979).

74. Nakhleh and Zureik, *Sociology of the Palestinians*, 12.

75. "Women's Role in Arab Society: Resume of the Speech Delivered in Arabic by Mrs. A. S. Khalidi," Ruth Frances Woodsmall Papers, 1863-1968, of Sophia Smith Collection, Women's History Archive, Smith College Special Collections, box 31, folder 2.

Chapter 1. Empire

1. Wadih Boustany [Wadi' al-Bustani] to John Lubbock, November 19, 1910, British Library, London (BL), Avebury Papers, MS 49676 f. 208.

2. Boustany to Lubbock, November 19, 1910.

3. Wadi' al-Bustani, "Muqaddima," in *Masarrat al-Hayat*, by Jon Lubbuk (Cairo: Matba'at al-Ma'arif, 1911), 11. Bustani wrote an article from London introducing Lubbock's life and work to Arab readers: "Lurd Afbury," *al-Zahra'*, September 1, 1911, 387–92.

4. Sulayman himself traveled to India (as well as Iraq and Iran) in the 1880s on business ventures. Albert Hourani, *Islam in European Thought* (Cambridge: Cambridge University Press, 1991), 176.

5. Mark Patton, *Science, Politics and Business in the Work of Sir John Lubbock: A Man of Universal Mind* (Hampshire: Ashgate, 2007), 223.

6. John Lubbock, *The Pleasures of Life* (Philadelphia: Henry Altemus, 1894), x.

7. For how these particular texts gained their currency in European culture see, among many other studies, Raymond Schwab, *The Oriental Renaissance: Europe's Rediscovery of India and the East, 1680-1880* (1950; New York: Columbia University Press, 1984); and Dorothy Matilda Figueira, *Translating the Orient: The Reception of Sakuntala in Nineteenth-Century Europe* (Albany: State University of New York Press, 1991).

8. Empire's centrality in the making of modern British literary and cultural institutions and sensibilities was among the central concerns of postcolonial studies and therefore constitutes a massive body of work produced over several decades; see, for example, Benita Parry, *Delusions and Discoveries: Studies on India in the British Imagination, 1880-1930* (Berkeley: University of California Press, 1972); Edward Said, *Culture and Imperialism* (New York: Knopf, 1993); and Catherine Hall, *Civilizing Subjects: Metropole and Colony in the English Imagination 1830-1867* (Chicago: University of Chicago Press, 2002). On the question of the English language and pedagogy specifically, see Gauri Viswanathan, *Masks of Conquest: Literary Study and British Rule in India* (New York: Columbia University Press, 1989); and Sanjay Seth, *Subject Lessons: The Western Education of Colonial India* (Durham, NC: Duke University Press, 2007).

9. Tomoko Masuzawa, *The Invention of World Religions: Or, How European Universalism Was Preserved in the Language of Pluralism* (Chicago: University of Chicago Press, 2005), 260; and Arie L. Molendijk, *Friedrich Max Müller and the Sacred Books of the East* (Oxford: Oxford University Press, 2016), 57–58.

10. Wadi' al-Bustani, "al-Ustadh Margoliouth," *al-Zuhoor*, October 1, 1911, 413–15.

11. Aamir Mufti, *Forget English! Orientalisms and World Literatures* (Cambridge, MA: Harvard University Press, 2016), 11. On Arab intellectuals' schooling in Orientalism, see Ronen Raz, "The Transparent Mirror: Arab Intellectuals and Orientalism, 1798–1950" (PhD diss., Princeton University, 1997); Marwa Elshakry, *Reading Darwin in Arabic, 1860–1950* (Chicago: University of Chicago Press, 2013); Anne-Laure Dupont, "How Should the History of the Arabs be Written? The Impact of European Orientalism in Jurji Zaidan Work," in *Jurji Zaidan: Contributions to Modern Arab Thought and Literature: Proceedings of a Symposium, The Library of Congress*, ed. George C. Zaidan and Thomas Philipp (Bethesda: The Zaidan Foundation, 2013), 85–122; and the relevant chapters of Susannah Heschel and Umar Ryad, eds., *The Muslim Reception of European Orientalism: Reversing the Gaze* (New York: Routledge, 2019).

12. John Yohannan, *Persian Poetry in England and America: A 200-Year History* (Delmar, NY: Caravan Books, 1977), 199.

13. Wadi' al-Bustani, "Muqaddima," in *Rub'iyat 'Umar al-Khayyam* (Cairo: Matba'at al-Ma'arif, 1912), 5.

14. Yaseen Noorani, "Translating World Literature into Arabic and Arabic into World Literature: Sulayman al-Bustani's al-Ilyadha and Ruhi al-Khalidi's Arabic Rendition of Victor Hugo," in *Migrating Texts: Circulating Translations around the Ottoman Mediterranean*, ed. Marilyn Booth (Edinburgh: Edinburgh University Press, 2019), 243.

15. John M. Willis, "Making Yemen Indian: Rewriting the Boundaries of Imperial Arabia," *International Journal of Middle East Studies* 41, no. 1 (2009): 24. On the place of the Arabian Peninsula in the British imperial history of the Indian Ocean, see the relevant chapters in Rosie Bsheer, *Archive Wars: The Politics of History in Saudi Arabia* (Stanford, CA: Stanford University Press, 2020); and Laleh Khalili, *Sinews of War and Trade: Shipping and Capitalism in the Arabian Peninsula* (London: Verso, 2020).

16. Wadi' al-Bustani, "Dibajat al-Mu'arib," in al-Bustani, *al-Mahabharata: Al-Malhama al-Hinduwiyya* (Beirut: Jam'iyat Mutakharrijyi al-Jam'iah al-Amirkiyah fi Beirut, 1952), 10.

17. On Tagore's trip to Egypt, see Ahmad Muhammad Ahmad 'Abd al-Rahman, "Rihlat Taghur ila Misr," *Thaqafatul Hind* 62, no. 4 (2011): 85–100; on Iraq, see Salma al-Youzbaki, "Tagore in Iraq: Poet and Educator," *Bulletin of the College of Arts, University of Baghdad* 20 (1977): 149–65.

18. "Taghur fi al-lugha al-ʿarabiyya," *al-Risala*, November 10, 1941, 1387.

19. Khuri-Makdisi, *Eastern Mediterranean and Global Radicalism*, 44.

20. Rabindranath Taghur, "Ila Buhayrati: Min Diwan al-Bustani," trans. Wadiʿ al-Bustani, *al-Funun*, May 1918, 318–19. On al-Funun, see Richard Alan Popp, "Al-Funun: The Making of an Arab-American Literary Journal" (PhD diss., Georgetown University, 2000).

21. Mikhail Naʿimy, "Fi ʿAlam al-Taʾlif: Al-Bustani," *al-Funun*, June 1918, 462.

22. Naʿimy, "Fi ʿAlam al-Taʾlif," 463.

23. Wadiʿ al-Bustani, "ʿAnd Rabindranath Taghur," *al-Hilal*, June 1916, 716. Earlier, in May 1916, *al-Hilal* published an article of Bustani's on Tagore that included translations of three of Tagore's poems into Arabic.

24. al-Bustani, "ʿAnd Rabindranath Taghur," 719–20.

25. See Michael Collins's well-researched study of Tagore's connections with the British and the circumstances of his being awarded the Nobel Prize: "History and the Postcolonial: Rabindranath Tagore's Reception in London, 1912–1913," *International Journal of the Humanities* 4, no. 9 (2007): 71–83.

26. Rabindranath Tagore, *Journey to Persia and Iraq: 1932* (Kolkata: Visva-Bharati, 2003), 107.

27. Tagore, *Journey to Persia and Iraq*, 110.

28. Edward Said, *Orientalism* (New York: Vintage, 1978), 224.

29. Tagore, *Journey to Persia and Iraq*, 23–24.

30. Priya Satia, *Spies in Arabia: The Great War and the Cultural Foundations of Britain's Covert Empire in the Middle East* (Oxford: Oxford University Press, 2009), 258.

31. Rabindranath Tagore, "Message to Iraq Air Force," in *The English Writings of Rabindranath Tagore: A Miscellany* (New Delhi: Sahitya Akademi, 1996), 798.

32. Tagore, *Journey to Persia and Iraq*, 25.

33. Caren Kaplan, *Aerial Aftermaths: Wartime from Above* (Durham, NC: Duke University Press, 2018), 32.

34. Abd al-Rahman Yaghi, *Hayat al-adab al-Filastini al-hadith min awwal al-nahda hatta al-nakba* (Beirut: al-Maktab al-Tijari lil-tabiʿah wal-nashr wal-tawziʿ, 1968), 176.

35. W. F. Boustany [Wadiʿ al-Bustani], *The Quatrains of War* (Transvaal: Dewittekrans, 1915), 7.

36. Boustany, *Quatrains of War*, 10.

37. Bustani, *Al-Filastiniyyat*, 82.

38. Milhim Ibrahim al-Bustani, *Al-Salsibil* (Jouniyeh: n.p., 1968), 191.

39. Laura Robson, *Colonialism and Christianity in Mandate Palestine* (Austin: University of Texas Press, 2011), 9. See also Noah Haiduc-Dale, *Arab Christians in British Mandate Palestine: Communalism and Nationalism, 1917-1948* (Edinburgh: Edinburgh University Press, 2013); and Nicholas E. Roberts, *Islam under the Palestine Mandate: Colonialism and the Supreme Muslim Council* (London: I. B. Tauris, 2017).

40. Ussama Makdisi, *Age of Coexistence: The Ecumenical Frame and the Making of the Modern Arab World* (Oakland: University of California Press, 2019).

41. Wadi' al-Bustani, "Kulina Muslimin," *al-Zahra'*, March 1, 1925, 183–85.

42. Thomas Hippler, *Governing from the Skies: A Global History of Aerial Bombing* (New York: Verso, 2017), 71.

43. al-Bustani, "Kulina Muslimun," 185.

44. al-Bustani, "Kulina Muslimun," 184.

45. Khalid Sulaiman, *Palestine and Modern Arab Poetry* (London: Zed, 1984), 21.

46. Bustani, *Al-Falistinyyat* (Beirut: Dar al-Tiba'a wal-Nashr al-Sharqiyya, 1946). The book is dedicated to "the friend of the Arabs," Frances Emily Newton, an English missionary expelled from Palestine by the British in 1938 for writing against British colonial practices in the Mandate. Bustani translated her memoirs into Arabic and served as her lawyer.

47. Bustani, *Al-Falistiniyyat*, 202.

48. Bustani, *Al-Falistiniyyat*, 205.

49. Nicholas E. Roberts, "Making Jerusalem the Centre of the Muslim World: Pan-Islam and the World Islamic Congress of 1931," *Contemporary Levant* 4, no. 1 (2019): 52–63.

50. Bustani, *Al-Falistiniyyat*, 205.

51. Maoz Azaryahu and Yitzhak Reiter, "The Geopolitics of Interment: An Inquiry into the Burial of Muhammad Ali in Jerusalem, 1931," *Israel Studies* 20, no. 1 (Spring 2015): 49. In general, the authors construe any support or good feeling expressed in the Arab press regarding Ali's burial as evidence of al-Husseini's propaganda, never the possibility that Palestinians felt any Eastern or anticolonial solidarity despite their differences with al-Husseini.

52. Sulayman Jubran, *Nazra jadidah 'ala al-shi'r al-filastini fi 'ahd al-intidab* (Haifa: Dar al-Huda, 2006), 50.

53. Ghassan Kanafani, "Thawra 1936-39 fi Filastin: Khalfiyyat wa tafasil wa tahlil," *Shu'un Filastiniyya* 6 (1972): 57. Bustani himself is the source of this exchange, which is recounted in Bustani, *Al-Falistiniyyat*, 114.

54. A. L. Tibawi, *Anglo-Arab Relations and the Question of Palestine, 1921-1921* (London: Luzac and Company, 1978), 270.

55. "Summary of the Proceedings of the Sixth Palestine Arab Congress," British National Archives (TNA), Kew, CO 733/47/Appendix 6. That same year Bustani was part of the Palestinian delegation to London.

56. W. F. Boustany [Wadiʿ al-Bustani], *Palestine Mandate: Invalid and Impracticable: A Contribution of Arguments and Documents towards the Solution of the Palestine Problem* (Beirut: American Press, 1936).

57. Boustany, *Palestine Mandate*, 71.

58. Boustany, *Palestine Mandate*, 129.

59. *Al-Hilal*, February 1937, 472-73; and *al-Mashriq*, January-March 1937, 145-46.

60. In 1921 the British administration established what were called simply the Jerusalem Law Classes. In a building that once housed Russian pilgrims to the Holy City, Arabs and Jews would spend their evenings studying the new law of the land, an Orientalist amalgamation of what British administrators imagined Ottoman law to be and English legal norms. The curriculum was developed by the attorney general of Mandate Palestine, Norman Bentwich, a British Zionist who had previously been posted in Cairo. Taught at night so officials could attend, the law classes were a five-year program of instruction, which provided a diploma that allowed one to practice law in the Mandate. See H. Kantrovich, "The Jerusalem Law Classes," *Journal of the Society of Public Teachers of Law* (1937): 46; Donald M. Reid, *Lawyers and Politics in the Arab World, 1880-1960* (Minneapolis: Bibliotheca Islamica, 1981), 297-98; Assaf Likhovski, *Law and Identity in Mandate Palestine* (Chapel Hill: University of North Carolina Press, 2006), 112-14; and Robson, *Colonialism and Christianity in Mandate Palestine*, 51-54.

61. Munir Fakher Eldin, "Communities of Owners: Land Law, Governance, and Politics in Palestine, 1858-1948" (PhD diss. New York University, 2008), 59. See also Munir Fakher Eldin, "British Framing of the Frontier in Palestine, 1918-1923: Revisiting Colonial Sources on Tribal Insurrection, Land Tenure, and the Arab Intelligentsia," *Jerusalem Quarterly* 60 (2014): 42-58.

62. Chaim Weizmann, *Trial and Error: The Autobiography of Chaim Weizmann* (Philadelphia: The Jewish Publication Society of America, 1949), 2:276. Bustani went on to translate Weizmann's autobiography into Arabic.

63. In order of appearance: Bernard Wasserstein, "'Clipping the Claws of Colonisers': Arab Officials in the Government of Palestine, 1917-48," *Middle*

Eastern Studies 13, no. 2 (May 1977): 191n32; Philip Graves, *Palestine, the Land of Three Faiths* (London: Jonathan Cape, 1923), 11; Gershon Agronsky, "Inquiry Commission to Examine Grand Mufti Monday in Own Home," *Jewish Daily Bulletin*, December 1, 1929; "Note by Herbert Samuel," July 21, 1923, National Archives, Kew, CO 733/54/427; and M. Perlmann, "Chapters of Arab Jewish Diplomacy, 1918–22," *Jewish Social Studies* 6, no. 2 (April 1944): 131.

64. Al-Jahiz, "al-Adab wal-fan fi al-usbu': Ijtima' ma' al-ustadh Wadi' al-Bustani," *al-Risala* 15 (March 31, 1947): 376.

65. Fu'ad al-Bustani, "Qissat al-Mu'arib," in al-Bustani, *al-Mahabharata: Al-Malhama al-Hinduwiyya*, 8.

66. Sheldon Pollock, "Future Philology? The Fate of a Soft Science in a Hard World," *Critical Inquiry* 35, no. 4 (2009), 956. See also Pollock, "Towards a Political Philology: D. D. Kosambi and Sanskrit" *Economic and Political Weekly* (July 26, 2008), 52–59; Pollock, "Comparison without Hegemony," in *The Benefit of Broad Horizons: Intellectual and Institutional Preconditions for a Global Social Science*, ed. Barbro Klein and Hans Joas (Leiden: Brill, 2010): 185–204; Pollock, "Liberating Philology," *Verge: Studies in Global Asias* 1, no. 1 (2015): 16–21;and Pollock, "Conundrums of Comparison," *Know: A Journal on the Formation of Knowledge* 1, no. 2 (2017): 273–94. See also Edward Said, *Humanism and Democratic Criticism* (New York: Columbia University Press, 2004).

67. Edward Said, *The World, the Text, and the Critic* (Cambridge, MA: Harvard University Press, 1983), 5–9; and Emily Apter, "Global Translation: The 'Invention' of Comparative Literature, Istanbul, 1933," *Critical Inquiry* 29, no. 2 (2003): 253–81. For an important response to these accounts, see Nergis Erturk, *Grammatology and Literary Modernity in Turkey* (Oxford: Oxford University Press, 2011).

68. Erich Auerbach, *Mimesis: The Representation of Reality in Western Literature* (Princeton, NJ: Princeton University Press, 2003), 557.

69. Bustani, "Dibajat al-Mu'arib," 15.

70. It should be noted that Asian intellectuals made European Orientalist scholarship possible in their work as historians, translators, compilers, and assistants, what Mohamad Tavakoli-Targhi has called "Orientalism's genesis amnesia." Mohamed Tavakoli-Targhi, *Refashioning Iran: Orientalism, Occidentalism and Historiography* (New York: Palgrave, 2001), 18–34. Moreover, European insights into Asian languages were not particularly novel, as they were entering a space with its own established philological practice; see Rajeev Kinra, "This Noble Science: Indo-Persian Comparative Philology, c. 1000–1800 CE," in *South*

Asian Texts in History: Critical Engagements, ed. Sheldon Pollock, Yigal Bronner, Lawrence McCrea, and Whitney Cox (Ann Arbor: Association for Asian Studies, 2011), 359-85. See also Phillip B. Wagoner, "Precolonial Intellectuals and the Production of Colonial Knowledge," *Comparative Studies in Society and History* 45, no. 4 (2003): 783-814; Rama Mantena, *The Origins of Modern Historiography in India: Antiquarianism and Philology, 1780-1880* (New York: Palgrave, 2012); and Manan Ahmed Asif, "Quarantined Histories: Sindh and the Question of Historiography in Colonial India—Part II," *History Compass* 15, no. 8 (2017): 1-7.

71. Geographic proximity and historical affinity obviously do not necessarily produce empathetic observations; often they did not. Bustani's exemplary case, therefore, is instructive. For another perspective, see Juan R. I. Cole, "Mirror of the World: Iranian 'Orientalism' and Early 19th-century India," *Critique: Journal for Critical Studies of the Middle East*, 5, no. 8 (1996): 41-60.

72. On the history of colonialism and the social sciences, see these exemplary studies: Omnia El Shakry, *The Great Social Laboratory: Subjects of Knowledge in Colonial and Postcolonial Egypt* (Stanford, CA: Stanford University Press, 2007); and Durba Mitra, *Indian Sex Life: Sexuality and the Colonial Origins of Modern Social Thought* (Princeton, NJ: Princeton University Press, 2020).

73. Hourani, *Islam in European Thought*, 178.

74. For an analysis of the form of and motivations behind Dutt's Mahabharata and other texts, see Sheshalatha Reddy, "Romesh Chunder Dutt's Indian-English Epics and Epochs," *Journal of Commonwealth Literature* 47, no. 2 (2012): 245-63. The transformation of Brahminical texts like the Mahabharata and the Ramayana into "epics" and their role in the history of modern Indian literature and political thought has been the subject of important work. In a 1904 essay, Tagore himself succinctly registered this shift in literary conceptualizations: "Before the Ramayana and the Mahabharata came to be classified with the great poetical works of the world, they used to be designated as history. Now, having adjusted them against the literary treasures of foreign lands, we call them epics." Tagore, "The Ramayana," in *Selected Writings on Literature and Language*, ed. Sukanta Chaudhuri (New Delhi: Oxford University Press, 2001), 252. See also Simona Sawhney, *The Modernity of Sanskrit* (Minneapolis: University of Minnesota Press, 2009). For a classic study of the role of Hindu texts and concepts in the articulation of Indian nationalist thought, see Partha Chatterjee, "History and the Nationalization Of Hinduism," *Social Research* 59, no. 1 (1992): 111-49.

75. Bustani, "Dibajat al-Muʿarib," 16.

76. Bustani, "Dibajat al-Muʿarib," 17.

77. Bustani, "Dibajat al-Muʿarib," 5-6.

78. Bustani, "Dibajat al-Muʿarib," 15.

79. Wadiʿ al-Bustani, *Akhbar al-Ahala*, Indian Council for Cultural Relations Library (ICCR), New Delhi, 294.592 AKH/M-119.

80. Bustani, *Akhbar al-Ahala*, 16.

81. Franz Rosenthal, "On Some Epistemological and Methodological Presuppositions of Al-Biruni," in *The Commemoration Volume of Biruni International Congress* (Tehran: High Council for Culture and Art, 1973).

82. Bustani, "Dibajat al-Muʿarib," 23.

83. Kalidasa, *al-Shakuntala*, trans. Wadiʿ al-Bustani (New Delhi: Indian Council of Cultural Relations, 1966).

84. *Al-Ramayana*, trans. Wadiʿ al-Bustani (Abu Dhabi: Kalima/Indian Council for Cultural Relations, 2012).

85. Ibrahim al-ʿArayyed, "al-Shiʿr wa qadiyatu fi al-adab al-ʿarabi al-hadith," *Al-Abhath* 7, no. 2 (1954): 139–88. The only other scholarly mention of Bustani's Indology after his death is from a publication by the ICCR itself, and even then, it is exceedingly brief. M. S. Ashraf, "India in Arabic Literature," in *India and World Literature* (New Delhi: Indian Council for Cultural Relations, 1990), 211–18.

86. "Al-Falsifa al-Hindiyya al-Qadima," *Al-Risala*, Feburary 17, 1947, 209.

87. Moseh Yitah to Mr. T. Eshbal, February 9, 1949, Israel State Archives (ISA), 1329/19-C. The Ministry of Minority Affairs, the only Israeli ministry not based on a department within the Yishuv, would close in July 1949, scarcely a year after its founding.

88. Wadiʿ al-Bustani to Moshe Yitah, June 15, 1953. I thank Nora Boustany for sharing this document with me from her personal archive.

89. Wadiʿ al-Bustani, "ʿIrfan," *al-Adib*, no. 7 (July 1953): 6.

Chapter 2. Islam

1. Wilfred Cantwell Smith, *Islam in Modern History* (Princeton, NJ: Princeton University Press, 1957), 88–89.

2. Muhammad Marmaduke Pickthall, "Islamic Culture," *Islamic Culture* 1, no. 2 (April 1927), 281–82. Text of lectures delivered in Madras in 1927.

3. Mushir Hosain Kidwai, *Pan-Islamism* (London: Lusac and Company, 1908), 5–6.

4. Quoted in Nikki Keddie, "The Pan-Islamic Appeal: Afghani and Abdülhamid II," *Middle Eastern Studies* 3, no. 1 (1966), 56.

5. Gail Minault, *The Khilafat Movement: Religious Symbolism and Political Mobilization in India* (New York: Columbia University Press, 1982).

6. Michael O'Sullivan, "Pan-Islamic Bonds and Interest: Ottoman Bonds, Red Crescent Remittances and the Limits of Indian Muslim capital, 1877–1924," *Indian Economic & Social History Review* 55, no. 2 (2018): 183–220. See also Takashi Oishi, "Muslim Merchant Capital and the Relief Movement for the Ottoman Empire in India, 1876-1924," *Journal of the Japanese Association for South Asian Studies* 11 (1999): 71–103.

7. Juan Cole, "'Indian Money' and the Shi'i Shrine Cities of Iraq, 1786–1850," *Middle Eastern Studies* 22, no. 4 (1986): 461–80; and Michael Christopher Low, "Empire and the Hajj: Pilgrims, Plagues, and Pan-Islam under British Surveillance, 1865–1908," *International Journal of Middle East Studies* 40, no. 2 (2008): 269–90.

8. Sir Sayyid Ahmad Khan, "The Views of Sir Syed on the Caliphate," in *Writings and Speeches of Sir Syed Ahmad Khan*, ed. Shan Mohammad (Bombay: Nachiketa Publications, 1972), 256. Khan's views on the caliphate conformed with British views; see Syed Tanvir Wasti, "Sir Syed Ahmad Khan and the Turks," *Middle Eastern Studies* 46, no. 4 (2010): 529–42; and Azmi Ozcan, *Pan-Islamism: Indian Muslims, the Ottomans and Britain (1877-1924)* (Leiden: Brill, 1997), 106–7n86.

9. For a survey of European approaches to Islam in the nineteenth and twentieth centuries in particular, see David Motadel, "Islam and the European Empires," *Historical Journal* 55, no. 3 (2012): 831–56. See also the related volume, David Motadel, ed., *Islam and the European Empires* (Oxford: Oxford University Press, 2014), especially the chapters by Umar Ryad and Faisel Davji, which focus on the question of Pan-Islam and British imperial thought, respectively.

10. Ozcan, *Pan-Islamism*, 13. For a thorough reading of a unique travelogue written by one of Tipu Sultan's emissaries as well as a study of how the Ottoman correspondence with Tipu reveals their sense of superiority to the Indian monarch, see Sanjay Subrhamanyam and Muzaffar Alam, *Indo-Persian Travels in the Age of Discoveries, 1400–1800* (Cambridge: Cambridge University Press, 2007), 313–27.

11. Ozcan, *Pan-Islamism*, 16.

12. Cemil Aydin, *The Idea of the Muslim World: A Global Intellectual History* (Cambridge, MA: Harvard University Press, 2017), 55.

13. Valentine Chirol, *Pan-Islamism* (London: Central Asian Society, 1906), 1.

14. "Editorial," *Moslem World* 1, no. 2 (1911), 97.

15. E. M. Wherry, C. G. Myirea, and S. M. Zwemer, eds., *Lucknow, 1911: Being Papers Read and Discussions on the Training of Missionaries, and Literature for Muslims at the General Conference on Missions to Muslims Held at Lucknow, Jan. 23-28, 1911* (London: Christian Literature Society for India, 1911), 46.

16. Selim Deringil, *The Well-Protected Domains: Ideology and the Legitimation of Power in the Ottoman Empire, 1876-1909* (Cambridge: Cambridge University Press, 1998), 66.

17. Umar Ryad, "Muslim Response to Missionary Activities in Egypt: With a Special Reference to the Al-Azhar High Corps of 'Ulamâ (1925-1935)," in *New Faith in Ancient Lands: Western Missions in the Middle East in the Nineteenth and Early Twentieth Centuries*, ed. Heleen Murre-van den Berg (Leiden: Brill, 2007); Ussama Makdisi, *Artillery of Heaven: American Missionaries and the Failed Conversion of the Middle East* (Ithaca, NY: Cornell University Press, 2009); and Beth Baron, *The Orphan Scandal: Christian Missionaries and the Rise of the Muslim Brotherhood* (Stanford, CA: Stanford University Press, 2014).

18. Wherry, Myirea, and Zwemer, *Lucknow, 1911*, 8-9.

19. Brian Stanley, *The World Missionary Conference, Edinburgh 1910* (Grand Rapids, MI: Eerdmans Publishing, 2009).

20. Wherry, Myirea, and Zwemer, *Lucknow, 1911*, 10.

21. Wherry, Myirea, and Zwemer, *Lucknow, 1911*, 37.

22. Wherry, Myirea, and Zwemer, *Lucknow, 1911*, 38.

23. Heather J. Sharkey, *American Evangelicals in Egypt: Missionary Encounters in an Age of Empire* (Princeton: Princeton University Press, 2008), 93.

24. Wherry, Myirea, and Zwemer, *Lucknow, 1911*, 59.

25. Quoted in A. L. Tibawi, *British Interests in Palestine 1800-1901: A Study of Religious and Educational Enterprise* (Oxford: Oxford University Press, 1961), 259.

26. P. J. E. Damishky [Dimishky], "The Moslem Population in Bombay," *Moslem World* 1, no. 2 (1911): 117-30. For a historical study of Bombay's transnational Muslim worlds, see Nile Green, *Bombay Islam: The Religious Economy of the West Indian Ocean, 1840-1915* (Cambridge: Cambridge University Press, 2011).

27. *World Missionary Conference, 1910 (To Consider Missionary Problems in Relation to the Non-Christian World): The Record of the Conference Together with Addresses Delivered at the Evening Meetings* (Edinburgh: Oliphant, Anderson, & Ferrier, 1910), 251-52.

28. Malcolm White, "Anglican Pioneers of the Ottoman Period: Sketches from the CMS Archives of Some Arab Lives Connected with the Early Days of the Diocese of Jerusalem," *St. Francis Magazine* 8, no. 2 (2012): 303-4.

29. J. R. Longley Hall, "Excerpts from the Annual Letters: Palestine," *Church Missionary Intelligencer and Record*, March 1882, 155. On Palestine in Smith's work, see Iain D. Campbell, "In Search of the Physical: George Adam Smith's Journeys to Palestine and Their Importance," *History and Anthropology* 13, no. 4 (2002): 291-99.

30. George Adam Smith, "Palestine," *Church Missionary Intelligencer*, August 1904, 604.

31. *Crockford's Clerical Directory* (Oxford: Oxford University Press, 1935), 355.

32. Edwin James to the Secretary of the Society for the Propagation of the Gospel, July 2, 1909, Bodleian Library, Oxford University (hereafter Bodleian), Papers of the United Society for the Propagation of the Gospel (hereafter USPG Papers), CLS/4. Mar. 1902–Dec. 1909, Bombay, vol. 3, 89.

33. Edwin Jones to Secretary of the SPG, March 18, 1910, Bodleian, USPG Papers, CLS/4. Mar. 1902–Dec. 1909, Bombay, vol. 3, 141a.

34. N. S. Glazebrook to Secretary of the SPG, January 31, 1910, Bodleian, USPG Papers, CLS/4. Mar. 1902–Dec. 1909, Bombay, vol. 3, 137. "Native agents" were customarily paid less than Westerners. Ussama Makdisi notes that in Beirut, Butrus al-Bustani was paid $300 a year, while American missionaries were paid "at least twice as much, and often several times as much, a year." *Artillery of Heaven*, 193.

35. Stuart Hall, "Race, Articulation and Societies Structured in Dominance," in *Sociological Theories: Race and Colonialism* (Paris: UNESCO, 1980), 341.

36. Wherry, Myirea, and Zwemer, *Lucknow, 1911*, 89.

37. Wherry, Myirea, and Zwemer, *Lucknow, 1911*, 90.

38. See, for example, the case of Edward Blyden, who was forced to flee Liberia for a time when he was accused of adultery. Hollis Lynch, *Edward Wilmot Blyden: Pan-Negro Patriot, 1832–1912* (Oxford: Oxford University Press, 1967), 88.

39. Dimishky and Edwin Jones both make this claim and attribute it to Dimishky's fluency in Urdu. Nevertheless, this conflation, of Urdu and Islam, is not without its problems. Others within the SPG (and other missions in Bombay) knew Marathi and other Indian languages that were also intelligible to some Muslims in the city.

40. Edwin Jones to Secretary of the SPG, December 17, 1910, Bodleian, USPG Papers, CLS/4. Mar. 1902–Dec. 1909, Bombay, vol. 3, 165b.

41. Paul Dimishky to Lord Bishop H. H. Montgomery, April 29, 1911, Bodleian, USPG Papers, CLS/4. Mar. 1902–Dec. 1909, Bombay, vol. 3, 189a.

42. Damishky, "Moslem Population of Bombay," 130.

43. Paul Dimishky to Lord Bishop H. H. Montgomery, May 12, 1911, Bodleian, USPG Papers, CLS/4. Mar. 1902–Dec. 1909, Bombay, vol. 3, 183.

44. Damishky, "Muslim Population in Bombay," 129.

45. Despite the institution's significance, surprisingly little scholarly work has been devoted to Al-Azhar's modern past in the English-language historiography. A

classic sweeping account of Al-Azhar from its founding until the twentieth century is Bayard Dodge, *Al-Azhar: A Millennium of Muslim Learning* (Washington, DC: The Middle East Institute, 1961). For a historical overview of the ulema's transformation from the eighteenth to the twentieth centuries, see the chapters by Afaf Lutfi al-Sayyid Marsot and Daniel Crecelius in *Scholars, Saints, and Sufis*, ed. Nikki Keddie (Berkeley: University of California Press, 1972). A fine study of Al-Azhar's relationship to Shiism that informs this work is Rainer Brunner, *Islamic Ecumenism in the 20th Century: The Azhar and Shiism Between Rapprochement and Restraint* (Leiden: Brill, 2004).

46. In the decades to come, the ascendance of Saudi Arabia's Islamic University of Medina would challenge Al-Azhar's position; see Michael Farquhar, *Circuits of Faith: Migration, Education, and the Wahhabi Mission* (Stanford, CA: Stanford University Press, 2016).

47. Har Dayal, *Forty-Four Months in Germany and Turkey, February 1915 to October 1918: A Record of Personal Impressions* (London: P. S. King & Son, 1920), 43.

48. Dayal, *Forty-Four Months in Germany and Turkey*, 39

49. Mona Hassan, *Longing for the Lost Caliphate: A Transregional History* (Princeton, NJ: Princeton University Press, 2017), 194.

50. Hassan, *Longing for the Lost Caliphate*, 209.

51. Arthur Goldschmidt, *Biographical Dictionary of Modern Egypt* (Boulder: Lynne Rienner, 2000), 123.

52. Israel Gershoni and James Janowski, *Redefining the Egyptian Nation, 1930–1945* (Cambridge: Cambridge University Press, 1995), 160–61.

53. Cited in Bhagawan Das, ed., *Thus Spoke Amebedkar* (Bangalore: Ambedkar Sahithya Prakashana, n.d.), 4:108.

54. Anupuma Rao, *The Caste Question: Dalits and the Politics of Modern India* (Berkeley: University of California Press, 2009), 119–20.

55. Das, ed., *Thus Spoke Amebedkar*, 4:47.

56. Christophe Jaferlot, *Dr. Ambedkar and Untouchability: Fighting the Indian Caste System* (New York: Columbia University Press, 2005), 124.

57. Al-Baʿtha al-Azhariyya ila al-Hind, *Dirasa li-ahwal al-tawaʾif wa-al-hayʾat al-Islamiyya bi-al-Hind wa-bahth fi shuʾun al-manbudhin wa-mablagh istiʿdadihim li-iʿtinaq al-Islam* (Cairo: Maktaba al-Hijaziyya, 1938), 4.

58. Al-Baʿtha al-Azhariyya, *Dirasa li-ahwal*, 5.

59. Al-Baʿtha al-Azhariyya, *Dirasa li-ahwal*, 6.

60. Al-Baʿtha al-Azhariyya, *Dirasa li-ahwal*, 5. See also Abd al-Aziz Al-Thaʿalabi, *Masʾalat al-Manbudhin fi al-Hind* (Beirut: Dar al-Gharb al Islami,

1984); and "Al-Imam al-Zanjani: Taqrir Manhaj al-Baʿtha Al-Azhariyya ila al-Hind," *Al-Ahram*, November 11, 1936.

61. Brunner, *Islamic Ecumenism in the 20th Century*, 108.

62. Al-Thaʿalabi, *Masʾalat al-Manbudhin fi al-Hind*, 6-7.

63. Zvi Ben-Dor Benite, "Taking ʿAbduh to China: Chinese Egyptian Intellectual Contact in the Early Twentieth Century," in *Global Muslims in the Age of Steam and Print*, ed. James Gelvin and Nile Green (Berkeley: University of California Press, 2014), 258-59.

64. Intelligence Bureau, Home Department, New Delhi to W. A. Smart, "Note on the visit of the Al-Azhar delegation to India," April 7, 1937, British National Archives (hereafter TNA), FO 141/649.

65. "Moslem Mission to India Leaving Egypt To-Day," *Manchester Guardian*, December 2, 1936, 6.

66. Al-Baʿtha al-Azhariyya, *Dirasa li-ahwal*, 14-15, 64.

67. Al-Baʿtha al-Azhariyya, *Dirasa li-ahwal*, 14-15.

68. TNA, FO 141/649.

69. "Egyptian Mission On Education In India," *Times of India*, March 12, 1937, 19.

70. Al-Baʿtha al-Azhariyya, *Dirasa li-ahwal*, 86.

71. Al-Baʿtha al-Azhariyya, *Dirasa li-ahwal*, 84.

72. Al-Baʿtha al-Azhariyya, *Dirasa li-ahwal*, 71-73.

73. Bernard Cohn, *Colonialism and Its Forms of Knowledge: The British in India* (Princeton, NJ: Princeton University Press, 1996), 72-73; and Ronald Inden, *Imagining India* (Oxford: Basil Blackwell, 1990), 49-84.

74. Al-Baʿtha al-Azhariyya, *Dirasa li-ahwal*, 97-98.

75. Al-Baʿtha al-Azhariyya, *Dirasa li-ahwal*, 10.

76. Al-Baʿtha al-Azhariyya, *Dirasa li-ahwal*, 13.

77. Al-Baʿtha al-Azhariyya, *Dirasa li-ahwal*, 26.

78. Al-Baʿtha al-Azhariyya, *Dirasa li-ahwal*, 30.

79. Al-Baʿtha al-Azhariyya, *Dirasa li-ahwal*, 31.

80. Al-Baʿtha al-Azhariyya, *Dirasa li-ahwal*, 30.

81. TNA, FO 141/649:

82. TNA, FO 141/649:

83. Frantz Fanon, *Black Skin, White Masks* (1952; London: Pluto Press, 2008), 69.

84. Fanon, *Black Skin, White* Masks, 69. Emphasis in original.

85. Al-Baʿtha al-Azhariyya, *Dirasa li-ahwal*, 6.

Chapter 3. Asia

1. Hawa ʾ Idris, *Ana wa al-Sharq* (Cairo: Muʾassasat al-Marʾa wa al-Dhakira, 2016), 111.

2. "Mr. Jinnah's Views: Egyptian Paper's Criticism," *Times of India*, December 19, 1946, 3. On the Wafd's links with the Congress, see Noor-Aiman Khan, *Egyptian-Indian Nationalist Collaboration and the British Empire* (New York: Palgrave Macmillan, 2011).

3. "Mr. Jinnah Meets with Nokrashy Pasha: Political Situation Discussed," *Times of India*, December 18, 1946, 1.

4. *Hindustan Times*, December 24, 1946.

5. Quoted in Nicholas Mansergh, *The Commonwealth and the Nations* (London: Royal Institute of International Affairs, 1948), 100.

6. Idris, *Ana wal-Sharq*, 113.

7. Abd al-Wahab al-Azzam, "Rihla ila al-Hind," *al-Risala* 730 (June 30, 1947): 720.

8. Abd al-Wahab al-Azzam, "Min al-adab al-Hindi al-Islami," *al-Thaqafa* 1 (January 3, 1939), 39–40; and al-Azzam, "Min al-adab al-Hindi al-Islami," *al-Thaqafa* 6 (February 6, 1939): 26–27.

9. Hanan Hammad, "From Orientalism to Khomeinism: A Century of Persian Studies in Egypt," *Alif: Journal of Comparative Poetics* 35 (May 2015), 35.

10. Of these six, three produced work reflecting on the conference. Besides Azzam's travelogues and Hawa ʾ Idriss's memoirs discussed below, Taqi al-Din al-Sulh wrote a long article for the Egyptian paper *Akhbar al-Youm* about the conference, largely about his meeting with Gandhi and Indian perceptions of Gandhi. Taqi al-Din al-Sulh, "Fi al-Hind ʿand Ghandhi," in *Taqi al-Din al-Sulh: Sirat Hayat wa Kifah*, ed. ʿUmar Zayn (Beirut: Shikat al-Matbaʿa lil-tawziʿ walnashr, 2007), 148–59. We may have had more from Sulh had his journal not been stolen from his hotel room during the course of the conference. "Theft in Arab League Observer's Room," *Dawn*, April 5, 1947, 1.

11. G. H. Jansen, *Afro-Asia and and Non-Alignment* (London: Faber and Faber, 1966), 51.

12. "Guests of Nehru," *Economist*, March 29, 1947, 452.

13. M. N. Roy, *Asia and the World: A Manifesto Issued on the Occasion of the Asian Relations Conference* (n.p.: Radical Democratic Party, 1947), 1.

14. Roy, *Asia and the World*, 5.

15. Cemil Aydin, *The Idea of the Muslim World: A Global Intellectual History* (Cambridge, MA: Harvard University Press, 2017), 181.

16. Jansen, *Afro-Asia and and Non-Alignment*, 48.

17. British Legation, Beirut to Foreign Office, January 20, 1947, TNA, FO 371/63539.

18. External Affairs Department to British Legation, Beirut, December 12, 1946, TNA, FO 371/63539.

19. "Autour du prochain Congrès Asiatique: La Ligue Arabe n'y assisterait qu'a titre 'd'obervateur,'" *Le Progrès Égyptien*, January 18, 1947.

20. "Organizers' Open Anti-Arab Attitude: Mostafa Momen's Protest Against Jewish Propaganda," *Dawn*, April 2, 1947, 8.

21. Edward Atiyah, "The Palestine Question," *India Quarterly* 2, no. 4 (1946): 340–45; and Burhan Dajani, "National Movement for Freedom in Syria and Palestine," *India Quarterly* 3, no. 2 (1947): 135–43.

22. "New Delhi Talks Open Today: Pan-Asiatic Conference," *Palestine Post*, March 23, 1947, 3.

23. Batavia to Foreign Office, February 28, 1947, TNA, FO/371/63539

24. Indian Council of World Affairs to M. R. Jayakar, M. R. Jayakar Papers, National Archives of India, reel 127.

25. TNA, FO/371/63539, March 12, 1947.

26. Khalil Mardem Bey, "Athar al-Hind fi al-Thaqafa al-Arabiyya," *Majallat al-Majma' al-'Ilmi al-'Arabi*, January 1, 1949, 42.

27. Idris, *Ana wal-Sharq*, 113.

28. Abd al-Wahab al-Azzam, "Rihla ila al-Hind 2," *al-Risala* 731 (July 7, 1947), 753. British reports detail that the Indonesian leader faced logistical challenges getting to Delhi, hence the need for the private plane.

29. Abd al-Wahab al-Azzam, "Rihla ila al-Hind 4, al-Muslimin fi al-Mu'tamar," *al-Risala* 733 (July 21, 1947), 806.

30. "Egyptian Visitor's Views: Hindu Propaganda in Action," *Dawn*, March 22, 1947, 2.

31. "Foreign Muslim Visitors to Be Politically Doped: Congress Emissaries in Middle East Countries," *Dawn*, March 23, 1947, 2.

32. Idris, *Ana wal-Sharq*, 168.

33. Quoted in "We Muslims Are One," *Islamic Culture* 21, no. 3 (July 1947): 305.

34. "We Muslims Are One," 306.

35. TNA, FO 371 63539.

36. *Asian Relations: Report of the Proceedings and Documents of the First Asian Relations Conference, New Delhi, March–April 1947* (New Delhi: Asian Relations Organization, 1948), 293–98.

37. "Secret Weekly Political Intelligence Summaries, August 1946–November 1947," British Library: India Office Records and Private Papers, IOR/L/PS/12/1167.

38. *Asian Relations*, 43.

39. *Asian Relations*, 63.

40. *Asian Relations*, 64.

41. Idris, *Ana wal-Sharq*, 118.

42. Idris, *Ana wal-Sharq*, 117.

43. TNA, FO/371/63541.

44. *Asian Relations*, 65.

45. Idris, *Ana wal-Sharq*, 135.

46. *Asian Relations*, 72.

47. *Asian Relations*, 72–73.

48. Idris, *Ana wal-Sharq*, 137.

49. Abe Bailey and P. N. S. Mansergh, "The Inter-Asian Relations Conference," April 6, 1947, TNA, FO/371/63541.

50. Jansen, *Afro-Asia and and Non-Alignment*, 55.

51. *Asian Relations*, 79.

52. Jawaharlal Nehru, in *Selected Works of Jawaharlal Nehru*, ed. M. Chalapathi Rau, H. Y. Sharada Prasad, B. R. Nanda, and Sarvepalli Gopal (New Delhi: Orient Longman, 1982), 15:522–23.

53. T. K. Venkatram, *Racial Problems* (New Delhi: Indian Council of World Affairs, 1947), 5.

54. Kalidas Nag, *New Asia* (Calcutta: Prajna Bharati, 1947), 52.

55. Nag, *New Asia*, 56.

56. Nag, *New Asia*, 57

57. Idris, *Ana wal-Sharq*, 138.

58. Abd al-Wahab al-Azzam, "Rihla ila al-Hind 3, al-Yahud fi al Mu'tamar," *al-Risala* 732 (July 14, 1947), 775.

59. Al-Azzam, "Rihla ila al-Hind 3," 776.

60. "Breeze in Asian Conference: Clash of Views on Palestine," *Times of India*, March 26, 1947, 7.

61. P. R. Kumaraswamy, *India's Israel Policy* (New York: Columbia University Press, 2010), 187.

62. Kumaraswamy, *India's Israel Policy*, 188; G. H. Jansen, *Zionism, Israel and Asian Nationalism* (Beirut: Institute for Palestine Studies, 1971), 210. See also As'ad Abd Al-Rahman, *Al-taslil al-Isra'ili fi Asya: Al-Hind wa Isra'il* (Beirut: Markaz al-Dirasat, Munazzamat al-Tahrir al-Falistini, 1967).

63. For summaries of these positions, see Leonard A. Gordon, "Indian Nationalist Ideas About Palestine and Israel," *Jewish Social Studies* 37, nos. 3/4 (1975): 221–34; Upendra N. Mishra, "India's Policy Towards the Palestinian Question," *International Affairs* 21, no. 2 (1982): 101–15; and S. P. Singh, "Indo-Arab Relations in the Light of the Palestine Problem (1930 to 1945)," *Proceedings of the Indian History Congress* 65 (2004): 1025–30. For a valuable critical account of official Indian positions on the Palestine question, see Azad Essa, *Hostile Homelands: The New Alliance Between India and Israel* (London: Pluto Press, 2023).

64. Elizabeth Armstrong, "Before Bandung: The Anti-Imperialist Women's Movement in Asia and the Women's International Democratic Federation," *Signs: Journal of Women in Culture and Society* 41, no. 2 (2016): 305–31.

65. *The All-India Women's Conference, Eighteenth Session, Hyderabad (Sind), December 28, 1945 to January 1, 1946*, 16.

66. *All-India Women's Conference*, 82.

67. Margot Badran, *Feminists, Islam, and Nation: Gender and the Making of Modern Egypt* (Princeton, NJ: Princeton University Press, 1995), 224. See also Ellen Fleischmann, *The Nation and Its New Women: The Palestinian Women's Movement, 1920–1948* (Berkeley: University of California Press, 2003).

68. Quoted in Badran, *Feminists, Islam, and Nation*, 233.

69. Quoted in Leila J. Rupp, "Challenging Imperialism in International Women's Organizations, 1888–1945," *NWSA Journal* 8, no. 1 (Spring 1996), 14.

70. Amina al-Saʻid, *Mushahadat fi al-Hind* (Cairo: Dar al-Maʻarif, 1946), 55.

71. *All-India Women's Conference*, 31.

72. *All-India Women's Conference*, 82.

73. Najma Heptulla, *Indo-West Asian Relations: The Nehru Era* (Bombay: Allied Publishers, 1991), 146–54; and Kumarswamy, *India's Israel Policy*, 44–67.

74. *All-India Women's Conference*, 2.

75. Saʻid, *Mushahadat fi al-Hind*, 57.

76. See chapters 8 and 12 of her incredible memoirs, Kamaladevi Chattopadhyaya, *Inner Recesses, Outer Spaces: Memoirs* (New Delhi: Navrang, 1986).

77. Saʻid, *Mushahadat fi al-Hind*, 77–78.

78. *All-India Women's Conference*, 79.

79. *All-India Women's Conference*, 82.

80. For the Egyptian case see Laura Bier, *Revolutionary Womanhood: Feminisms, Modernity, and the State in Nasser's Egypt* (Stanford, CA: Stanford University Press, 2011). For an important account of how some feminist energies where transferred to the production of "status of women" reports and their

particular social scientific view, see Durba Mitra, "The Report, or, Whatever Happened to Third World Feminist Theory?," *Signs* 48, no. 3 (2023): 557–584. It should be noted that the only significant publication produced by the short-lived Asian Relations Organization (the institutional product of the 1947 conference) was an early instantiation of one of these reports published in cooperation with UNESCO. See A. Appadorai, ed., *Status of Women in South Asia* (Calcutta: Orient Longmans, 1954). The book contains papers delivered at a seminar on the subject convened in New Delhi in December and January 1952–53.

81. Cynthia Nelson, *Doria Shafik: A Woman Apart* (Gainesville: University of Florida Press, 1996), 222–24. See also Shafik's account of her travels to South Asia in Doria Shafik, *Rihlati hawla al-ʿalam* (Cairo: Matabiʿ Sharikat al-Iʿlanat al-Sharqiyya, 1955).

82. Quoted in Cynthia Nelson, "Satyagraha: Gandhi's Influence on an Egyptian Feminist," in *Investigating the South-South Dimension of Modernity and Islam*, ed. Helmut Buchholt and George Stauth (Hamburg: Lit Verlag, 2000), 107.

83. Nelson, "Satyagraha," 110.

84. Nelson, "Satyagraha," 108.

85. Nelson, *Doria Shafik*.

86. Abd al-Wahab al-Azzam, "Rihla ila al-Hind 6," *al-Risala* 740 (September 8, 1947).

87. Abd al-Wahab al-Azzam, "Rihla ila al-Hind 18," *al-Risala* 763 (February 2, 1948), 191.

88. al-Azzam, "Rihla ila al-Hind 18," 192. I have rendered the poem literally.

89. Taomo Zhou, "Global Reporting from the Third World: The Afro-Asian Journalists' Association, 1963–1974," *Critical Asian Studies* 51, no. 2 (2019), 179.

90. Ummah Staff Reporter, "An Historic Moot at Bandung," *Ummah* 1, no. 12 (April 1965): 16–22, 26–27.

91. Sukarno, *Islam Must Fight Colonialism: Inaugural Address by President Sukarno, African-Asian Islamic Conference, Bandung, 6th March 1965* (n.p.: Executive Command, Tenth Anniversary, First Asian-African Conference, n.d.), 9.

92. Sukarno, *Islam Must Fight Colonialism*, 9.

93. See Saad S. Khan, *Reasserting Internationalism: A Focus on the Organization of the Islamic Conference and Other Islamic Institutions* (Oxford: Oxford University Press, 2001), 67–69.

94. Gurbachan Singh, the Indian ambassador to Morocco at the time, recounts in detail the travails of the Indian delegation in the following oral history: Singh, "India at the Rabat Islamic Summit (1969)," *Indian Foreign Affairs Journal* 1, no. 2 (2006): 105–20.

95. "Declaration of the Rabat Islamic Summit Conference," https://www.oic-oci.org/archive/english/conf/is/1/DecReport-1st%20IS.htm.

96. Jacob Landau, *The Politics of Pan-Islam: Ideology and Organization* (Oxford: Oxford University Press, 1990), 288.

Chapter 4. Nonalignment

1. S. Maqbul Ahmad, ed., *India and the Arab World: Proceedings of the Seminar on India and the Arab World* (New Delhi: Indian Council for Cultural Relations, 1965), 32–33.

2. Maulana Abul Kalam Azad, "Presidential Address," *Indo-Asian Culture* 6, no. 4 (1958), 437. The ICCR did not start its English-language journal *Indo-Asian Culture* until 1952.

3. Azad, "Presidential Address," 437.

4. The recent and first biography of Husain does not corroborate this anecdote. Tantalizingly little is known about Husain's time in Cairo, and this biography unfortunately does not reveal much in the way of new information. N. S. Vinodh, *A Forgotten Ambassador in Cairo: The Life and Times of Syud Hossain* (New Delhi: Simon and Schuster India, 2020).

5. Azad, "Presidential Address," 438. Azad was a vocal opponent of partition; his autobiographical account of the partition's making is essential reading. Abul Kalam Azad, *India Wins Freedom* (New Delhi: Orient Longman, 1988).

6. K. M. Panikkar, *An Autobiography* (Madras: Oxford University Press, 1977), 247.

7. Mona Abaza, "East Is East? Where Does the East Begin for Egyptian Liberal Intellectuals?," *IAS Newsletter* 29 (November 2002): 20.

8. I have drawn here from the accounts provided in the early chapters of D. N. Sharma, *Afro-Asian Group in the U.N.* (Allahabad: Chaitanya Publishing House, 1969); G. H. Jansen, *Afro-Asia and Non-Alignment* (London: Faber and Faber, 1966); and Robert W. MacDonald, *The League of Arab States: A Study in the Dynamics of Regional Organization* (Princeton: Princeton University Press, 1965), ch. 5. Also useful is Luthi's critical examination of the Arab League. Lorenz Luthi, *Cold Wars: Asia, the Middle East, Europe* (Cambridge: Cambridge University Press, 2020), 42–67.

9. Muhammad Fadl Al-Jamali, "Arab Struggle: Experience of Mohammed Fadhel Jamali, 1943–1958" (unpublished manuscript, Widener Library, Harvard University, 1974). Al-Jamali was a fervent anti-communist. His Lebanese counterpart Charles Malik recalled that at the Bandung conference itself,

"It was [Jamali] who mentioned communism or international communism by name; others beat around the bush, at least so far as calling this thing by its proper name was concerned." Quoted in Elizabeth Bishop, "'Asia and Adjacent Areas': Mohammed Fadhel Jamali's Cold War Experiences," *Auto/Fiction* 1, no. 2 (2014): 62.

10. Rami Ginat, *Syria and the Doctrine of Arab Neutralism: From Independence to Dependence* (Brighton: Sussex Academic Press, 2005), 13.

11. Abd al-Rahman Azzam, "The Arab League in World Unity," in *Contemporary Arab Thought*, ed. Anour Abdel-Malek (London: Zed, 1980), 143.

12. The finest account of Nasser and Arab debates about the left and non-alignment that takes seriously Arab thought remains Anouar Abdel-Malek, *Egypt: Military Society* (Vintage: New York, 1968), especially chapters 5 and 6.

13. On Ben Barka, see this important chapter: Nathaniel George, "Travelling Theorist: Mehdi Ben Barka and Morocco from Anti-colonial Nationalism to the Tricontinental," in *The Arab Lefts: Histories and Legacies, 1950s-1970s*, ed. Laure Guirguis (Edinburgh: Edinburgh University Press, 2020), 127-47.

14. Malek Bennabi, *L'Afro-Asiatisme: Conclusions sur la Conference de Bandoeng* (Cairo: Imprimerie Misr, 1956), 165.

15. Fayez A. Sayegh, "Anatomy of Neutralism—A Typological Analysis," in *The Dynamics of Neutralism in the Arab World: A Symposium*, ed. Sayegh (San Francisco: Chandler Publishing, 1964), 23.

16. Samir Amin, "The Countries of the South Must Take Their Own Independent Initiatives," in *Samir Amin: Pioneer of the Rise of the South* (Cham: Springer, 2014), 72.

17. K. M. Panikkar, "The Twentieth Century in Asian and World History," *India Quarterly* 12, no. 3 (1956), 246.

18. Edward Said, *The Question of Palestine* (New York: Vintage, 1992), 219.

19. Quoted in Monhem Naim Nassereddine, "The Progressive Socialist Party of Lebanon: A Study of Its Origins, Organization, and Leadership" (MA thesis, Oklahoma State University, 1967), 106.

20. Stuart Hall, "Life and Times of the First New Left," *New Left Review* 61 (2010), 182.

21. Clovis Maksoud, *Min zawaya al-dhakira* (Beirut: al-Dar al-Arabiyya lil 'uloom al-nashrun, 2014), 56-57. See also Mélanie Torrent, *Algerian Independence and the British Left: Solidarities and Resistance in a Decolonising World* (London: Bloomsbury, 2024), 89.

22. Maksoud, *Min zawaya al-dhakira*, 66.

23. Maksoud, *Min zawaya al-dhakira*, 61.

24. Clovis Maksoud, "Socialism in the Arab World," *Oxford Clarion* Trinity Term (1954), 16-19.

25. Maksoud, *Min zawaya al-dhakira*, 118-19.

26. Maksoud, *Min zawaya al-dhakira*, 101.

27. Maksoud speculates that the establishment of the office in Delhi and Maksoud's appointment to the position were the work of R. K. Nehru, a prominent Indian diplomat who was the Indian ambassador to the United Arab Republic from 1958 to 1961, and whom Maksoud had met in India. Maksoud, *Min zawaya al-dhakira*, 121-22.

28. Clovis Maksoud, *Ma'na al-Hiyad al-Ijabi* (Beirut: Dar al-'Ilm lil Malayin, 1960), 85.

29. Clovis Maksoud, *On Non-Alignment* (New Delhi: League of Arab States Mission, 1966), 31.

30. "Non-Alignment Is Only a Plan of Action," *Times of India*, 9.

31. Maksoud, *Ma'na al-Hiyad al-Ijabi*, 7.

32. Maksoud, *Ma'na al-Hiyad al-Ijabi*, 103.

33. Maksoud, *Min zawaya al-dhakira*, 98.

34. Maksoud, interview with Jean Krasno, August 11, 1997, Yale-UN Oral History Project, 2.

35. Rehman Sobhan, *Untranquil Recollections: The Years of Fulfilment* (New Delhi: Sage, 2016), 371.

36. Maksoud, himself, during his time in India, would regularly make statements supporting Indian and Pakistani rapprochement.

37. K. K. Sastry, "Bangla centre in Beirut to close down," *Times of India*, March 28, 1972, 9.

38. Srinath Raghavan, *1971: A Global History of the Creation of Bangladesh* (Cambridge, MA: Harvard University Press, 2013), 182-83. Today of course India and Israel are in full embrace, and India is Israel's largest purchaser of arms.

39. Abdel-Malek, *Egypt*, 232.

40. MacDonald, *League of Arab States*, 138.

41. J. Anthony Lukas, "India Recognizes Arab League, Becoming First Nation to Do So," *New York Times*, July 14, 1965, 8.

42. Maksoud wrote often about Arab politics for these periodicals. See his essays on nonalignment Indian and Arab relations: "Reflections on Indian-Arab Relations," *Indian Foreign Affairs* 1, no. 2 (1958): 57-59; "India and the Arabs," *Link*, February 1, 1959, 28-29; "The Roots," *Seminar* 45 (May 1965): 13-16; and "Perspectives on Indian-Arab Relations," *Foreign Affairs Reports* 17, no. 4 (April 1966): 1-9.

43. See references to Maksoud's home in the memoirs of his friends: Karan Singh, *Heir Apparent: An Autobiography* (New Delhi: Oxford University Press, 1982), 126; and Raj Thapar, *All These Years: A Memoir* (New Delhi: Seminar Publications, 1991), 194–97.

44. M. S. Khan, "Indo-Arab Cultural Relations during the Last Decade: A Re-Examination," in *Contemporary West Asian Scene: A Selection of Papers Presented at a Seminar Held at Aligarh*, ed. Arif. H. Rizvi (Aligarh: Centre for West Asian Studies, Aligarh Muslim University, 1980), 240.

45. Pothan Joseph, "These Chimerical Stunts," *Swarajya*, November 13, 1965, 2.

46. *Al-Arab*, 9, no. 6, June 1970.

47. *Al-Arab*, 8, no. 7, July 1969.

48. *Palestine: A Symposium* (New Delhi: The League of Arab States Mission, 1969).

49. P. R. Kumaraswamy, "K. M. Panikkar and Indo-Israeli Relations," *International Studies* 32, no. 2 (1995): 327–37.

50. Panikkar, *Autobiography*, 249.

51. Panikkar, *Autobiography*, 249.

52. Ahmed Qasim Gouda, "Hatha al-Majalla," *Sawt al-Sharq* 1 (October 1952): 1. See Gouda's travelogue: Ahmad Qasim Gouda, *Marid min al-Sharq* (Cairo: Matbaʿat Jaridat al-Misri, 1950).

53. *Asian Relations: Report of the Proceedings and Documents of the First Asian Relations Conference, New Delhi, March–April 1947* (New Delhi: Asian Relations Organization, 1948), 22–23.

54. Ahmad, *India and the Arab World*, 8.

55. Humayun Kabir, "Indo-Arab Relations," *Indo-Asian Culture* 16, no. 4 (1967), 185.

56. Ahmad, *India and the Arab World*, 8. Elsewhere, he would wax poetic about Nehru's life and anti-colonial legacy. Omar Abou Risha, "Nehru: Man of Two Cultures and One World," in *Nehru and the Modern World* (New Delhi: Indian National Commission for Co-operation with Unesco, 1967), 17–22.

57. Abou Risha, "al-Amakin al-Hindiyya," "Taʾir al-Bajaʿ," and "Hub al-Ard," in *al-Hind fi al-shiʿr al-ʿArabi*, ed. Suhayb ʿAlam (Rampur: Raza Rampur Library, 2010), 186–90.

58. Badiʿ Haqqi, "Omar Abou Risha wal-Dhikrayat," *al-ʿArabi*, March 1994.

59. Ahmad, *India and the Arab World*, 39.

60. Ahmad, *India and the Arab World*, 40.

61. Clovis Maksoud, "Inaugural speech by the Chief Representative of the Arab League, Dr. Clovis Maksoud," *Arab Observer*, May 2, 1966, 12.

62. Ahmad, *India and the Arab World*, 173–74.

63. Clovis Maksoud, *The Arab Image* (New Delhi: Acharya Ramlochan Publishing House, 1963), 100.

64. Maksoud, *Arab Image*, 51.

65. Clovis Maksoud, in Maksoud and V. V. Ramana Murti, *Gandhi and the Violence of Zionism* (New Delhi: League of Arab States Mission, [1966]), 7–8.

66. Maksoud, *Gandhi and the Violence of Zionism*, 8.

67. Boutros Ghali, "al-siyasa wal-istratijiyya fi al muhit al-Hindi," *al-Siyasa al-Dawliyya* 2 (1966): 62–73. The journal was a publication of the Al-Ahram Center for Political and Strategic Studies, which Boutrous Ghali was a key part of (as was Maksoud for a period). The center's activities are in need of a serious study. For a brief and unsatisfactory view, see chapter 6 of Raymond William Baker, *Sadat and After: Struggles for Egypt's Political Soul* (Cambridge, MA: Harvard University Press, 1990).

68. Boutros-Ghali, "al-siyasa wal-istratijiyya fi al muhit al-Hindi," 62.

69. Boutros-Ghali, "al-siyasa wal-istratijiyya fi al muhit al-Hindi," 63.

70. Boutros-Ghali, "al-siyasa wal-istratijiyya fi al muhit al-Hindi," 66.

71. Boutros Ghali, "The Suez Canal and Indian Ocean Strategy," *SWASIA North Africa* 1, no. 27 (August 2, 1974): 1. First published in Arabic in *al-Ahram al-Iqtisadi*, June 15, 1974.

72. Isabel Hofmyer, "Against the Global South," in *The Global South and Literature*, ed. Russell West-Pavlov (Cambridge: Cambridge University Press, 2018), 307–14.

73. Underwood, "New SIS Center Highlights South," *The Eagle*, September, 7, 1986. A4.

74. United Nations Archive, Conference Proceedings, "Environmental Challenges and the Global South," April 13-14, 1992, S-1086, box 108, file 2, Boutros Boutros-Ghali Papers.

75. Clovis Maksoud, "Redefining Non-Alignment: The Global South in the New Global Equation," in *Altered States: A Reader in the New World Order*, ed. Phyllis Bennis and Michel Moushabeck (New York: Olive Branch Press, 1993), 33.

76. Maksoud, "Redefining Non-Alignment," 37.

77. Norman Palmer, "Note on the First Asian History Congress," *Asian Survey* 1, no. 12 (1962): 39.

78. Richard Wright, *The Color Curtain: A Report on the Bandung Conference* (New York: World Publishing Company, 1956), 82.

79. K. S. Lal, *Studies in Asian History: Proceedings of the Asian History Congress, 1961* (Bombay: Asia Publishing House for the Indian Council for Cultural Relations, 1969), 524.

80. Lal, *Studies in Asian History*, 525.

81. Lal, *Studies in Asian History*, 525.

82. K. M. Panikkar, "Presidential Address," *Proceedings of the Indian History Congress* 18 (1955), 20.

83. Walter Rodney, *A History of the Guyanese Working People, 1881–1905* (Baltimore, MD: Johns Hopkins University Press, 1981), 268.

Chapter 5. Area

1. M. L. Roy Choudhury, introduction to *Egypt in 1945*, ed. Choudhury (Calcutta: University of Calcutta, 1946). Choudhury would later also travel to Afghanistan and write an English-language account of that journey, *Romance of Afghanistan* (Calcutta: Indian Book Concern, 1961). The book bears some resemblance to Syed Mujtaba Ali's famous (and famously hilarious) 1947 travelogue about Afghanistan, *Deshe Bideshe*. See Syed Mujtaba Ali, *In a Land Far From Home: A Bengali in Afghanistan*, trans. Nazes Afroz (New Delhi: Speaking Tiger, 2015). Although not detailed in this chapter, Ali's career—as a scholar of Islamic studies and an administrator in the Indian Council for Cultural Relations—corresponds strongly with the history recounted here. On his life and engagement with West Asia, see Supriya Chaudhuri, "The Traveller as Internationalist: Syed Mujtaba Ali," in *The Form of Ideology and the Ideology of Form: Cold War, Decolonization and Third World Print Cultures*, ed. Francesca Orsini, Neelam Srivastava, and Laetitia Zecchini (Cambridge, UK: Open Book Publishers, 2022), 31–66.

2. Partha Chatterjee, "The Disciplines in Colonial Bengal," in *Texts of Power: Emerging Disciplines in Colonial Bengal*, ed. Chatterjee (Minneapolis: University of Minnesota Press, 1995), 10.

3. Projit Bihari Mukharji, "The Bengali Pharaoh: Upper-Caste Aryanism, Pan-Egyptianism, and the Contested History of Biometric Nationalism in Twentieth-Century Bengal," *Comparative Studies in Society and History* 59, no. 2 (2017): 446–76.

4. Makhan Lal Roy Choudhury, *Misara Dayeri* (Calcutta: Pratulchandra Ghosh, 1948), 2:91.

5. "Dr. M. L. Roy Choudhury," *Calcutta Review*, May 1945, 78

6. Mandakranta Bose, "The Tragedy of the Roy Choudhurys," accessed August 16, 2023, https://www.pastconnect.net/the-tragedy-of-the-roy-choudhurys/.

7. "Cultural Activities," *Islamic Culture* 19, no. 1 (January 1945), 97.

8. Makhan Lal Roy Choudhury, trans., *Al-Kita: Tarjumah al-kitab al muqaddas 'and al-Hindus*. Calcutta: M/S Thacker Spink, 1951.

9. M. L. Roy Choudhury, *The State and Religion in Mughal India* (Calcutta: Indian Publicity Society, 1951), 343.

10. Muhammad Ajmal Khan, "Qism al-'Uloom al-Islamiya bi Jami'at Washwa Baharti bil Binghal," *Thaqafat al-Hind* 12, no. 3 (July 1961): 32. On Hyderabad's global Islamic connections see Eric Lewis Beverley, *Hyderabad, British India, and the World: Muslim Networks and Minor Sovereignty, c. 1850-1950* (Cambridge: Cambridge University Press, 2015).

11. Azizul Haque, "The Vice Chancellor's Speech," in *The Indian Annual Register: An Annuel Digest of Public Affairs of India Recording the Nation's Activites each year in matters Political, Economic, Industrial, Social Etc.* Vol. 1, *January–June 1940*, ed. Nirpendra Nath Mitra (Calcutta: The Annual Register Office, 1940), 430.

12. University of Calcutta, *Development of Post-Graduate Studies in Arts and Letters in the University of Calcutta (1907-48)* (Calcutta: University of Calcutta Press, 1949), 35.

13. While I am not equipped to do so, Habibullah is deserving of serious and thorough study. A partisan of the organized Left in pre-Partition Bengal, he did his doctorate on early Islam in India and later translated al-Biruni's *Tarkih al-Hind* into Bengali from the Arabic. For a sense of his historical and political attitudes, see A. B. M. Habibullah, "Presidential Address," *Proceedings of the Indian History Congress* 13 (1950): 137-41.

14. P. N. Banerjee, "University of Calcutta and Islamic Studies," *Calcutta Review*, October 1949, 6. First broadcast on All-India Radio on August 11, 1949.

15. Bernard Cohn, *Colonialism and Its Forms of Knowledge: The British in India* (Princeton, NJ: Princeton University Press, 1996), 15.

16. William Fenton, *Area Studies in American Universities* (Washington, DC: American Council on Education, 1947), 11.

17. Fenton, *Area Studies in American Universities*, 3.

18. Ke Niu, "The SSRC and the Founding Movement of Area Studies in America, 1943-1953," *China International Strategy Review* 1 (2019): 283-309.

19. Zachary Lockman, *Field Notes: The Making of Middle East Studies in the United States* (Stanford, CA: Stanford University Press, 2016), 270n3.

20. Edward H. Berman, *The Influence of the Carnegie, Ford and Rockefeller Foundations on American Foreign Policy: The Ideology of Philanthropy* (Albany: State University of New York Press, 1983), 32.

21. Inderjeet Parmar, *Foundations of the American Century: The Ford, Carnegie, and Rockefeller Foundations in the Rise of the American Power* (New York: Columbia University Press, 2012), 118.

22. Kwame Nkrumah, "Address Delivered to Mark the Opening of the First International Congress of Africanists," in *The Proceedings of the First International Congress of Africanists*, ed. Lalage Brown and Micahel Crowder (Chicago: Northwestern University Press, 1964), 7.

23. Nkrumah, "Address Delivered to Opening of the First International Congress of Africanists," 10.

24. *Proceedings of the Twenty-Sixth International Congress of Orientalists* (New Delhi: Organising Committee XXVI International Congress of Orientalists, 1966), 43.

25. Edward [Édouard] Montet, "The Congress of Orientalists at Algiers," *Imperial and Asiatic Quarterly Review and Oriental and Colonial Record* 20, no. 39-40 (July-October 1905), 84.

26. Montet, "Congress of Orientalists," 84.

27. Montet, "Congress of Orientalists," 84.

28. "The International Congress of Orientalists," *Athenaeum*, no. 4046 (May 13, 1905), 594.

29. Ahmad Hilmi, "Muqadamit al-tab'a al-thaniya," in *al-Islam din al-Fitra*, by Abd al-Aziz Jawish (Cairo: Matba'at al-Hidaya, 1905), 20. On Hilmi's activities as an anti-colonial journalist, see Aaron G. Jakes, *Egypt's Occupation: Colonial Economism and the Crises of Capitalism* (Stanford, CA: Stanford University Press, 2020), ch. 4.

30. Hussein Omar, "Arabic Thought in the Liberal Cage," in *Islam After Liberalism*, ed. Faisal Devji and Zaheer Kazmi (Oxford: Oxford University Press, 2017), 34.

31. Anour Abdel-Malek, "Orientalism in Crisis," *Diogenes* 11, no. 44 (1963), 121.

32. Masha Kirasirova, "'Sons of Muslims' in Moscow: Soviet Central Asian Mediators to the Foreign East, 1955-1962," *Ab Imperio* 4 (2011): 106-32.

33. Basil Davidson, "The Africanists," *West Africa*, December 29, 1962, 1457.

34. Melville J. Herskovits, "The Development of Africanist Studies in Europe and America," in Brown and Crowder, *Proceedings of the First International Congress of Africanists*, 30.

35. Nkrumah, "Address Delivered to Opening of the First International Congress of Africanists," 8.

36. I. Potekhin, "Problems of Economic Independence of African Countries," in Brown and Crowder, *Proceedings of the First International Congress of Africanists*, 183.

37. "Symposium on Role of Oriental Studies in the Humanities," in *Proceedings of the Twenty-Sixth International Congress of Orientalists*, 77.

38. Issa G. Shivji, "The Metamorphosis of the Revolutionary Intellectual," *Agrarian South: Journal of Political Economy* 7:3 (2018), 399.

39. Azizul Haque, "Note by the Hon'ble Sir M. Azizul Haque," in *Report of the Kamal Yar Jung Education Committee* (Calcutta: n.p., 1942), 280.

40. *Report of the University Education Commission (December 1948–August 1949)* (New Delhi: Ministry of Education and Culture, 1950), 1:101

41. A.A. Fyzee, "The Study of Modern Arabic," note attached to letter from R. K. Nehru to Humayun Kabir, August 20, 1952, F-18-6-53, Ministry of Education, National Archives of India (NAI).

42. Zakir Husain to Abul Kalam Azad, March 18, 1953, F-18-6-53, Ministry of Education, NAI.

43. Husain to S. S. Bhatnagar, April 16, 1953, F-18-6-53, Ministry of Education, NAI.

44. Typescript note from Ministry of External Affairs, F-18-6-53, Ministry of Education, NAI.

45. R. K. Nehru to Kabir, April 16, 1953 F-18-6-53, F-18-6-53, Ministry of Education, NAI.

46. R. K. Nehru to Ministry of Education, July 10, 1953, F-18-6-53, Ministry of Education, NAI.

47. Zakir Husain to Abul Kalam Azad, September 1, 1953, F-18-6-53, Ministry of Education, NAI.

48. Ale Ahmad Suroor, "Alim Sahib," in *Alim Sahib*, ed. Muhammad Salim Qidwai (Aligarh: Idara 'uloom Islamiyya: Aligarh Muslim Universati, 1995), 75

49. Sajjad Zaheer, *The Light: A History of the Movement for Progressive Literature in the Indo-Pakistan Subcontinent*, trans. Amina Azfar (Oxford: Oxford University Press, 2006), 253.

50. Ralph Russel, "Urdu and I," *Annual of Urdu Studies* 11 (1996), 26.

51. Carlo Coppola, "Interview with Ali Sardar Jafri," *Journal of Urdu Studies* 1 (2020), 94n2.

52. Suroor, "Alim Sahib," 68.

53. Abdul Aleem, "Marksism aur adab," in Qidwai, *Alim Sahib*, 313–28.

54. Suroor, "Alim Sahib," 70.

55. Riaz al-Rahman Sherwani, "Professor Abdul Alim," in Qidawi, *Alim Sahib*, 100–104.

56. Abdul Aleem, "Preface," *Bulletin of the Institute of Islamic Studies* 1 (1957).

57. Jamila Majid, "Humaray abba," in Qidwai, *Alim Sahib*, 33.

58. Note by B. N. Nanda, July 6, 1953, F-18-6-53, Ministry of Education, NAI.

59. Kavita Datla, *The Language of Secular Islam: Urdu Nationalism and Colonial Hyderabad* (Honolulu: University of Hawai'i Press, 2013).

60. Taylor C. Sherman, *Muslim Belonging in Secular India: Negotiating Citizenship in Postcolonial Hyderabad* (Cambridge: Cambridge University Press, 2015), 57.

61. Note by Humayun Kabir, July 20, 1953, F-18-6-53, Ministry of Education, NAI.

62. "Kul hind 'ulum islami confrens," *Majjala i 'Ulum i Islamiya* 1, no. 2 (December 1960): 218–19.

63. Abdul Aleem, "Some Aspects of Islamic Studies in India," *Bulletin of the Institute of Islamic Studies*, nos. 8/9 (1964/1965): 2.

64. Aleem, "Some Aspects of Islamic Studies in India," 3.

65. K. M. Panikkar, *An Autobiography* (Madras: Oxford University Press, 1977), 341.

66. Panikkar, *Autobiography*, 342.

67. M. C. Chagla, *Roses in December: An Autobiography* (Bombay: Bharatiy Vidya Bhavan, 1973), 378.

68. Pratinav Anil, *Another India: The Making of the World's Largest Muslim Minority, 1947-77* (Oxford: Oxford University Press, 2023), 303.

69. Laurence Gautier, "Crisis of the 'Nehruvian Consensus' or Pluralization of Indian Politics? Aligarh Muslim University and the Demand for Minority Status," *South Asia Multidisciplinary Academic Journal* 22 (2019), http://journals.openedition.org/samaj/6493.

70. Maqbul Ahmad, *Barg-i gull: Khud navisht savanih, safar namah, ta'limi khidmat, aur silsilah-yi nasab* (Mumbai: Qazi Sayyid Mahtab Ahmad Husaini, 2001), 52.

71. Ahmad, *Barg-i gull*, 55.

72. Ahmad, *Barg-i gull*, 165.

73. David Lelyveld, *Aligarh's First Generation: Muslim Solidarity in British India* (Princeton, NJ: Princeton University Press, 1978), 131.

74. Nicola Ziadeh, *Hawla al-'alam fi sab'a wa sittin 'aman: Rihlat muthaqqaf shami fi asya wa urubba wal-shamal al-Ifriqi, 1916–1992*. (Beirut: al-Mu'assasa al-'Arabiyya lil-Dirasat wal-Nashr, 2007), 343.

75. Hafsa Kanjwal, *Colonizing Kashmir: State-Building under Indian Occupation* (Stanford, CA: Stanford University Press, 2023).

76. Ahmad, *Barg-I gull*, 16. The details about Ahmad's early life in this paragraph and the paragraph that follows are also from Ahmad, *Barg-i gull*, 12–21.

77. Ahmad, *Barg-i gull*, 112.

78. Masʿudurrahman Khan Nadvi, *Profaisar Sayyid Maqbul Ahmad, hayat va khidmat* (Patna: Khuda Baksh Oriental Library, 1999), 77–78. This text compiles and contextualizes excerpts from Ahmad's diaries, which the author had access to.

79. Ahmad, *Barg-i gull*, 126.

80. Ahmad, *Barg-i gull*, 126—27.

81. On these efforts, see Hana Sleiman, "History Writing and History Making in Twentieth Century Beirut" (PhD diss., University of Cambridge, 2021).

82. Ziadeh, *Hawla al-ʿalam fi sabʿa wa sittin ʿaman*, 341.

83. Nicola Ziadeh, "Speech," in *Al-Masudi Millenary Commemoration Volume*, ed. S. Maqbul Ahmad and A. Rahman (Aligarh: Institute of Islamic Studies, Aligarh Muslim University and the Indian Society for the History of Science, 1960), 142.

84. "Extract from a Letter by the late Maulana Abul Kalam Azad to the Vice Chancellor, Aligarh Muslim University," in Ahmad and Rahman, *Al-Masudi Millenary Commemoration Volume*, 130.

85. Maqbul Ahmad, *Indo-Arab Relations* (New Delhi: Indian Council for Cultural Relations, 1969), ix.

86. Ahmad, *Indo-Arab Relations*, 165.

87. Ahmad, *Indo-Arab Relations*, xi.

88. On the founding of the school, see the official account produced from internal documents by the ICWA: T.C. A. Raghavan and Vivek Mishra, *Sapru House: A Story of Institution-Building in World Affairs* (New Delhi: Indian Council of World Affairs, 2021), especially chs. 3–5. See also V. M. Reddi, "Area Studies in India," *Proceedings of the Indian History Congress* 40 (1979): 925-31; and the accounts of key leaders in the school's development, A. Appadorai and M. S. Rajan (the first and second directors of the school, respectively), collected in M. S. Rajan, ed., *International and Area Studies in India* (New Delhi: Lancers Books, 1997). Important work seeking to historicize the discipline of international relations in colonial and postcolonial India has also examined the activities of the ICWA and related efforts. See Vineet Thakur and Alexander E. Davis, "A Communal Affair over International Affairs: The Arrival of IR in Late Colonial India," *South Asia: Journal of South Asian Studies* 40, no. 4 (2017): 689-705;

and Raphaëlle Khan, "Disrupting the Empire and Forging IR: The Role of India's Early Think Tanks in the Decolonisation Process, 1936-1950s," *International History Review* 44, no. 4 (2022): 836-55. On JNU, see the first chapter of Gyan Prakash, *Emergency Chronicles: Indira Gandhi and Democracy's Turning Point* (Princeton, NJ: Princeton University Press, 2019); and Neeladri Bhattacharya, Kunal Chakrabarti, S. Gunasekaran, Janaki Nair, and Joy L. K. Pachuau, *JNU Stories: The First 50 Years* (New Delhi: Aleph, 2020).

89. Raghavan and Vivek Mishra, *Sapru House*, 70; and M. S. Agwani, *Life in Academia: A Memoir* (New Delhi: Har-Anand Publications, 2013), 68.

90. 'Abid Suhail, *'Abdul 'Alim* (New Delhi: Sahtiya Akademi, 2008), 105-6.

91. This paragraph is drawn from Agwani, *Life in Academia*, 9-43.

92. Agwani, *Life in Academia*, 68.

93. M. S. Agwani, "A Preliminary Note on Libraries and Archives in Egypt and Libya," *International Studies* (October 1959): 201-3.

94. Agwani, *Life in Academia*, 69.

95. Albert Hourani, introduction to *The United States and the Arab World, 1945-1952*, by Mohammed Shafi Agwani (Aligarh: Institute of Islamic Studies, Aligarh Muslim University, 1955). On Hourani see Walid Khalidi, "On Albert Hourani, the Arab Office, and the Anglo-American Committee of 1946," *Journal of Palestine Studies* 35, no. 1 (2005): 60-79; and Roger Owen, "Albert Hourani and the Making of Modern Middle East Studies in the English-Speaking World: A Personal Memoir," in *Arabic Thought Beyond the Liberal Age: Towards an Intellectual History of the Nahda*, ed. Jens Hanssen and Max Weiss (Cambridge: Cambridge University Press, 2016), 41-61.

96. Valentine Chirol, *The Middle Eastern Question: Or, Some Political Problems of Indian Defence* (London: John Murray, 1903) 5.

97. Hourani, introduction. Emphasis in original.

98. M. S. Agwani, "Key Note Address," in *Contemporary West Asian Scene: A Selection of Papers Presented at a Seminar Held at Aligarh*, ed. Arif H. Rizvi (Aligarh: Centre of West Asian Studies, Aligarh Muslim University, 1980), 16.

99. Agwani, "Key Note Address," 17.

100. Agwani, "Key Note Address," 17.

Epilogue

1. M. S. Agwani, "The Palestine Conflict from an Asian Perspective," in *The Transformation of Palestine*, ed. Ibrahim Abu-Lughod (Evanston: Northwestern University Press, 1971), 443; and M. S. Agwani, *Asia and Palestine* (New Delhi:

League of Arab States Mission, n.d.). All quotes are from the article version, although the pamphlet is nearly identical except for some minor changes in diction.

2. Agwani, "Palestine Conflict from an Asian Perspective," 461–62.

3. M. S. Agwani, *Life in Academia: A Memoir* (New Delhi: Har-Anand Publications, 2013), 80.

4. David C. Gordon, *Self-Determination and History in the Third World* (Princeton, NJ: Princeton University Press, 1971), 23.

5. Gordon, *Self-Determination and History*, 23.

6. David C. Gordon, *Lebanon: The Fragmented Nation* (London: Croom Helm, 1980), 14. The biographical details presented here are summarized from the same source. See the laudatory account of Gordon's Lebanese career written by his son: Matthew Gordon, "The AUB History Department, 1970–1971: An Appreciation," in *One Hundred and Fifty*, ed. Nadia El Cheikh, Lina Choueiri, and Bilal Orfali (Beirut: American University of Beirut, 2016), 235–41.

7. Agwani, *Life in Academia*, 80.

8. Fred Moten, *Stolen Life* (Durham, NC: Duke University Press, 2018), 214.

Bibliography

Individual periodical articles and online sources are not listed in the bibliography.

Archives

Bodleian Library, Oxford University
British Library (BL), London
British National Archives (TNA), Kew
Indian Council for Cultural Relations Library (ICCR), New Delhi
Israel State Archives (ISA), Jerusalem
Library of Congress, Washington D.C.
National Archives of India (NAI), New Delhi
Special Collections, Smith College
United Nations Archives, New York City
Widener Library, Harvard University

Periodicals

Arabic titles are alphabetized by the main word in the title, not by the definite article *al-*.

al-Abhath (Beirut)
al-Adab (Beirut)
al-Adib (Beirut)
al-Ahram (Cairo)
al-'Arabi (Kuwait)

Amrita Bazar Patrika (Cairo)
The Athenaeum (London)
Bulletin of the Institute of Islamic Studies (Aligarh)
The Calcutta Review (Calcutta)
The Church Missionary Intelligencer and Record (London)
Dawn (Lahore)
The Economist (London)
Filistin (Jaffa)
al-Funun (New York)
Hamizrah Hahedesh (Jerusalem)
al-Hilal (Cairo)
Hindustan Times (New Delhi)
The Imperial and Asiatic Quarterly Review and Oriental and Colonial Record (London)
India Quarterly (New Delhi)
Indo-Asian Culture (New Delhi)
Islamic Culture (Hyderabad)
Jewish Daily Bulletin (New York)
Le Progrès Égyptien (Cairo)
Majallat al-Majmaʿ al-ʿIlmi al-ʿArabi (Damascus)
The Manchester Guardian (Manchester)
al-Mashriq (Beirut)
The Moslem World (London)
New Outlook (Tel Aviv)
The Palestine Post (Jerusalem)
Présence Africaine (Paris)
al-Risala (Cairo)
al-Risala al-Jadida (Cairo)
Sawt al-Sharq (Cairo)
al-Siyasa al-Dawliyya (Cairo)
al-Thaqafa (Cairo)
Thaqafat al-Hind (New Delhi)
al-Thaqafa al-Wataniyya (Beirut)
Times of India (New Delhi)
Ummah (Karachi)
al-Urwa (Bombay)
West Africa (London)

Women of the Whole World (Berlin)
al-Zahra' (Cairo)
al-Zuhoor (Cairo)

Reports and Proceedings

Afro-Asian People's Conference: Held at Cairo from 26 December 1957 to 1st January 1958; Inaugural Addresses, Resolutions, Closing Addresses. Cairo: Permanent Secretariat of the Afro-Asian Peoples' Solidarity Organization, 1958.

Ahmad, S. Maqbul, ed. *India and the Arab World: Proceedings of the Seminar on India and the Arab World.* New Delhi: Indian Council for Cultural Relations, 1965.

Ahmad, S. Maqbul, and A. Rahman, eds. *Al-Masudi Millenary Commemoration Volume: Aligarh; Institute of Islamic Studies.* Aligarh Muslim University and the Indian Society for the History of Science, 1960.

al-Ba'tha al-Azhariyya ila al-Hind. *Dirasa li-ahwal al-tawa'if wa-al-hay'at al-Islamiyya bi-al-Hind wa-bahth fi shu'un al-manbudhin wa-mablagh isti'dadihim li-i'tinaq.* Cairo: al-Maktaba al-Hijaziyya, 1938.

The All-India Women's Conference, Eighteenth Session, Hyderabad (Sind), December 28, 1945 to January 1, 1946. N.p.: All-India Women's Conference, n.d.

Appadorai, A. ed. *Status of Women in South Asia.* Calcutta: Orient Longmans, 1954.

Asia-Africa Speaks from Bandung. Jakarta: Ministry of Foreign Affairs Republic of Indonesia, 1955.

Asian Relations: Report of the Proceedings and Documents of the First Asian Relations Conference, New Delhi, March–April 1947. New Delhi: Asian Relations Organization, 1948.

Brown, Lalage, and Michael Crowder, eds. *The Proceedings of the First International Congress of Africanists.* Chicago: Northwestern University Press, 1964.

India and the Arab World: A Symposium. Bombay: Indo-Arab Society, 1955.

Lal, K. S. *Studies in Asian History: Proceedings of the Asian History Congress, 1961.* Bombay: Asia Publishing House for the Indian Council for Cultural Relations, 1969.

Mu'tamar al-udaba' al-'arab al-thani. Damascus: Ittihad al-Udaba' al-'Arab, 1956.

Proceedings of the Twenty-Sixth International Congress of Orientalists. New Delhi: Organising Committee XXVI International Congress of Orientalists, 1966.

Report of the Kamal Yar Jung Education Committee. Calcutta: n.p., 1942.

The Report of the University Education Commission (December 1948–August 1949). New Delhi: Ministry of Education and Culture, 1950.

Rizvi, Arif H., ed. *Contemporary West Asian Scene: A Selection of Papers Presented at a Seminar Held at Aligarh*. Aligarh: Centre for West Asian Studies, Aligarh Muslim University, 1980.

Sayegh, Fayez, ed. *The Dynamics of Neutralism in the Arab World: A Symposium*. San Francisco: Chandler Publishing, 1964.

University of Calcutta. *Development of Post-Graduate Studies in Arts and Letters in the University of Calcutta (1907–48)*. Calcutta: University of Calcutta Press, 1949.

Wherry, E. M., C. G. Myirea, and S. M. Zwemer, eds. *Lucknow, 1911: Being Papers Read and Discussions on the Training of Missionaries, and Literature for Muslims at the General Conference on Missions to Muslims Held at Lucknow, Jan. 23–28, 1911*. London: Christian Literature Society for India, 1911.

World Missionary Conference, 1910 (to Consider Missionary Problems in Relation to the Non-Christian World): The Record of the Conference Together with Addresses Delivered at the Evening Meetings. Edinburgh: Oliphant, Anderson, & Ferrier, 1910.

Other Sources

Abaza, Mona. "East Is East? Where Does the East Begin for Egyptian Liberal Intellectuals?" *IAS Newsletter* 29 (November 2002): 20.

'Abd al-Rahman, Ahmad Muhammad Ahmad. "Rihlat Taghur ila Misr." *Thaqafatul Hind* 62, no. 4 (2011): 85–100.

'Abd al-Rahman, As'ad. *Al-Tasallul al-Isra'ili fi Asiya: al-Hind wa Isra'il*. Beirut: Markaz al-Dirasat, Munazimat al-Tahrir al-Falistini, 1967.

Abdel-Malek, Anour, ed. *Contemporary Arab Thought*. London: Zed, 1980.

Abdel-Malek, Anour. *Egypt: Military Society*. New York: Vintage, 1968.

Abdel-Malek, Anour. "Orientalism in Crisis." *Diogenes* 11, no. 44 (1963).

Abdel-Malek, Anour. "'Ishtu Marhalat Siyaghat al-Khat al-am lil-Haraka al-Wataniyya al-Misriyya." In *Takwin: Hayat al-Mufakirin wal-Uduba' wal-Fananin bi Qalamihim*. Cairo: Dar al-Hilal, 1998.

Abou Risha, Omar. "Nehru: Man of Two Cultures and One World." In *Nehru and the Modern World*. New Delhi: Indian National Commission for Co-operation with Unesco, 1967.

Abourahme, Nasser. "Revolution after Revolution: The Commune as Line of Flight in Palestinian Anticolonialism." *Critical Times* 4, no. 3 (2022): 445–75.

Abu-Lughod, Ibrahim. "The Pitfalls of Palestiniology." *Arab Studies Quarterly* 3, no. 4 (1981) : 403–11.

Abu-Lughod, Ibrahim, ed. *The Transformation of Palestine*. Evanston, IL: Northwestern University Press, 1971.

Agwani, M. S. *Asia and Palestine*. New Delhi: League of Arab States Mission, n.d.

Agwani, M. S. *Life in Academia: A Memoir*. New Delhi: Har-Anand Publications, 2013.

Agwani, M. S. "A Preliminary Note on Libraries and Archives in Egypt and Libya." *International Studies* (October 1959): 201–3.

Agwani, Mohammed Shafi. *The United States and the Arab World, 1945–1952*. Aligarh: Institute of Islamic Studies, Aligarh Muslim University, 1955.

Ahmad, Eqbal. "An Address in Gaza." In *The Selected Writings of Eqbal Ahmed*, edited by Carollee Bengelsoorf, Margaret Cerullo, and Yogesh Chandrani. New York: Columbia University Press, 2006.

Ahmad, Maqbul. *Barg-i gull: Khud navisht savanih, safar namah, ta ʿlimi khidmat, aur silsilah-yi nasab*. Mumbai: Qazi Sayyid Mahtab Ahmad Husaini, 2001.

Ahmad, Maqbul. *Indo-Arab Relations*. New Delhi: Indian Council for Cultural Relations, 1969.

Ahmed Asif, Manan. "Quarantined Histories: Sindh and the Question of Historiography in Colonial India—Part II." *History Compass* 15, no. 8 (2017): 1–7.

ʿAlam, Suhayb, ed. *al-Hind fi al-shiʿr al-ʿArabi*. Rampur: Raza Rampur Library, 2010.

Alkalimat, Abd-al Hakimu Ibn [Abdul Alkalimat]. "Common Problems, Common Solutions: Toward a Pan-African Ideology." *Journal of Black Poetry* 1, no. 14 (1970–71): 23–30.

Alshehabi, Omar Hesham. "Policing Labour in Empire: The Modern Origins of the Kafala Sponsorship System in the Gulf Arab States." *British Journal of Middle Eastern Studies* 48, no. 2 (2021): 291–310.

Amin, Samir. "The Countries of the South Must Take Their Own Independent Initiatives." In *Samir Amin: Pioneer of the Rise of the South*. Cham: Springer, 2014.

Anil, Pratinav. *Another India: The Making of the World's Largest Muslim Minority, 1947-77*. Oxford: Oxford University Press, 2023.

Apter, Emily. "Global *Translatio*: The 'Invention' of Comparative Literature, Istanbul, 1933." *Critical Inquiry* 29, no. 2 (2003): 253–81.

Armstrong, Elizabeth. "Before Bandung: The Anti-Imperialist Women's Movement in Asia and the Women's International Democratic Federation." *Signs: Journal of Women in Culture and Society* 41, no. 2 (2016): 305–31.

Asad, Talal. Response in "Indigenous Anthropology in Non-Western Countries: A Further Elaboration." *Current Anthropology* 21, no. 5 (1980): 662.

Auerbach, Erich. *Mimesis: The Representation of Reality in Western Literature*. Princeton, NJ: Princeton University Press, 2003.

Aydin, Cemil. *The Idea of the Muslim World: A Global Intellectual History*. Cambridge, MA: Harvard University Press, 2017.

Azad, Abul Kalam. *India Wins Freedom*. New Delhi: Orient Longman, 1988.

Azaryahu, Maoz, and Yitzhak Reiter. "The Geopolitics of Interment: An Inquiry into the Burial of Muhammad Ali in Jerusalem, 1931." *Israel Studies* 20, no. 1 (Spring 2015): 31–56.

Azeb, Sophia. "Crossing the Saharan Boundary: *Lotus* and the Legibility of Africanness." *Research in African Literatures* 50, no. 3 (2019): 91–117.

Badran, Margot. *Feminists, Islam, and Nation: Gender and the Making of Modern Egypt*. Princeton, NJ: Princeton University Press, 1995.

Baghoolizadeh, Beeta. *The Color Black: Enslavement and Erasure in Iran*. Durham, NC: Duke University Press, 2024.

Bahl, Aditya. "Green, Red: From *Pragati* to *Jujhar* in the Cold War Punjab." In *The Oxford Companion to Modern Indian Literatures*, edited by Ulka Anjaria and Anjali Nerlekar. Oxford: Oxford University Press, 2024.

Baker, Raymond William. *Sadat and After: Struggles for Egypt's Political Soul*. Cambridge, MA: Harvard University Press, 1990.

Barakat, Rana. "Lifta, the Nakba, and the Museumification of Palestine's History." *Native American and Indigenous Studies* 5, no. 2 (2018): 1–15.

Baron, Beth. *The Orphan Scandal: Christian Missionaries and the Rise of the Muslim Brotherhood*. Stanford, CA: Stanford University Press, 2014.

Bawalsa, Nadim. *Transnational Palestine: Migration and the Right of Return before 1948*. Stanford, CA: Stanford University Press, 2022.

Bier, Laura. *Revolutionary Womanhood: Feminisms, Modernity, and the State in Nasser's Egypt*. Stanford, CA: Stanford University Press, 2011.

Benite, Zvi Ben-Dor. "Taking 'Abduh to China: Chinese Egyptian Intellectual Contact in the Early Twentieth Century." In *Global Muslims in the Age of Steam and Print*, edited by James Gelvin and Nile Green. Berkeley: University of California Press, 2014.

Bennabi, Malek. *L'Afro-Asiatisme: Conclusions sur la Conference de Bandoeng*. Cairo: Imprimerie Misr, 1956.

Berman, Edward H. *The Influence of the Carnegie, Ford and Rockefeller Foundations on American Foreign Policy: The Ideology of Philanthropy*. Albany: State University of New York Press, 1983.

Bhattacharya, Neeladri, Kunal Chakrabarti, S. Gunasekaran, Janaki Nair, and Joy L. K. Pachuau. *JNU Stories: The First 50 Years*. New Delhi: Aleph, 2020.

Bishara, Fahad. *A Sea of Debt: Law and Economic Life in the Western Indian Ocean, 1780–1950*. Cambridge: Cambridge University Press, 2017.

Bishop, Elizabeth. "'Asia and Adjacent Areas'; Mohammed Fadhel Jamali's Cold War Experiences." *Auto/Fiction* 1, no. 2 (2014): 62.

Boustany [Wadiʿ al-Bustani], W. F. *The Palestine Mandate: Invalid and Impracticable; A Contribution of Arguments and Documents towards the Solution of the Palestine Problem*. Beirut: American Press, 1936.

Boustany [Wadiʿ al-Bustani], W. F. *The Quatrains of War*. Transvaal: n.p., 1915.

Brunner, Rainer. *Islamic Ecumenism in the 20th Century: The Azhar and Shiism between Rapprochement and Restraint*. Leiden: Brill, 2004.

Bsheer, Rosie. *Archive Wars: The Politics of History in Saudi Arabia*. Stanford, CA: Stanford University Press, 2020.

Buck-Morss, Susan. *Thinking Past Terror: Islamism and Critical Theory on the Left*. London: Verso, 2006.

al-Bustani, Milhim Ibrahim. *Al-Salsibil*. Jounieh: n.p., 1968.

al-Bustani, Wadiʿ. *Al-Falistinyyat*. Beirut: Dar al-Tibaʿa wal-Nashr al-Sharqiyya, 1946.

al-Bustani, Wadiʿ. *Al-Mahabharata: Al-Malhama al-Hinduwiyya*. Beirut: Jamʿiyat Mutakharrijyi al-Jamʿiah al-Amirkiyah fi Beirut, 1952.

al-Bustani, Wadiʿ, trans. *Al-Ramayana*. Abu Dhabi: Kalima/Indian Council for Cultural Relations, 2012.

al-Bustani, Wadiʿ. "Muqaddima," In *Masarrat al-Hayat*, edited by Jon Lubbuk. Cairo: Matbaʿat al-Maʿarif, 1911.

al-Bustani, Wadiʿ. "Muqaddima." In *Rubaʿiyat ʿUmar al-Khayyam*. Cairo: Matbaʿat al-Maʿarif, 1912.

Butalia, Urvashi. *The Other Side of Silence: Voices from the Partition of India*. New Delhi: Penguin Books, 1998.

Cabral, Amilcar. *Unity and Struggle: Speeches and Writings of Amilcar Cabral*. New York: Monthly Review Press, 1979.

Campbell, Iain D. "In Search of the Physical: George Adam Smith's Journeys to Palestine and Their Importance." *History and Anthropology* 13, no. 4 (2002): 291–99.

Chandra, Satish. "A Note on the Decentring of History and Apprehension by All People of Their History." *Diogenes* 20, no. 77 (1972): 92–109.

Chagla, M. C. *Roses in December: An Autobiography*. Bombay: Bharatiy Vidya Bhavan, 1973.

Chatterjee, Partha. "History and the Nationalization of Hinduism." *Social Research* 59, no. 1 (1992): 111–49.

Chatterjee, Partha, ed. *Texts of Power: Emerging Disciplines in Colonial Bengal.* Minneapolis: University of Minnesota Press, 1995.

Chatterji, Joya. *Bengal Divided: Hindu Communalism and Partition, 1932–1947.* Cambridge: Cambridge University Press, 1994.

Chattopadhyaya, Kamaladevi. *Inner Recesses, Outer Spaces: Memoirs.* New Delhi: Navrang, 1986.

Chaudhuri, K. N. *Trade and Civilisation in the Indian Ocean: An Economic History from the Rise of Islam to 1750.* Cambridge: Cambridge University Press, 1985.

Chaudhuri, Supriya. "The Traveller as Internationalist: Syed Mujtaba Ali." In *The Form of Ideology and the Ideology of Form: Cold War, Decolonization and Third World Print Cultures*, edited by Francesca Orsini, Neelam Srivastava, and Laetitia Zecchini. Cambridge, UK: Open Book Publishers, 2022.

Chirol, Valentine. *The Middle Eastern Question: Or, Some Political Problems of Indian Defence.* London: John Murray, 1903.

Chirol, Valentine. *Pan-Islamism.* London : Central Asian Society, 1906.

Cleary, Joe. *Literature, Partition and the Nation-State Culture and Conflict in Ireland, Israel and Palestine.* Cambridge: Cambridge University Press, 2001.

Cohn, Bernard. *Colonialism and Its Forms of Knowledge: The British in India.* Princeton, NJ: Princeton University Press, 1996

Cole, Juan R. I. "'Indian Money' and the Shi'i shrine Cities of Iraq, 1786–1850." *Middle Eastern Studies* 22, no. 4 (1986): 461–80.

Cole, Juan R. I. "Mirror of the World: Iranian 'Orientalism' and Early 19th-century India." *Critique: Journal for Critical Studies of the Middle East* 5, no. 8 (1996): 41–60.

Collins, Michael. "History and the Postcolonial: Rabindranath Tagore's Reception in London, 1912–1913." *International Journal of the Humanities* 4, no. 9 (2007): 71–83.

Coppola, Carlo. "Interview with Ali Sardar Jafri." *Journal of Urdu Studies* 1 (2020): 90–126.

Crockford's Clerical Directory. Oxford: Oxford University Press, 1935.

Daftary, Farhad. *Historical Dictionary of the Ismailis.* Lanham, MD: Scarecrow Press, 2012.

Das, Bhagawan, ed. *Thus Spoke Ambedkar.* Vol. 4. Bangalore: Ambedkar Sahithya Prakashana, n.d.

Das Gupta, Ashin. "India and the Indian Ocean in the Eighteenth Century." In *The World of the Indian Ocean Merchant, 1500–1800: Collected Essays of Ashin Das Gupta*. New Delhi: Oxford University Press, 2001.

Datla, Kavita. *The Language of Secular Islam: Urdu Nationalism and Colonial Hyderabad*. Honolulu: University of Hawai'i Press, 2013.

Dayal, Har. *Forty-Four Months in Germany and Turkey, February 1915 to October 1918: A Record of Personal Impressions*. London: P. S. King & Son, 1920.

Deringil, Selim. *The Well-Protected Domains: Ideology and the Legitimation of Power in the Ottoman Empire, 1876–1909*. Cambridge: Cambridge University Press, 1998.

Devji, Faisal. *Muslim Zion: Pakistan as a Political Idea*. Cambridge, MA: Harvard University Press, 2013.

Djagalov, Rossen. *From Internationalism to Postcolonialism: Literature and Cinema between the Second and the Third Worlds*. Montreal: McGill-Queen's University Press, 2020.

Dodge, Bayard. *Al-Azhar: A Millennium of Muslim Learning*. Washington, DC: The Middle East Institute, 1961.

Doumani, Beshara. "Rediscovering Ottoman Palestine: Writing Palestinians into History." *Journal of Palestine Studies* 21, no. 2 (1992): 5–28.

Du Bois, W. E. B. *The World and Africa: An Inquiry into the Part Which Africa Has Played in World History*. New York: International Publishers, 1946.

Dubnov, Arie. "Notes on the Zionist Passage to India, or: The Analogical Imagination and Its Boundaries." *Journal of Israeli History* 35, no. 2 (2016): 177–214.

Dubnov, Arie, and Laura Robson. *Partitions: A Transnational History of Twentieth-Century Territorial Separatism*. Stanford, CA: Stanford University Press, 2019.

Dupont, Anne-Laure. "How Should the History of the Arabs Be Written? The Impact of European Orientalism in Jurji Zaidan Work." In *Jurji Zaidan: Contributions to Modern Arab Thought and Literature; Proceedings of a Symposium, The Library of Congress*, edited by George C. Zaidan and Thomas Philipp. Bethesda: The Zaidan Foundation, 2013.

El Shakry, Omnia. *The Great Social Laboratory: Subjects of Knowledge in Colonial and Postcolonial Egypt*. Stanford, CA: Stanford University Press, 2007.

El Shakry, Omnia. "'History without Documents': The Vexed Archives of Decolonization in the Middle East." *American Historical Review* 120, no. 3 (2015): 920–34.

Elhalaby, Esmat. *Arab Archives and Asian Histories*. World Humanities Report. CHCI, 2023.

Elhalaby, Esmat. "A Dying Postcolonialism." *Palestine Yearbook of International Law* 24 (2023): 155–64.

Elshakry, Marwa. *Reading Darwin in Arabic, 1860–1950*. Chicago: University of Chicago Press, 2013.

Erekat, Noura. *Justice for Some: Law and the Question of Palestine*. Stanford, CA: Stanford University Press, 2019.

Erturk, Nergis. *Grammatology and Literary Modernity in Turkey*. Oxford: Oxford University Press, 2011.

Eslava, Luis, Michael Fakhri, and Vasuki Nesiah, eds. *Bandung, Global History, and International Law: Critical Pasts and Pending Futures*. Cambridge: Cambridge University Press, 2017.

Essa, Azad. *Hostile Homelands: The New Alliance Between India and Israel*. London: Pluto Press, 2023.

Faiz A. *Faiz: The Living Word*. Tunis: Lotus Books, 1987.

Fakher Eldin, Munir. "British Framing of the Frontier in Palestine, 1918–1923: Revisiting Colonial Sources on Tribal Insurrection, Land Tenure, and the Arab Intelligentsia." *Jerusalem Quarterly* 60 (2014): 42–58.

Fakher Eldin, Munir. "Communities of Owners: Land Law, Governance, and Politics in Palestine, 1858–1948." PhD diss., New York University, 2008.

Fanon, Frantz. *Black Skin, White Masks*. Translated by Charles Lam Markmann. London: Pluto Press, 2008.

Fanon, Frantz. *The Wretched of the Earth*. Translated by Constance Farrington. New York: Grove Press, 1963.

Farquhar, Michael. *Circuits of Faith: Migration, Education, and the Wahhabi Mission*. Stanford, CA: Stanford University Press, 2016.

Fejzula, Merve. "Gendered Labour, Negritude and the Black Public Sphere." *Historical Research* 95, no. 269 (2022): 423–46.

Fenton, William. *Area Studies in American Universities*. Washington, DC: American Council on Education, 1947.

Figueira, Dorothy Matilda. *Translating the Orient: The Reception of Sakuntala in Nineteenth-Century Europe*. Albany: State University of New York Press, 1991.

First, Ruth. *The Barrel of a Gun: Political Power in Africa and the Coup d'etat in Africa*. London: Allen Lane, 1970.

Fischbach, Michael. *Black Power and Palestine: Transnational Countries of Color*. Stanford, CA: Stanford University Press, 2018.

Fleischmann, Ellen. *The Nation and Its New Women: The Palestinian Women's Movement, 1920-1948*. Berkeley: University of California Press, 2003.

Gautier, Laurence. "Crisis of the 'Nehruvian Consensus' or Pluralization of Indian Politics? Aligarh Muslim University and the Demand for Minority Status." *South Asia Multidisciplinary Academic Journal* 22 (2019). http://journals.openedition.org/samaj/6493.

George, Nathaniel. "Travelling Theorist: Mehdi Ben Barka and Morocco from Anti-colonial Nationalism to the Tricontinental." In *The Arab Lefts: Histories and Legacies, 1950s-1970s*, edited by Laure Guirguis. Edinburgh: Edinburgh University Press, 2020.

Gershoni, Israel, and James Janowski, *Redefining the Egyptian Nation, 1930-1945*. Cambridge: Cambridge University Press, 1995.

Ghazal, Amal. *Islamic Reform and Arab Nationalism: Expanding the Crescent from the Mediterranean to the Indian Ocean 1880s-1930s*. London: Routledge, 2010.

Ginat, Rami. *Syria and the Doctrine of Arab Neutralism: From Independence to Dependence*. Brighton: Sussex Academic Press, 2005.

Goebel, Michael. *Anti-Imperial Metropolis: Interwar Paris and the Seeds of Third World Nationalism*. Cambridge: Cambridge University Press, 2015.

Goldschmidt, Arthur. *Biographical Dictionary of Modern Egypt*. Boulder: Lynne Rienner, 2000.

Gordon, David C. *Lebanon: The Fragmented Nation*. London: Croom Helm, 1980.

Gordon, David C. *Self-Determination and History in the Third World*. Princeton, NJ: Princeton University Press, 1971.

Gordon, Leonard. "Indian Nationalist Ideas about Palestine and Israel." *Jewish Social Studies* 37, nos. 3/4 (1975): 221-34.

Gordon, Matthew. "The AUB History Department, 1970-1971: An Appreciation." In *One Hundred and Fifty*, edited by Nadia El Cheikh, Lina Choueiri, and Bilal Orfali. Beirut: American University of Beirut, 2016. 235-241.

Gouda, Ahmad Qasim. *Marid min al-Sharq*. Cairo: Matbaʿat Jaridat al-Misri, 1950.

Graves, Philip. *Palestine, the Land of Three Faiths*. London: Jonathan Cape, 1923.

Green, Nile, ed. "Arabic as a South Asian Language." *International Journal of Middle East Studies* 55, no. 1 (2023): 106-70.

Green, Nile. *Bombay Islam: The Religious Economy of the West Indian Ocean, 1840-1915*. Cambridge: Cambridge University Press, 2011.

Greenberg, Jonathan. "Generations of Memory: Remembering Partition in India/Pakistan and Israel/Palestine." *Comparative Studies of South Asia, Africa and the Middle East* 25, no. 1 (2005): 89-110.

Gulihot, Nicholas, ed. *The Invention of International Relations Theory: Realism, the Rockefeller Foundation, and the 1954 Conference on Theory*. New York: Columbia University Press, 2011.

Habibullah, A. B. M. "Presidential Address." *Proceedings of the Indian History Congress* 13 (1950): 137–41.

Haiduc-Dale, Noah. *Arab Christians in British Mandate Palestine: Communalism and Nationalism, 1917–1948*. Edinburgh: Edinburgh University Press, 2013.

Halim, Hala. "*Lotus*, the Afro-Asian Nexus, and Global South Comparatism." *Comparative Studies of South Asia, Africa and the Middle East* 32, no. 3 (2012): 563–83.

Halim, Hala. "'A Theatre—or, More Aptly, a Laboratory': India in the 1940s Egyptian Left as an Antecedent of Bandung Internationalism." *Comparative Literature Studies* 59, no. 1 (2022): 49–76.

Hall, Catherine. *Civilizing Subjects: Metropole and Colony in the English Imagination 1830–1867*. Chicago: University of Chicago Press, 2002.

Hall, Stuart. "Life and Times of the First New Left." *New Left Review* 61 (2010): 182.

Hall, Stuart. "Race, Articulation and Societies Structured in Dominance." In *Sociological Theories: Race and Colonialism*. Paris: UNESCO, 1980.

Hammad, Hanan. "From Orientalism to Khomeinism: A Century of Persian Studies in Egypt." *Alif: Journal of Comparative Poetics* 35 (May 2015): 32–51.

Haque, Azizul. "The Vice Chancellor's Speech." In *The Indian Annual Register: An Annual Digest of Public Affairs of India Recording the Nation's Activities Each Year in Matters Political, Economic, Industrial, Social Etc.* Vol. 1, *January–June 1940*, edited by Nirpendra Nath Mitra. Calcutta: The Annual Register Office, 1940.

Harrison, Olivia C. *Transcolonial Maghreb: Imagining Palestine in the Era of Decolonization*. Stanford, CA: Stanford University Press, 2015.

Hassan, Mona. *Longing for the Lost Caliphate: A Transregional History*. Princeton, NJ: Princeton University Press, 2017.

Heschel, Susannah, and Umar Ryad, eds. *The Muslim Reception of European Orientalism: Reversing the Gaze*. New York: Routledge, 2019.

Heptulla, Najma. *Indo-West Asian Relations: The Nehru Era*. Bombay: Allied Publishers, 1991.

Hippler, Thomas. *Governing from the Skies: A Global History of Aerial Bombing*. New York: Verso, 2017.

Ho, Engseng. *The Graves of Tarim: Genealogy and Mobility across the Indian Ocean*. Berkeley: University of California Press, 2006.

Hofmyer, Isabel. "Against the Global South." In *The Global South and Literature*, edited by Russell West-Pavlov. Cambridge: Cambridge University Press, 2018.

Hooper, Matthew S. *Slaves of One Master Globalization and Slavery in Arabia in the Age of Empire*. New Haven, CT: Yale University Press, 2015.

Hourani, Albert. *Islam in European Thought*. Cambridge: Cambridge University Press, 1991.

Ibn Duraid [Muhammad ibn al-Hasan]. *Al-maqsurah*. Translated by Muhammad Ibrahim Dar. Bombay: Indo-Arab Cultural Society, 1947.

Idris, Hawa'. *Ana wal-Sharq*. Cairo: Mu'assasat al-Mar'a wal-Dhakira, 2016.

Inden, Ronald. *Imagining India*. Oxford: Basil Blackwell, 1990.

Jabary Salamanca, Omar, Mezna Qato, Kareem Rabie, and Sobhi Samour. "Past Is Present: Settler Colonialism in Palestine." *Settler Colonial Studies* 2, no. 1 (2012): 1–8.

Jabbari, Alexander. *The Making of Persianate Modernity: Language and Literary History between Iran and India*. Cambridge: Cambridge University Press, 2023.

Jacquemond, Richard. *Conscience of the Nation: Writers, State, and Society in Modern Egypt*. Translated by David Tresilian. Cairo: American University in Cairo Press, 2008.

Jaferlot, Christophe. *Dr. Ambedkar and Untouchability: Fighting the Indian Caste System*. New York: Columbia University Press, 2005.

Jakes, Aaron. *Egypt's Occupation: Colonial Economism and the Crises of Capitalism*. Stanford, CA: Stanford University Press, 2020.

James, C. L. R. "The Destiny of the Negro: An Historical Overview." In *C.L.R. James on the "Negro Question"*, edited by Scott McLemee. Jackson: University of Mississippi, 1996.

Jansen, G. H. *Afro-Asia and Non-Alignment*. London: Faber and Faber, 1966.

Jansen, G. H. *Zionism, Israel and Asian Nationalism*. Beirut: Institute of Palestine Studies, 1971.

Jawish, Abd al-Aziz. *Al-Islam din al-Fitra*. Cairo: Matba'at al-Hidaya, 1905.

Jordan, June. *On Call: Political Essays*. Boston: South End Press, 1985.

Jubran, Sulayman. *Nazra jadida 'ala al-shi'r al-filastini fi 'ahd al-intidab*. Haifa: Dar al-Huda, 2006.

Jules-Rosette, Bennetta. "Conjugating Cultural Relations: *Présence Africaine*." In *The Surreptitious Speech: Présence Africaine and the Politics of Otherness 1947–1987*, edited by V. Y. Mudimbe. Chicago: University of Chicago Press, 1992.

Kalidasa. *Al-Shakuntala*. Translated by Wadi' al-Bustani. New Delhi: Indian Council of Cultural Relations, 1966.

Kalisman, Hilary Falb. "'A World of Tomorrow': Diaspora Intellectuals and Liberal Thought in the 1950s." *Journal of Palestine Studies* 50, no. 2 (2021): 92–107.

Kanafani, Ghassan. "Thawra 1936–39 fi Filastin: Khalifat wa tafasil wa tahlil." *Shu'un Filastiniyya* 6 (1972): 45–77.

Kanjwal, Hafsa. *Colonizing Kashmir: State-Building under Indian Occupation*. Stanford, CA: Stanford University Press, 2023.

Kantrovich, H. "The Jerusalem Law Classes." *Journal of the Society of Public Teachers of Law* (1937): 46–49.

Kaplan, Caren. *Aerial Aftermaths: Wartime from Above*. Durham, NC: Duke University Press, 2018.

Karl, Rebecca. *Staging the World: Chinese Nationalism at the Turn of the Twentieth Century*. Durham, NC: Duke University Press, 2002.

Kattan, Victor, and Amit Rajan. *The Breakup of India and Palestine: The Causes and Legacies of Partition*. Manchester: Manchester University Press, 2023.

Keddie, Nikki. *An Islamic Response to Imperialism: Political and Religious Writings of Sayyid Jamal ad-Din "al-Afghani"*. Berkeley: University of California Press, 1968.

Keddie, Nikki. "The Pan-Islamic Appeal: Afghani and Abdülhamid II." *Middle Eastern Studies* 3, no. 1 (1966): 46–67.

Keddie, Nikki, ed. *Scholars, Saints, and Sufis*. Berkeley: University of California Press, 1972.

Khalidi, Tarif. "Palestinian Historiography: 1900–1948." *Journal of Palestine Studies* 10, no. 3 (1981): 59–76.

Khalidi, Walid. "On Albert Hourani, the Arab Office, and the Anglo-American Committee of 1946." *Journal of Palestine Studies* 35, no. 1 (2005): 60–79.

Khalidi, Walid. "Palestine and Palestine Studies: One Century after World War I and the Balfour Declaration," *Journal of Palestine Studies* 44, no. 1 (2014): 137–47.

Khalil, Osamah. *America's Dream Palace: Middle East Expertise and the Rise of the National Security State*. Cambridge, MA: Harvard University Press, 2016.

Khalili, Laleh. *Sinews of War and Trade: Shipping and Capitalism in the Arabian Peninsula*. London: Verso, 2020.

Khan, Noor-Aiman. *Egyptian-Indian Nationalist Collaboration and the British Empire*. New York: Palgrave Macmillan, 2011.

Khan, Raphaëlle. "Disrupting the Empire and Forging IR: The Role of India's Early Think Tanks in the Decolonisation Process, 1936–1950s." *International History Review* 44, no. 4 (2022): 836–55.

Khan, Saad S. *Reasserting Internationalism: A Focus on the Organization of the Islamic Conference and Other Islamic Institutions.* Oxford: Oxford University Press, 2001.

Khuri-Makdisi, Ilham. *The Eastern Mediterranean and the Making of Global Radicalism, 1860–1914.* Berkeley: University of California Press, 2010.

Kidwai, Mushir Hosain. *Pan-Islamism.* London: Lusac and Company, 1908.

Kiernan, Victor. *The Lords of Human Kind.* Boston: Little, Brown, 1969.

Kinra, Rajeev. "This Noble Science: Indo-Persian Comparative Philology, c. 1000–1800 CE." In *South Asian Texts in History: Critical Engagements with Sheldon Pollock.* Edited by Yigal Bronner, Lawrence McCrea, and Whitney Cox. Ann Arbor: Association for Asian Studies, 2011.

Kirasirova, Masha. "'Sons of Muslims' in Moscow: Soviet Central Asian Mediators to the Foreign East, 1955–1962." *Ab Imperio* 4 (2011): 106–32.

Kotb, Sayed. *Social Justice in Islam.* Translated by John B. Hardie. Washington, DC: American Council of Learned Societies, 1953.

Kracuer, Sigfried. *History, the Last Things before the Last.* New York: Oxford University Press, 1969.

Kumaraswamy, P. R. *India's Israel Policy.* New York: Columbia University Press, 2010.

Kumaraswamy, P. R. "K. M. Panikkar and Indo-Israeli Relations." *International Studies* 32, no. 2 (1995): 327–37.

Lamming, George. *The Pleasures of Exile.* Ann Arbor: University of Michigan Press, 1992.

Landau, Jacob. *The Politics of Pan-Islam: Ideology and Organization.* Oxford: Oxford University Press, 1990.

Laroui, Abdallah. *The Crisis of the Arab Intellectual: Traditionalism or Historicism?* Translated by Diarmid Cammell. Berkeley: University of California Press, 1976.

Lee, Christopher J., ed. *Making a World after Empire: The Bandung Moment and Its Political Afterlives.* Athens: Ohio University Press, 2010.

Lelyveld, David. *Aligarh's First Generation: Muslim Solidarity in British India.* Princeton, NJ: Princeton University Press, 1978.

Lewis, Su Lin. "Conferencing: The Global South as Public and Counterpublic." *American Historical Review* 129, no. 2 (2024): 587–94.

Likhovski, Assaf. *Law and Identity in Mandate Palestine*. Chapel Hill: University of North Carolina Press, 2006.

Lockman, Zachary. *Field Notes: The Making of Middle East Studies in the United States*. Stanford, CA: Stanford University Press, 2016.

Low, Michael Christopher. "Empire and the Hajj: Pilgrims, Plagues, and Pan-Islam under British Surveillance, 1865-1908." *International Journal of Middle East Studies* 40, no. 2 (2008): 269-90.

Lubbock, John. *The Pleasures of Life*. Philadelphia: Henry Altemus, 1894.

Lubin, Alex. "Locating Palestine in Pre-1948 Black Internationalism." *Souls: A Critical Journal of Black Politics, Culture, and Society* 9, no. 2 (2007): 95-108.

Luthi, Lorenz. *Cold Wars: Asia, the Middle East, Europe*. Cambridge: Cambridge University Press, 2020.

Lynch, Hollis. *Edward Wilmot Blyden: Pan-Negro Patriot, 1832-1912*. Oxford: Oxford University Press, 1967.

MacDonald, Robert W. *The League of Arab States: A Study in the Dynamics of Regional Organization*. Princeton, NJ: Princeton University Press, 1965.

Makdisi, Ussama. *Age of Coexistence: The Ecumenical Frame and the Making of the Modern Arab World*. Oakland: University of California Press, 2019.

Makdisi, Ussama. *Artillery of Heaven: American Missionaries and the Failed Conversion of the Middle East*. Ithaca, NY: Cornell University Press, 2009.

Maksoud, Clovis. *The Arab Image*. New Delhi: Acharya Ramlochan Publishing House, 1963.

Maksoud, Clovis. "India and the Arabs." *Link*, February 1, 1959, 28-29.

Maksoud, Clovis. Interview with Jean Krasno. August 11, 1997. Yale-UN Oral History Project.

Maksoud, Clovis. *Ma'na al-Hiyad al-Ijabi*. Beirut: Dar al-'Ilm lil Malayin, 1960.

Maksoud, Clovis. *Min zawaya al-dhakira: Mahattat rihla fi qitar al-'uruba*. Beirut: al-Dar al-'Arabiyya lil-'Ulum Nashirun, 2014.

Maksoud, Clovis. *On Non-Alignment*. New Delhi: League of Arab States Mission, 1966.

Maksoud, Clovis. "Perspectives on Indian-Arab Relations." *Foreign Affairs Reports* 17, no. 4 (April 1966): 1-9.

Maksoud, Clovis. "Redefining Non-Alignment: The Global South in the New Global Equation." In *Altered States: A Reader in the New World Order*, edited by Phyllis Bennis and Michel Moushabeck. New York: Olive Branch Press, 1993.

Maksoud, Clovis. "Reflections on Indian-Arab Relations," *Indian Foreign Affairs* 1, no. 2 (1958): 57-59.

Maksoud, Clovis. "The Roots," *Seminar* 45 (May 1965): 13-16.

Maksoud, Clovis. "Socialism in the Arab World." *Oxford Clarion* Trinity Term (1954): 16-19.

Maksoud, Clovis, and V. V. Ramana Murti. *Gandhi and the Violence of Zionism.* New Delhi: League of Arab States Mission, [1966].

Mansergh, Nicolas. *The Commonwealth and the Nations.* London: Royal Institute of International Affairs, 1948.

Mantena, Rama. *The Origins of Modern Historiography in India: Antiquarianism and Philology, 1780-1880.* New York: Palgrave, 2012.

Masuzawa, Tomoko. *The Invention of World Religions: Or, How European Universalism Was Preserved in the Language of Pluralism.* Chicago: University of Chicago Press, 2005.

Mathew, Johan. *Margins of the Market Trafficking and Capitalism across the Arabian Sea.* Oakland: University of California Press, 2016.

Maurya, Abhai, ed. *India and World Literature.* New Delhi: Indian Council for Cultural Relations, 1990.

McLemee, Scott. ed., *C. L. R. James on the "Negro Question."* Jackson: University of Mississippi Press, 1996.

Mejcher-Atassi, Sonja. *An Impossible Friendship: Group Portrait, Jerusalem before and after 1948.* New York: Columbia University Press, 2024.

Mignolo, Walter. "Delinking: The Rhetoric of Modernity, the Logic of Coloniality and the Grammar of De-Coloniality." *Cultural Studies* 21, no. 2 (2007): 449-514.

Minault, Gail. *The Khilafat Movement: Religious Symbolism and Political Mobilization in India.* New York: Columbia University Press, 1982.

Mishra, Upendra N. "India's Policy towards the Palestinian Question." *International Affairs* 21, no. 2 (1982): 101-15.

Miskovic, Natasa, Harald Fischer-Tiné, and Nada Boskovska, eds. *The Non-Aligned Movement and the Cold War: Delhi-Bandung-Belgrade.* London: Routledge, 2014.

Mitra, Durba. "The Report, or, Whatever Happened to Third World Feminist Theory?" *Signs* 48, no. 3 (2023): 557-84.

Mitra, Durba. *Indian Sex Life: Sexuality and the Colonial Origins of Modern Social Thought.* Princeton, NJ: Princeton University Press, 2020.

Mohammad, Shan, ed. *Writings and Speeches of Sir Syed Ahmad Khan.* Bombay: Nachiketa Publications, 1972.

Molendijk, Arie L. *Friedrich Max Müller and the Sacred Books of the East.* Oxford: Oxford University Press, 2016.

Mondlane, Eduardo. *The Struggle for Mozambique.* London: Penguin, 1970.

Montet, Edward [Édouard]. "The Congress of Orientalists at Algiers." *Imperial and Asiatic Quarterly Review and Oriental and Colonial Record* 20, nos. 39–40 (July–October 1905): 84.

Mor, Jessica Sites. *South-South Solidarity and the Latin American Left*. Madison: University of Wisconsin Press, 2022.

Morsi, Eman. "Cuba in Arabic and the Limits of Third World Solidarity." *Global South* 13, no. 1 (2019): 145–77.

Motadel, David. "Islam and the European Empires." *Historical Journal* 55, no. 3 (2012): 831–56.

Motadel, David, ed. *Islam and the European Empires*. Oxford: Oxford University Press, 2014.

Moten, Fred. *Stolen Life*. Durham, NC: Duke University Press, 2018.

Mufti, Aamir. *Forget English! Orientalisms and World Literatures*. Cambridge, MA: Harvard University Press, 2016.

Mujtaba Ali, Syed. *In a Land Far from Home: A Bengali in Afghanistan*. Translated by Nazes Afroz. New Delhi: Speaking Tiger, 2015.

Mukharji, Projit Bihari. "The Bengali Pharaoh: Upper-Caste Aryanism, Pan-Egyptianism, and the Contested History of Biometric Nationalism in Twentieth-Century Bengal." *Comparative Studies in Society and History* 59, no. 2 (2017): 446–76.

Nadvi, Mas'udurrahman Khan. *Profaisar Sayyid Maqbul Ahmad, hayat va khidmat*. Patna: Khuda Baksh Oriental Library, 1999.

Nag, Kalidas. *New Asia*. Calcutta: Prajna Bharati, 1947.

Nakhleh, Khalil and Elia Zureik, eds. *The Sociology of the Palestinians*. London: Croom Helm, 1980.

Nassar, Maha. *Brothers Apart: Palestinian Citizens of Israel and the Arab World*. Stanford, CA: Stanford University Press, 2017.

Nassereddine, Monhem Naim. "The Progressive Socialist Party of Lebanon: A Study of Its Origins, Organization, and Leadership." MA thesis, Oklahoma State University, 1967.

Nehru, Jawaharlal. *Selected Works of Jawaharlal Nehru*. Edited by M. Chalapathi Rau, H. Y. Sharada Prasad, B. R. Nanda, and Sarvepalli Gopal. 15 vols. New Delhi: Orient Longman, 1982.

Nelson, Cynthia. *Doria Shafik: A Woman Apart*. Gainesville: University of Florida Press, 1996.

Nelson, Cynthia. "Satyagraha: Gandhi's Influence on an Egyptian Feminist." In *Investigating the South-South Dimension of Modernity and Islam*, edited by Helmut Buchholt and George Stauth. Hamburg: Lit Verlag, 2000.

Niu, Ke. "The SSRC and the Founding Movement of Area Studies in America, 1943–1953." *China International Strategy Review* 1 (2019): 283–309.

Noorani, Yaseen. "Translating World Literature into Arabic and Arabic into World Literature: Sulayman al-Bustani's al-Ilyadha and Ruhi al-Khalidi's Arabic Rendition of Victor Hugo." In *Migrating Texts: Circulating Translations around the Ottoman Mediterranean*, edited by Marilyn Booth. Edinburgh: Edinburgh University Press, 2019.

Norton, Anne. *On the Muslim Question*. Princeton, NJ: Princeton University Press, 2013.

Oishi, Takashi. "Muslim Merchant Capital and the Relief Movement for the Ottoman Empire in India, 1876–1924." *Journal of the Japanese Association for South Asian Studies* 11 (1999): 71–103.

Omar, Hussein. "Arabic Thought in the Liberal Cage." In *Islam after Liberalism*, edited by Faisal Devji and Zaheer Kazmi. Oxford: Oxford University Press, 2017.

O'Sullivan, Michael. "Pan-Islamic Bonds and Interest: Ottoman Bonds, Red Crescent Remittances and the Limits of Indian Muslim Capital, 1877–1924." *Indian Economic & Social History Review* 55, no. 2 (2018): 183–220.

Owen, Roger. "Albert Hourani and the Making of Modern Middle East Studies in the English-Speaking World: A Personal Memoir." In *Arabic Thought Beyond the Liberal Age: Towards an Intellectual History of the Nahda*, edited by Jens Hanssen and Max Weiss. Cambridge: Cambridge University Press, 2016.

Ozcan, Azmi. *Pan-Islamism: Indian Muslims, the Ottomans and Britain (1877–1924)*. Leiden: Brill, 1997.

Pabón, Maru. "In Search of the 'Voice of the People': Mahmoud Darwish's Third-Worldist Genres." *Middle Eastern Literatures* 25, no. 2 (2022): 168–86.

Padmore, George. *The Life and Struggles of Negro Toilers*. London: Red International of Labour of Unions Magazine for the International Trade Union Committee of Negro Workers, 1931.

Palestine: A Symposium. New Delhi: The League of Arab States Mission, 1969.

Palmer, Norman. "Note on the First Asian History Congress." *Asian Survey* 1, no. 12 (1962): 39–40.

Pandey, Gyanendra. *Remembering Partition: Violence, Nationalism and History in India*. Cambridge: Cambridge University Press, 2001.

Panikkar, K. M. *An Autobiography*. Madras: Oxford University Press, 1977.

Panikkar, K. M. "Presidential Address." *Proceedings of the Indian History Congress* 18 (1955): 20.

Pappé, Ilan, Tariq Dana, and Nadia Naser-Najjab. "Palestine Studies, Knowledge Production, and the Struggle for Decolonisation." *Middle East Critique* (May 12, 2024): 1–21.

Parmar, Inderjeet. *Foundations of the American Century: The Ford, Carnegie, and Rockefeller Foundations in the Rise of the American Power*. New York: Columbia University Press, 2012.

Parry, Benita. *Delusions and Discoveries: Studies on India in the British Imagination, 1880–1930*. Berkeley: University of California Press, 1972.

Patton, Mark. *Science, Politics and Business in the Work of Sir John Lubbock: A Man of Universal Mind*. Hampshire: Ashgate, 2007.

Penslar, Derek. "Zionism, Colonialism and Postcolonialism." *Journal of Israeli History* 20, no. 2-3 (2001): 84–98.

Perlmann, M. "Chapters of Arab Jewish Diplomacy, 1918–22." *Jewish Social Studies* 6, no. 2 (April 1944): 123–54.

Pollock, Sheldon. "Comparison Without Hegemony." In *The Benefit of Broad Horizons: Intellectual and Institutional Preconditions for a Global Social Science*, edited by Barbro Klein and Hans Joas. Leiden: Brill, 2010.

Pollock, Sheldon. "Conundrums of Comparison." *Know: A Journal on the Formation of Knowledge* 1, no. 2 (2017): 273–94.

Pollock, Sheldon. "Future Philology? The Fate of a Soft Science in a Hard World." *Critical Inquiry* 35, no. 4 (2009): 931–61.

Pollock, Sheldon. "Liberating Philology." *Verge: Studies in Global Asias* 1, no. 1 (2015): 16–21.

Pollock, Sheldon. "Towards a Political Philology: D. D. Kosambi and Sanskrit." *Economic and Political Weekly*, July 26, 2008, 52–59.

Popp, Richard Alan. "*Al-Funun*: The Making of an Arab-American Literary Journal." PhD diss., Georgetown University, 2000.

Prakash, Gyan. *Emergency Chronicles: Indira Gandhi and Democracy's Turning Point*. Princeton, NJ: Princeton University Press, 2019.

Prashad, Vijay. *The Darker Nations: A People's History of the Third World*. New York: The New Press, 2007.

Qato, Mezna. "Forms of Retrieval: Social Scale, Citation, and the Archive on the Palestinian Left." *International Journal of Middle East Studies* 51, no. 2 (2019): 312–15.

Qidwai, Muhammed Salim, ed. *Alim Sahib*. Aligarh: Idara uloom Islamiyya, Aligarh Muslim Universati, 1995.

Raghavan, Srinath. *1971: A Global History of the Creation of Bangladesh*. Cambridge, MA: Harvard University Press, 2013.

Raghavan, T. C. A., and Vivek Mishra. *Sapru House: A Story of Institution-Building in World Affairs*. New Delhi: Indian Council of World Affairs, 2021.

al-Rahman, Asʿad. *Al-taslil al-Isra'ili fi Asya: Al-Hind wa Isra'il*. Beirut: Markaz al-Dirassat, Munazimat al-Tahrir al-Falistini, 1967.

Rajan, M. S., ed. *International and Area Studies in India*. New Delhi: Lancers Books, 1997.

Rao, Anupuma. *The Caste Question: Dalits and the Politics of Modern India*. Berkeley: University of California Press, 2009.

Raz, Ronen. "The Transparent Mirror: Arab Intellectuals and Orientalism, 1798–1950." PhD diss., Princeton University, 1997.

Reddi, V. M. "Area Studies in India." *Proceedings of the Indian History Congress* 40 (1979): 925–31.

Reddy, Sheshalatha. "Romesh Chunder Dutt's Indian-English Epics and Epochs." *Journal of Commonwealth Literature* 47, no. 2 (2012): 245–63.

Reid, Donald M. *Lawyers and Politics in the Arab World, 1880–1960*. Minneapolis: Bibliotheca Islamica, 1981.

Retort. *Afflicted Powers: Capital and Spectacle in a New Age of War*. London: Verso, 2005.

Roberts, Nicholas E. *Islam under the Palestine Mandate: Colonialism and the Supreme Muslim Council*. London: I. B. Tauris, 2017.

Roberts, Nicholas E. "Making Jerusalem the Centre of the Muslim World: Pan-Islam and the World Islamic Congress of 1931." *Contemporary Levant* 4, no. 1 (2019): 52–63.

Robson, Laura. *Colonialism and Christianity in Mandate Palestine*. Austin: University of Texas Press, 2011.

Rodney, Walter. *A History of the Guyanese Working People, 1881–1905*. Baltimore, MD: Johns Hopkins University Press, 1981.

Rodney, Walter. *The Russian Revolution: A View from the Third World*. London: Verso, 2018.

Rodrigues, Shaunna. "The Place of Political Membership: Abul Kalam Azad's Critique of Borders and Nations." *Comparative Studies of South Asia, Africa and the Middle East* 41, no. 3 (2021): 378–88.

Rosenthal, Franz. "On Some Epistemological and Methodological Presuppositions of Al-Biruni." In *The Commemoration Volume of Biruni International Congress*. Tehran: High Council for Culture and Art, 1973.

Roy, M. N. *Asia and the World: A Manifesto Issued on the Occasion of the Asian Relations Conference*. N.p.: Radical Democratic Party, 1947.

Roy Choudhury, M .L., ed. *Egypt in 1945*. Calcutta: University of Calcutta, 1946.
Roy Choudhury, M. L. *The State and Religion in Mughal India*. Calcutta: Indian Publicity Society, 1951.
Roy Choudhury, Makhan Lal, trans. *Al-Kita: Tarjumah al-kitab al muqaddas 'and al-Hindus*. Calcutta: M/S Thacker Spink, 1951.
Roy Choudhury, Makhan Lal. *Misara Dayeri*. Calcutta: Pratulchandra Ghosh, 1948.
Roy Choudhury, Makhan Lal. *Romance of Afghanistan*. Calcutta: Indian Book Concern, 1961.
Rupp, Leila J. "Challenging Imperialism in International Women's Organizations, 1888–1945." *NWSA Journal* 8, no. 1 (Spring 1996): 8–27.
Russel, Ralph. "Urdu and I." *Annual of Urdu Studies* 11 (1996): 26.
Ryad, Umar. "Muslim Response to Missionary Activities in Egypt: With a Special Reference to the Al-Azhar High Corps of 'Ulama' (1925–1935)." In *New Faith in Ancient Lands: Western Missions in the Middle East in the Nineteenth and Early Twentieth Centuries*, edited by Heleen Murre-van den Berg. Leiden: Brill, 2007.
Šabaseviciute, Giedre. *Sayyid Qutb: An Intellectual Biography*. Syracuse: Syracuse University Press, 2021.
Sabbagh-Khoury, Areej. *Colonizing Palestine: The Zionist Left and the Making of the Palestinian Nakba*. Stanford, CA: Stanford University Press, 2023.
al-Said, Amina. *Mushahadat fi al-Hind*. Cairo: Dar al-Maʿarif, 1946.
Said, Edward. *Culture and Imperialism*. New York: Knopf, 1993.
Said, Edward. *The End of the Peace Process: Oslo and After*. New York: Pantheon, 2000.
Said, Edward. *Humanism and Democratic Criticism*. New York: Columbia University Press, 2004.
Said, Edward. "The Intellectual Origins of Imperialism and Zionism." *Gazelle Review* 2 (1977): 47–52.
Said, Edward (). *Orientalism*. New York: Vintage, 1978.
Said, Edward. *The Question of Palestine*. New York: Vintage, 1992.
Said, Edward. *Representations of the Intellectual*. New York: Vintage, 1996.
Said, Edward. *The World, the Text, and the Critic*. Cambridge, MA: Harvard University Press, 1983.
Sajdi, Dana. "The Pasha's New Clothes: The History Section (*tārīkh*)." In *The Library of Aḥmad Pasha al-Jazzār: Book Culture in Late Ottoman Palestine* edited by Said Aljoumani, Guy Burak, and Konrad Hirschler. Leiden: Brill 2025.
Salkey, Andrew. *Havana Journal*. Harmondsworth: Penguin, 1971.

Satia, Priya. *Spies in Arabia: The Great War and the Cultural Foundations of Britain's Covert Empire in the Middle East.* Oxford: Oxford University Press, 2009.

Sawhney, Simona. *The Modernity of Sanskrit.* Minneapolis: University of Minnesota Press, 2009.

Schaar, Stuart. *Eqbal Ahmad: Critical Outsider in a Turbulent Age.* New York: Columbia University Press, 2015.

Schwab, Raymond. *The Oriental Renaissance: Europe's Rediscovery of India and the East, 1680–1880.* New York: Columbia University Press, 1984.

Seikaly, Sherene. "The Matter of Time." *American Historical Review* 124, no. 5 (2019): 1681–1688.

Seth, Sanjay. *Subject Lessons: The Western Education of Colonial India.* Durham, NC: Duke University Press, 2007.

Shafik, Doria. *Rihlati hawla al-'alam.* Cairo: Matabi' Sharikat al-I'lanat al-Sharqiyya, 1955.

Shafir, Gershon. *Land, Labor and the Origins of the Israeli-Palestinian Conflict, 1882–1914.* Cambridge: Cambridge University Press, 1989.

Shahbaz, Haider. "Fahmida Riaz's *Āwāz*: Translation and Solidarities in the Global South." In *Translation and Decolonisation: Interdisciplinary Approaches*, edited by Claire Chambers and Ipek Demir. New York: Routledge, 2024.

Sharkey, Heather J. *American Evangelicals in Egypt: Missionary Encounters in an Age of Empire.* Princeton, NJ: Princeton University Press, 2008.

Sharma, D. N. *Afro-Asian Group in the U.N.* Allahabad: Chaitanya Publishing House, 1969.

Sheriff, Abdul. *Slaves, Spices and Ivory in Zanzibar: Integration of an East African Commercial Empire into the World Economy, 1770–1873.* London: James Currey, 1987.

Sherman, Taylor C. *Muslim Belonging in Secular India: Negotiating Citizenship in Postcolonial Hyderabad.* Cambridge: Cambridge University Press, 2015.

Shivji, Issa. "The Metamorphosis of the Revolutionary Intellectual." *Agrarian South: Journal of Political Economy* 7, no. 3 (2018): 399.

Siegel, Benjamin. "The Kibbutz and the Ashram: Sarvodaya Agriculture, Israeli Aid, and the Global Imaginaries of Indian Development," *American Historical Review* 125, no. 4 (2020): 1175–1204.

Sikainga, Ahmad Alawad. *Slaves into Workers Emancipation and Labor in Colonial Sudan.* Austin: University of Texas Press, 1996.

Silber, Irwin. ed. *Voices of National Liberation: The Revolutionary Ideology of the "Third World" as Expressed by Intellectuals and Artists at the Cultural Congress of Havana, January 1968.* New York: Central Book, 1970.

Singh, Gurbachan. "India at the Rabat Islamic Summit (1969)." *Indian Foreign Affairs Journal* 1, no. 2 (2006): 105-20.

Singh, Karan. *Heir Apparent: An Autobiography*. New Delhi: Oxford University Press, 1982.

Singh, S. P. "Indo-Arab Relations in the Light of the Palestine Problem (1930 to 1945)." *Proceedings of the Indian History Congress* 65 (2004): 1025-30.

Singham, A. W., and Tran Van Dinh. *From Bandung to Colombo: Conferences of the Non-aligned Countries, 1955-75*. New York: Third Press Review, 1976.

Sleiman, Hana. "History Writing and History Making in Twentieth Century Beirut." PhD diss., University of Cambridge, 2021.

Sleiman, Hana. "The Paper Trail of a Liberation Movement." *Arab Studies Journal* 24, no. 1 (2016): 42-67.

Sleiman, Hana, and Kaoukab Chebaro. "Narrating Palestine: The Palestinian Oral History Archive Project." *Journal of Palestine Studies* 47, no. 2 (2018): 63-76.

Smith, Wilfred Cantwell. *Islam in Modern History*. Princeton, NJ: Princeton University Press, 1957.

Sobhan, Rehman. *Untranquil Recollections: The Years of Fulfilment*. New Delhi: Sage, 2016.

Stanley, Brian. *The World Missionary Conference, Edinburgh 1910*. Grand Rapids, MI: Eerdmans, 2009.

Subrhamanyam, Sanjay, and Muzaffar Alam. *Indo-Persian Travels in the Age of Discoveries, 1400-1800*. Cambridge: Cambridge University Press, 2007.

Suhail, 'Abid. *'Abdul 'Alim*. New Delhi: Sahtiya Akademi, 2008.

Sukarno. *Islam Must Fight Colonialism: Inaugural Address by President Sukarno, African-Asian Islamic Conference, Bandung, 6th March 1965*. N.p.: Executive Command, Tenth Anniversary, First Asian-African Conference, n.d.

Sulaiman, Khalid. *Palestine and Modern Arab Poetry*. London: Zed, 1984.

Tagore, Rabindranath. *Journey to Persia and Iraq: 1932*. Kolkata: Visva-Bharati, 2003.

Tagore, Rabindranath. "Message to Iraq Air Force." In *The English Writings of Rabindranath Tagore: A Miscellany*. New Delhi: Sahitya Akademi, 1996.

Tagore, Rabindranath. "The Ramayana." In *Selected Writings on Literature and Language*, edited by Sukanta Chaudhuri. New Delhi: Oxford University Press, 2001.

Takriti, Abdel Razzaq. "The Kurd and the Wind: The Politics and Poetics of Palestinian-Kurdish Affiliation." In *The Political and Cultural History of Kurds*, vol.2, edited by Amir Harrak. New York: Peter Lang, 2021.

Takriti, Abdel Razzaq. *Monsoon Revolution: Republicans, Sultans, and Empires in Oman, 1965-1976*. Oxford: Oxford University Press, 2013.

Tavakoli-Targhi, Mohamed. *Refashioning Iran: Orientalism, Occidentalism and Historiography*. New York: Palgrave, 2001.

Al-Tha'alabi, Abd al-Aziz. *Mas'alat al-Manbudhin fi al-Hind*. Beirut: Dar al-Gharb al-Islami, 1984.

Thakur, Vineet, and Alexander E. Davis. "A Communal Affair over International Affairs: The Arrival of IR in Late Colonial India." *South Asia: Journal of South Asian Studies* 40, no. 4 (2017): 689-705.

Thapar, Raj. *All These Years: A Memoir*. New Delhi: Seminar Publications, 1991.

Thomson, Sorcha, and Pelle Valentin Olsen. *Palestine in the World International Solidarity with the Palestinian Liberation Movement*. London: I. B. Tauris, 2023.

Tibawi, A. L. *Anglo-Arab Relations and the Question of Palestine, 1914-1921*. London: Luzac and Company, 1978.

Tibawi, A. L. *British Interests in Palestine 1800-1901: A Study of Religious and Educational Enterprise*. Oxford: Oxford University Press, 1961.

Torrent, Mélanie. *Algerian Independence and the British Left: Solidarities and Resistance in a Decolonising World*. London: Bloomsbury, 2024.

Venkatram, T. K. *Racial Problems*. New Delhi: Indian Council of World Affairs, 1947.

Vinodh, N. S. *A Forgotten Ambassador in Cairo: The Life and Times of Syud Hossain*. New Delhi: Simon and Schuster India, 2020.

Viswanathan, Gauri. *Masks of Conquest: Literary Study and British Rule in India*. New York: Columbia University Press, 1989.

Von Eschen, Penny. *Race against Empire: Black Americans and Anticolonialism, 1937-1957*. Ithaca: Cornell University Press, 1997.

Von Eschen, Penny. *Satchmo Blows Up the World: Jazz Ambassadors Play the Cold War*. Cambridge, MA: Harvard University Press, 2004.

Wagoner, Phillip B. "Precolonial Intellectuals and the Production of Colonial Knowledge." *Comparative Studies in Society and History* 45, no. 4 (2003): 783-814.

Wallerstein, Immanuel. *The Modern-World System I: Capitalist Agriculture and the Origins of the European World-Economy in the Sixteenth Century*. New York: Academic Press, 1974.

Wasserstein, Bernard. "'Clipping the Claws of Colonisers': Arab Officials in the Government of Palestine, 1917-48." *Middle Eastern Studies* 13, no. 2 (May 1977): 171-94.

Wasti, Syed Tanvir. "Sir Syed Ahmad Khan and the Turks." *Middle Eastern Studies* 46, no. 4 (2010): 529–42.
Weizmann, Chaim. *Trial and Error: The Autobiography of Chaim Weizmann.* Vol. 2. Philadelphia: The Jewish Publication Society of America, 1949.
Willis, John. "Debating the Caliphate: Islam and Nation in the Work of Rashid Rida and Abul Kalam Azad." *International History Review* 32, no. 4 (2010): 711–32.
Willis, John M. "Making Yemen Indian: Rewriting the Boundaries of Imperial Arabia." *International Journal of Middle East Studies* 41, no. 1 (2009): 23–38.
Wright, Richard. *The Color Curtain: A Report on the Bandung Conference.* New York: World Publishing Company, 1956.
Yaghi, Abd al-Rahman. *Hayat al-adab al-Filastini al-hadith min awwal al-nahda hatta al-nakba.* Beirut: al-Maktab al-Tijari lil tibiʿa wal-nashr wal-tawziʿ, 1968.
Yaqub, Nadia. *Palestinian Cinema in the Days of Revolution.* Austin: University of Texas Press, 2018.
Yohannan, John. *Persian Poetry in England and America: A 200-Year History.* Delmar, NY: Caravan Books, 1977.
al-Youzbaki, Salma. "Tagore in Iraq: Poet and Educator." *Bulletin of the College of Arts, University of Baghdad* 20 (1977): 149–65.
Zaheer, Sajjad. *The Light: A History of the Movement for Progressive Literature in the Indo-Pakistan Subcontinent.* Translated by Amina Azfar. Oxford: Oxford University Press, 2006.
Zayn, ʿUmar, ed. *Taqi al-Din al-Sulh: Sirat Hayat wa Kifah.* Beirut: Shikat al-Matbuʿat lil-tawziʿ wal-nashr, 2007.
Zhou, Taomo. "Global Reporting from the Third World: The Afro-Asian Journalists' Association, 1963–1974." *Critical Asian Studies* 51, no. 2 (2019): 166–97.
Ziadeh, Nicola. *Hawla al-ʿalam fi sabʿa wa sittin ʿaman: Rihlat muthaqqaf shami fi asya wa ʾurubba wal-shamal al-Ifriqi, 1916–1992.* Beirut: al-Muʾassasa al-ʿArabiya lil-Dirasat wal-nashr, 2007.
Zureik, Elia. *The Palestinians in Israel: A Study in Internal Colonialism.* London: Routledge and Kegan Paul, 1979.

Index

Endnotes are indicated by "n" followed by the endnote number.

Abaza, Mona, 106-7
Abdel-Malek, Anouar, 18, 19-20, 22, 116, 140
Abdulhamid II, Sultan, 54, 57
al-Abhath (journal), 50
Abou Risha, Omar, 119-20
Abu Hakima, Ahmad Mustafa, 104-5
Abu-Laban, Baha, 166
Abu-Lughod, Ibrahim, 14-15, 161, 166
Achille, Louis, 20
al-Afghani, Jamal al-Din, 22, 54, 138
Afghanistan, 87, 124, 203n1
Africa: anthropology in Africanist studies, 141; conversion efforts in, 57, 59; First International Congress of Africanists, 136-37; Pan-Africanism, 18
Africanist Congress (1963), 25
Afro-Asianism, 107-11
Afro-Asian Solidarity Conference (1958), 24
Afro-Asian Women's Conference (1961), 5-6
Agwani, Mohmmed Shafi, 158-59, 161-63, 164

Ahmad, Eqbal, 12-13
Ahmad, Maqbul, 117, 148, 152, 154-57
Ahmed, Muhammad Habib, 71, 72-73, 130
"Akhbar al-Ahala" (al-Bustani), 49
Aleem, Abdul, 102, 146-48, 150-51, 156, 157-58
Algeria, 18, 21, 104, 108, 137-138
Ali, Asaf, 107
Ali, Syed Mujtaba, 203n1
Aligarh Muslim University (AMU): 1966 address by Clovis Maksoud, 120-21; Abdul Aleem and, 146-48; Azharite mission and, 72; conflicts over "Muslim" India, 148-53; Indo-Arab history, 154-60; Institute for Islamic Studies, establishment of, 142-46; visited by Mostafa Momin, 87
Alkalimat, Abdul, 179n67
All-Indian Islamic Studies Conference (1958), 150-51
All India Oriental Conference (1961), 150, 153
All India Student Federation, 158

[237]

All India Women's Conference (1945), 94-97
Ambedkar, Bhimrao Ramji, 69-70, 72, 73
American Council of Learned Societies (ACLS), 6, 134
American University (Washington), 123
American University of Beirut, 83, 111, 155, 163 *see also* Syrian Protestant College
American University of Cairo, 108
Amin, Samir, 109-10
Amrita Bazar Patrika (newspaper), 75
al-Anba' (magazine), 111
The Annihilation of Caste (Ambedkar), 69
Ansari (newspaper), 75
anthropology, 141
anti-imperial thought: author's approach, 3-8; characterized, 1-2, 22-27; decolonization today, 165-68; denigration of Afro-Asian thought, 161-64; distorted Palestinian histories, 12-16; Indo-Arab cultural solidarities, 8-12; international conferences, 16-22; nonalignment ideology and, 109-10, 121-22, 124-26. *See also* area knowledge; nonalignment; Pan-Asianism; Pan-Islamism; solidarity under imperialism
Al-'Arab (magazine), 117, 119
Arab Academy (Damascus), 83-84
Arabic: centrality to Christian missionary aims, 63, 65-66; Muslim reform movements and, 9-10; teaching of, in India, 143-44
The Arab Image (magazine), 121
Arab-Indian Friendship Association, 11

Arab League, 79, 83, 88, 107, 116-17
Arab nationalism, 111-12
'Arab-o-Hind ke Ta'luqqat (al-Nadwi), 156
Arab Women's Committee, 94-95
Arab Writers Congress (1956), 20-21
al-'Arayyed, Ibrahim, 50
area knowledge: Abdul Aleem and, 146-48; conflicts over "Muslim India," 148-53; Indo-Arab past and future, 154-60; Institute for Islamic Studies, establishment of, 142-46; Islamic study in India, 127-32; postwar knowledge efforts, 132-36; tensions and contradictions in, 24, 45, 136-42
Arida, Nasib, 33
Armaghan-i-Hijaz (The gift from Hijaz) (Iqbal), 99-100
Asad, Muhammad (Leopold Weiss), 9
Asad, Talal, 7
Ashby, Margery Corbett, 95
Asia and Western Dominance (Panikkar), 118
Asian-African Conference (1955), 11, 24, 25, 93, 101, 107, 125
Asian-African Islamic Conference (1965), 100
Asianism. *See* Pan-Asianism
Asian Relations Conference (1947): anxieties and controversies, 77-81; Arab participation in, 81-87; Nehru on isolationism, 119; Palestinian cause and, 88-93
Asian Relations Organization, 196n80
Atiyah, Edward, 83
Auerbach, Erich, 45-46
Azad, Abul Kalam, 72, 85, 105-6, 120, 143-44, 156
Al-Azhar mosque and seminary: Azharite mission to India, 66-73;

Azharite racial and religious prejudices, 73–75; lack of scholarship on, 190n45
al-'Azm, Khaled, 24
al-'Azzam, Abd Al-Rahman, 108
al-'Azzam, 'Abd al-Wahab, 79, 84–85, 86–87, 92–93, 98–100

al-Balagh (newspaper), 70, 73
Balfour Declaration (1917), 23, 37, 41, 42–43, 97
Balkan Wars (1912–13), 54
Bandung, 11, 24, 25, 93, 100, 101, 107, 125
Banerjee, P. N., 132
Bangladesh, 115, 132
al-Banna, Hassan, 78, 82
Barka, Mehdi Ben, 108
Al-Bayan fi i'jaz al-Qur'an (al-Khattabi), 148
Bayn al-Qasrayn (Palace Walk) (Mahfouz), 19
Bazzi, Ali, 113
al-Bedawi, Muhammed Ahmed, 71
Benares Hindu University (BHU), 152
Bennabi, Malek, 108
Bentwich, Norman, 43
Bergman, Hugo, 88–91
Berman, Edward H., 135
Bhandarkar Oriental Research Institute, 150
Bharat Varsha (magazine), 128
Bhatnagar, S. S., 144
Bint al-Nil (magazine), 97
Birla, G. D., 48
Al-Biruni, 49, 155, 159–60
Black Skin, White Masks (Fanon), 75
Blyden, Edward Wilmot, 5, 170n8, 190n38
Bombay University, 69, 154
Boutros-Ghali, Boutros, 122–23

Brandt, C.D.J., 158
Brown, W. Norman, 124
al-Bustani, Butrus, 23, 29, 190n34
al-Bustani, Sulayman, 29, 32, 47
al-Bustani, Wadi': as anti-colonial poet, 23, 37–44; Arabic translations and understandings of India, 31–35, 44–45, 47–50; later life, 50–52; writing to John Lubbock, 28–29; on writing under colonial rule, 46

Cabral, Amílcar, 2, 21
Cairo Caliphate Congress, 67
Calcutta University, 128, 131–32
Canaan, Tawfiq, 127–28
Carnegie family, 135
Center for the Study of the Global South, 123
Central Intelligence Agency (CIA), 133, 136, 157
Chagla, M. C., 151
Chamoun, Camille, 51
Chand, Tara, 156
Chandra, Satish, 24–25
Chatterjee, Partha, 128
Chattopadhyay, Kamaladevi, 10–11, 96–97
China, 2, 81, 114, 115
Chirol, Valentine, 56, 159
Choudhury, M. L. Roy, 127–30, 203n1
Choudhury, Rajendra Lal Roy, 129–30
Christianity: racist division of labor, 63–66; response to Islam's missionizing aims, 58–63
classical knowledge, 30, 133, 144
Cohn, Bernard, 133
Cold War: and Palestine in extant scholarship, 14; postwar knowledge effort, 133–34
Cole, G.D.H., 111

colonialism: al-Bustani as anti-colonial poet, 37–44; colonial conditions of canonicity, 30–31; history after, 119–24; settler colonialism, 165–66; varied responses to, 57–58. *See also* decolonization; imperialism
Comber, E. Philip, 65
communism, 18, 20, 108, 109–10, 134, 198n9
Communist Party of India, 147, 158
conferences, significance of, 16–22, 23–24. See also *specific conferences*
Congress for Cultural Freedom, 18, 136
Congress of Berlin (1878), 23
Congress of Black Writers and Artists (1956), 18–20
Congress of Cultural Freedom (CCF), 135–36
Congress of Orientalists (1960), 140
Congress of the Communist Party of the Soviet Union (1956), 140
Crisis of the Arab Intellectual (Laroui), 22
"cult of the Rubaiyat," 31
Cultural Congress of Havana (1968), 21
cultural decline, in colonial discourse, 30

Dajani, Burhan, 83
Damascus, 9, 20, 39, 61, 83,
Darwin, Charles, 28
Das Gupta, Ashin, 169n1
Davidson, Basil, 140
Dawn (newspaper), 85, 86
Dayal, Har, 67
Deccan Times, 87
"decolonial," 5
decolonization: anti-colonial thought, characterized, 1–2, 22–27; author's approach, 3–8; decolonization today, 165–68; denigration of Afro-Asian thought and, 24–26, 161–64; distorted Palestinian histories, 12–16; history after colonialism, 119–24; Indo-Arab cultural solidarities, 8–12; international conferences, 16–22; of the mind, 2, 5–6; Ruth First on, 21–22; Walter Mignolo on "delinking," 171n11; nonalignment ideology and, 109–10, 121–22, 124–26. *See also* area knowledge; nonalignment; Pan-Asianism; Pan-Islamism; solidarity under imperialism
Delhi University, 84
"delinking," 171n11
Der Islam (journal), 61
Dimishky, Hanna, 61–62
Dimishky, Paul, 60–66
Diop, Alioune, 18, 19–20
Direct Action Day (1946), 129–30
Dixon, Dean, 18
Du Bois, W.E.B., 18, 169n1
"Duranta Asha" (Wild hopes) (Tagore), 35
Dutt, Romesh, 47–48, 49

Eastern Women's Conference (1938), 95
Egypt: at 1947 Delhi conference, 88–89; at 1956 intellectual conferences, 18–21; Choudhury's engagement with, 127–29; feminist commitment to Palestine, 97–98; missionary training, Cairo, 59–60; nonalignment ideology and, 113, 116. *See also* Al-Azhar mosque and seminary
Egyptian Feminists Union, 77–79, 94–95

Faiz, Faiz Ahmed, 12, 146
al-Falistiniyyat (al-Bustani), 39
Fanon, Frantz, 16, 75, 125
Faris, Nabih Amin, 163
Faris, Shibli, 48
Farouk I, King of Egypt, 68-69
Fawzi, Hussein, 106-7
feminism: at 1947 Delhi conference, 77-79, 89-90; early 20th-century activism, 80; al-Khalidi on anti-imperial thought, 27; Palestinian cause and, 93-98; Yvonne Quilès on women's liberation, 5
Ferdowsi, 79
First, Ruth, 21
First International Congress of Africanists (1962), 136-37, 140
Ford Foundation, 133, 135, 140, 157
Forman Christian College, 99
France, 18-20, 39, 102
Fuad I, King of Egypt, 68
al-Funun (magazine), 33-34
Fyzee, Asaf Ali Asghar, 9, 143-45

Gairdner, W.H.T., 61
Gandhi, Mohandas, 48, 72, 97-98, 122
The Gardener (Tagore), 33
Gaza, 12, 167
General Conference on Missions to Muslims (1911), 58
Genet, Jean, 12
geography: Boutros-Ghali on the Indian Ocean, 122-23; the "global," 16, 167; "global South" and, 123-24; Indo-Arab history and, 155-56; "Muslim empire" ideology, 56; under nonalignment, 125-26; "White geographers," 51
George Washington University, 113
Germany, 67, 146
Ghalib, Mirza, 79

Gibb, Hamilton, 154
Gitanjali (Tagore), 120
global history, problems with, 13-16
"global South," nonalignment and, 123-24
Gordon, David, 163-64
Gouda, Ahmed Qasim, 118-19
Gramsci, Antonio, 45
Graves, Mortimer, 134
Great Britain: al-Bustani's critique of, 37-44; export of world literature, 30-31; "Muslim empire" ideology, 56; as observers of Pan-Islamism, 55; Tagore on occupation of Iraq, 35-37. *See also* imperialism
Grunebaum, Gustave Von, 22

Habibi, Emile, 45
Habibullah, A.B.M., 132, 204n13
Haddad, Azra, 51
Hajj, 59, 152
Hall, Stuart, 63, 112
al-Hamdani, H. F., 8, 10
Hamizrah Hehadash (The New East) (journal), 25
Haqqi, Badiʻ, 120
Haque, Azizul, 131
Hayter Report (University Grants Committee), 135
Hebrew University of Jerusalem, 25, 83, 88-89, 91
Hekmat, Ali Ashghar, 99
Herskovits, Melville, 140, 141
Heyd, Uriel, 25
Hilal, Jamil, 166
al-Hilal (journal), 34, 43
Hilmi, Ahmad, 139, 205n29
Hinduism: Arab understandings of, 34, 48-49; Eastern Women's Conference and, 96; efforts at Dalit conversion to Islam, 69-76

hinduwi ("Indian who is not a Muslim"), 34, 38, 44, 49
history: after colonialism, 119–24; challenges of Eurocentrism, 124–26; colonial condescension, 24–26, 161–64; distorted Palestinian histories, 12–16; Indo-Arab area studies, 127–32, 149–50, 154–60; of Indo-Arab relations, 104–5; methodological nationalism, 81; partition, historical treatment of, 170n6. *See also* area knowledge; knowledge; social sciences
Hitti, Philip, 9–10
Hourani, Albert, 47, 159–60, 209n95
Huque, Azizul, 131, 142
Hurewitz, J. C., 162–63, 164
Husain, Syed, 106
Husain, Zakir, 72, 143, 144–46, 148, 151
al-Husseini, Amin, 40, 41, 78, 118
Hyderabad, 53, 68, 72, 79, 130, 131, 149, 150
Hyderabad (Sind), 94–97

The Ideology of Philanthropy (Berman), 135
Idris, Hawa', 77–78, 79, 84–86, 88–90, 92
Iliad (Homer), 29, 32, 47
imperialism: beginnings of imperial knowledge, 133; Britain's "Muslim empire" ideology, 56; al-Bustani as anti-colonial poet, 37–44; colonial conditions of canonicity, 30–31; critical philology and, 44–50; impact on non-European interaction, 2–3; myth of imperial knowledge, 22; racial science, 59–61; relationship between knowledge and, 19; responses to colonialism, 57–58; Tagore on Iraq Mandate, 35–37. *See also* solidarity under imperialism
"Imperialism and Settler Colonialism in West Asia" (Hilal), 166
India: Arabic education in, criticisms of, 9; Arabic representations of, 28–35, 44–45, 47–50; Arab women's movement and, 93–98; Azharite delegation to, 66–73; Azharite denigration of, 73–76; al-'Azzam's engagement with, 79, 98–99; centrality to Pan-Islamism, 54–55; Christian response to Islamism in, 58–66; comparisons to Palestine, 88–92; conflicts over "Muslim India," 148–53; Direct Action Day (1946), 129–30; Indo-Arab relations after colonialism, 119–24; Indo-Arab relations under nonalignment, 104–7; Islamic studies in, 127–32, 154–60; Clovis Maksoud's engagement with, 113–18; representing anti-colonialism, 108; support for Bangladeshi independence, 115; Tagore on Iraq Mandate, 35–37. *See also* area knowledge; nonalignment; Pan-Asianism; Pan-Islamism; solidarity under imperialism
Indian Council for Cultural Relations (ICCR), 49–50, 104–105, 119–120, 121, 140, 156, 187n85, 198n2, 203n1
Indian Council of World Affairs (ICWA), 83, 84, 85, 157, 208n88
Indian History Congress (1955), 126
Indian National Congress, 78, 81, 96, 158
Indian Ocean, 2, 38, 56, 122–23, 148, 155
Indian revolt (1857), 55
Indian School of International Studies, 110, 113, 157, 158

Indian Socialist Party, 113
India Office, 31, 82
India Quarterly (journal), 83
Indo-Arab Cultural Society of Bombay, 8-10
Indo-Arab Relations (Ahmad), 156
Indo-Arab Society, 10-11
Indonesia, 87, 94, 100-102
Influence of Islam on Indian Culture (Chand), 156
Institute for Islamic Studies (AMU): Abdul Aleem and, 146-48; conflicts over "Islamic" nature of, 148-53; establishment of, 142-46
Institute for Oriental Studies, 79
International Congress of Orientalists (1964), 136-37
internationalism, 2, 97, 114, 122, 148, 167
International Monetary Fund, 162
International Women's Congress (1939), 95
Iqbal, Muhammad, 70-71, 72, 79, 99-100
Iraq: 1947 Asian Relations Conference and, 87; British imperialism in, 35-37; nonalignment in, 113
Islamic Culture (journal), 53, 130
Ismail Yusuf College, 154
isolationism, Asian, 119
Israel: 1947 Asian Relations Conference and, 88-93; denigration of Afro-Asian thought, 25-26, 161-63; Palestinian history and, 13-14, 15; as settler colonial nation, 165-66, 167-68. *See also* Palestine
Israeli archives, 82
Israeli Oriental Society, 25

al-Jamali, Muhammad Fadl, 107, 198n9

James, C.L.R., 21, 22, 178n57
James, Edwin, 62, 64
Jamia Millia Islamia, 72, 143, 146
al-Jami'a al-'Arabiyya (newspaper), 40
Jansen, G. H., 14, 80, 82, 90
Jauhar, Muhammad Ali, 40, 41
Jawaharlal Nehru University (JNU), 157, 160
Jawish, Abd al-Aziz, 138-39
Jewish Agency, 43, 117
al-Jibali, Ibrahim, 71
Jinnah, Muhammad Ali, 78, 82, 85, 143
Jones, William, 73-74
Jonnart, Charles, 138
Jordan, June, 16
Jubran, Suleiman, 41
Jumblatt, Kamal, 108, 111, 113
Jung, Ali Yavar, 151-52

Kabir, Humayun, 120, 137, 139-40, 144-145
Kalidiasi (poet and playwright), 30, 32
Kalila wa Dimna (unknown), 50
Kamal, Mustafa, 79
Kanafani, Ghassan, 41-42
Kapeliuk, Amnon, 26
Kashmir, 115, 143, 153
Kesteman, Francoise, 12
Khadduri, Majid, 87
al-Khalidi, 'Anbara Salam, 27
al-Khalidi, Walid, 112
Khan, Sayyid Ahmad, 54-55, 142, 152
al-Khattabi, *Al-Bayan fi i'jaz al-Qur'an*, 148
Khayyam, Omar, 30, 31-32, 51
Khuri, Raif, 20
Kidwai, Mushir Hosain, 54
Kiernan, Victor, 2-3
King Saud University, 100
Kissinger, Henry, 155

knowledge: anti-colonial sociology of Palestine, 26–27; critical philology, 44–50; denigration and condescension, 24–26, 161–64; for liberation vs. domination, 7; methodological nationalism, 81; myth of imperial knowledge, 22; racial science, 59–61; relationship between imperialism and, 19; Sanskritic knowledge, 30, 44–45, 47, 74, 132, 150; wartime knowledge efforts, 133–35. *See also* anti-imperial thought; area knowledge; history
Korean War (1950–53), 107
Kosambi, D. D., 45
Kracuer, Sigfried, 6
Kumaraswamy, P. R., 93

al-Lafi, Tariq, 8–9
L'Afro-Asiatisme (Bennabi), 108
Lamming, George, 24
Landau, Jacob, 103
language: Arabic translations, 28–35, 44–45, 47–50; centrality to missionary aims, 63, 65–66, 190n39; critical philology, 44–50; export of world literature and, 30; Muslim reform movements and, 9–10; teaching of Arabic in India, 143–44
Laroui, Abdallah, 22
Laws of Manu, 73–74
League of Nations, 43, 53
Lebanon, 39, 51–52, 83, 94, 104, 111, 113, 124
Les Cahiers de l'Est (journal), 111
literature: Arabic understandings of India, 28–35, 44–45, 47–50; al-Bustani as anti-colonial poet, 23, 37–44; colonial conditions of canonicity, 30–31; critical philology, 44–50. *See also* poetry; *and specific texts*
Lohia, Ram Manohar, 113
Lubbock, John, 28–30

madrasas (educational institutions), 9, 154
Mahabharata (Vyasa), 44, 46, 47–48, 50
Mahfouz, Naguib, 19
Majjalat al-Azhar (journal), 73
Maksoud, Clovis, 111–18, 120–23, 125, 154
Manchester Guardian (newspaper), 72
Manyar, Muhammad Zakariyya, 70
al-Maraghi, Mustafa, 67, 68–69, 76
March of India (magazine), 118
Mardem Bey, Khalil, 20, 83–84
Margoliouth, David, 31
Marx, Karl, 167
Marxism, 146, 147
al-Mashriq (journal), 43
Massachusetts Institute of Technology (MIT), 157
Al-Masudi, 155–56
Matzpen (anti-Zionist organization), 165
Ma'na al-Hiyad al-Ijabi (Maksoud), 113, 114
Ma'na al-Nakba (The Meaning of Disaster) (Zurayk), 163
Mehta, Hansa, 94
al-Melaiji, Hamid, 70
method, 5, 6, 13, 14, 25–26, 126, 160, 166–167
methodological nationalism, 81
Mignolo, Walter, 171n11
Mimesis (Auerbach), 45–46
Minault, Gail, 54
modernization theory, 134
Mokerjee, Radha Kumur, 130

Momin, Mustafa, 79, 83, 86, 87, 88
Mondlane, Edouardo, 4
Montet, Édouard, 138
Morocco, 87, 102, 197n94,
Moslem World (journal), 61, 65
Mozambique, 4
Mughal history, 130, 149–50
Muhammadan Anglo-Oriental College, 142 *see also* Aligarh Muslim University
Muller, Max, 31, 48
Mushahadat fi al-Hind (Said), 95
Muslim Brotherhood, 78, 82, 86
Muslim-Christian Association, 38
Muslim League, 78, 80, 83, 85, 90, 129

Nabrawi, Saiza, 95
Nadwatul Ulema (seminary), 72, 74
al-Nadwi, Sulieman, 156
Nag, Kalidas, 91–92
Nahda (Arab renaissance), 19, 22, 29, 33, 34, 38, 74, 77,
Naimy, Mikhail, 20, 33–34
al-Najjar, Abd al-Wahab, 71
al-Najjar, Muhammad Salah al-Din, 71, 72
Nakhleh, Khalil, 26–27
Nanda, B. N., 148–49
Nasser, Gamal Abdel, 20, 98, 108
National Association for the Advancement of Colored People (NAACP), 18
National Defense Education Act, 135
nationalism: anti-colonial, 41; Arab, 111–12; methodological, 81; nationalist internationalism, 148; nonalignment and, 121–22; pedagogical, 90
Nehru, Jawaharlal: 1947 Delhi conference and, 83, 86, 89–90; 1954 Indo-Arab Society inauguration, 10; on Asian isolationism, 119; criticisms of, 78, 81; feminist initiatives and, 98; on Indo-Arab cooperation, 129
Nehru, Rajen, 11
Nehru, Rameshwari, 97
Nehru, R. K., 11, 145
neutralism. *See* nonalignment
New Arab (magazine), 117
Nkrumah, Kwame, 136–37, 141
nonalignment: Arabs, Afro-Asia and, 107–11; Indo-Arab relations after colonialism, 119–24; Indo-Arab relations under, 104–7; Clovis Maksoud and, 111–15; print media, 116–19; production of new histories, 124–26

Olsavaanger, Immanual, 91
On Call (Jordan), 16
On Peace and Happiness (Lubbock), 29
Organization of the Islamic Conference (OIC), 102–3
Orientalism, 31, 39, 48–49, 50, 60, 106, 133, 138–40
Orientalist Congress (1964), 25–26, 136–37, 140
Osmania University, 149
Ottoman Empire, 43–44, 54–55, 57, 66–68
Oxford University, 31, 113

Pakistan: Bangladeshi independence and, 115; Indian and Egyptian freedom and, 78; in Islamic cultural scholarship, 99; Islamic solidarity with, 82, 145; Panikkar's meeting with Amin al-Husseini, 118; world perceptions of, post-partition, 105–6
Palestine: 1969 OIC declaration on, 102–3; Arab feminist commitment

Palestine (continued)
   to, 93–98; as Asian, 88–93;
   al-Bustani's critique of British
   Mandate, 37–44; al-Bustani's later
   life in, 50–52; calls for anti-colonial
   sociology of, 26–27; Christian
   missionary education in, 62;
   decolonization today and, 165–68;
   denigration of Afro-Asian thought
   and, 161–64; distorted histories of,
   12–16; global imaginary of liberation and, 2, 103; Indo-Arab
   relations, 127–28; nonalignment
   and, 110, 118. *See also* area
   knowledge; nonalignment;
   Pan-Asianism; Pan-Islamism;
   solidarity under imperialism
Palestine Liberation Organization
   (PLO), 12, 165
Palmer, Norman, 124–25
Pan-Africanism, 18, 24, 80; Nkrumah
   on how scholars can serve, 137
Pan-Asianism: 1947 Delhi conference
   and, 81–87; anxieties and controversies, 77–81; Arab feminist
   commitment to Palestine, 93–98;
   Nehru on Asian isolationism, 119;
   Palestine as Asian, 88–93; postwar
   decolonization and, 16; toward
   Islamic political geography, 98–103
Panikkar, K. M., 106, 110, 118, 119, 122,
   125–26, 151, 153,
Pan-Islamism: 1947 Delhi conference
   and, 81–87; Azharite mission to
   India, 66–73; Azharite racial and
   religious prejudices, 73–76; British
   preoccupations with, 40, 55–56;
   chimeric nature of, 53; Christian
   missionary response to, 58–63;
   Christian racial-religious order,
   63–66; in distorted representations

of Palestine, 13–14; India's function
   in, 54–55; Ottoman response to
   imperial Christianity, 57
partition: Abul Kalam Azad on, 105–6;
   al-Bustani's vision for unity, 50–52;
   historical treatment of, 170n6;
   impact on Aligarh Muslim University, 143; India on partition of
   Palestine, 93; Indo-Arab cultural
   solidarities, post-partition, 8–12
philanthropy, 135, 157
philology, 30, 44–50, 148, 157,
"The Pitfalls of Palestiniology"
   (Abu-Lughod), 14–15
The Pleasures of Exile (Lamming), 24
The Pleasures of Life (Lubbock),
   29–30, 31
poetry: al-'Azzam reflecting on Iqbal,
   99–100; al-Bustani as anti-colonial
   poet, 23, 37–44; work of Abou
   Risha, 120. *See also* al-Bustani,
   Wadi'; *and specific texts*
The Politics of Pan-Islam (Landau), 103
Pollock, Sheldon, 45
positive neutralism. *See* nonalignment
Potekhin, I. I., 140, 141
Presence Africaine (magazine), 18, 20
print media, nonalignment and, 116–19
The Problem of the Rupee (Ambedkar),
   69
Progressive Socialist Party (PSP)
   (Lebanon), 111, 113
Progressive Writers Association
   (PWA), 146–47

Quatrains of War (al-Bustani), 37
The Question of Palestine (Said), 110
Quilès, Yvonne, 5
Qur'an, 30
Qureshi, I. H., 84
Qutb, Sayyid, 6, 171n11

Radhakrishnan Commission, 143
al-Rahman, Asʿad ʿAbd, 14
Ramayana, 50
religion: Azharite mission to India, 66–73; Azharite religious prejudices, 73–75; Christian racial-religious order, 63–66; Christian response to Islamism in India, 58–66; in colonial discourse, 30; secularism, 120, 148–49, 151. *See also* Hinduism; Pan-Islamism
Renan, Ernest, 22
Revue du Monde Musulman (journal), 61
revolution: the 1919 (Egyptian), 19; the 1952 (Egyptian), 118; the African, 7 141; the Algerian, 18; the moon's, 28; the Russian, 62; the Third World's, 14, 110
Riddles in Hinduism (Ambedkar), 69
al-Risala (magazine), 44, 79, 85
al-Risala al-Jadida (magazine), 18–19, 50
Riyadh University, 100
Rockefeller Foundation, 6, 135, 157
Rodney, Walter, 23, 126
Rostow, Walt, 134
Roy, M. N., 81
Rubaiyat of Omar Khayyam (Khayyam), 30, 31, 51
Russo-Turkish War (1877), 54

Safi, Joseph Antoine, 62
Said, Edward, 1, 12, 15, 35, 45, 110
al-Said, Amina, 94–96
al-Said, Karima, 79, 89–90, 92, 93
Sakakini, Khalil, 23
Sakakini, Wadad, 20
Sanskritic knowledge, 30, 44–45, 47, 74, 132, 150
Saudi Arabia, 87, 100, 157,

Sawt al-Sharq (magazine), 118–19
Sayegh, Fayez, 109, 165
Sayigh, Rosemary, 12
School of Oriental Studies (London), 79
al-Sebaʿi, Yusif, 18–20
secularism, 120, 148–49, 151
Self-Determination and History in the Third World (Gordon), 163, 164
Seminar on India and the Arab World (1965), 104–5, 119
separation, Asian, 119
Sergius, Qommus, 40
The Settler-Colonial Phenomenon in Africa and the Middle East (Steven), 166
Settler Regimes in Africa and the Arab World (Abu-Lughod and Abu-Laban), 166
Shaarawi, Huda, 77–78, 80, 94–95
Shafik, Doria, 97–98
Shahnameh (Ferdowsi), 79
Shakuntala (Kalidiasi), 30, 32, 50
Sherwani, Riaz-ur-Rehman, 147
Shinar, Pessah, 25–26
Shivji, Issa, 142
Sinha, Sachchidananda, 130
Sixth Palestine Arab Congress (1923), 42
al-Siyasa al-Dawliya (magazine), 122
Smith, George Adam, 62
Smith, Wilfred Cantwell, 53
Sobhan, Rehman, 115
socialism, 96–97, 102, 111–13, 115, 120, 165
"Socialism in the Arab World" (Maksoud), 112
Social Justice in Islam (Qutb), 6
Social Science Research Council (SSRC), 134
social sciences: anthropology in Africanist studies, 141; calls for

social sciences (*continued*)
   anti-colonial sociology, 26–27;
   colonial condescension and
   denigration, 24–26, 161–64;
   methodological nationalism, 81;
   wartime knowledge effort, 133–35.
   See also area knowledge; history;
   knowledge
Society for the Propagation of the
   Gospel (SPG), 60, 64, 65
The Sociology of Palestinians (Nakhleh
   and Zureik), 26
solidarity under imperialism: Arabic
   representations of India, 28–35,
   47–50; al-Bustani as anti-colonial
   poet, 37–44; liberation philology,
   44–50; partition and, 50–52; Tagore
   on British presence in Iraq, 35–37
Soviet Union (USSR), 102, 109, 110,
   134–35, 140
spatiality, 122–23
Spinoza, Baruch, 45
Sputnik, 134
The Stages of Economic Growth
   (Rostow), 134
The State and Religion in Mughal India
   (Choudhury), 130
The Struggle for Mozambique
   (Mondlane), 4
Sudan, 20, 104, 112
Sukarno, 100–103
Sulaiman, Khalid, 39
al-Sulh, Taqi al-Din, 79, 85, 88, 90,
   193n10
Supreme Muslim Council, 38
Suroor, Ale Ahmad, 146
Swarajya (magazine), 117
Syria: 1956 Arab Writers Congress,
   20–21; nonalignment in, 113; revolt
   against French Mandate, 39

Syrian Protestant College, 29, 62, 163
   see also American University of
   Beirut

Tagore, Rabindranath, 33–37, 120, 131
Taj ul Masjid madrasa, 154
Tarkih al-Hind (al-Biruni), 160
Al-Tasallul al-Isra 'ili fi Asiya
   (al-Rahman), 14
Taylor, Charles, 112
al-Thaqafa (magazine), 79
Thaqafat al-Hind (journal), 105
al-Tha'alabi, Abd al-Aziz, 71
Third Force Association, 113
"Third World," term usage, 123
Tibawi, A. L., 42
Tibet, 81
Times of India, 72, 86
Tipu Sultan, 55
Tito, Josip Broz, 11, 112
Togan, Zeki Velidi, 137
The Transformation of Palestine
   (Abu-Lughod), 161
translations, Arabic, 28–35, 44–45,
   47–50
Transvaal, 37
Turkey, 87, 105, 146, 148

UN Commission on the Status of
   Women, 27
United Arab Republic (UAR), 11
United Nations, 22, 93, 107, 115, 123,
   161, 162
United Nations Educational,
   Scientific and Cultural Organiza-
   tion (UNESCO), 133, 140
United States, 100, 124–25, 133–35,
   140–41, 157, 160, 162
University of Ghana, 136
University of Rajasthan, 158

University of Utrecht, 158
al-Urwa (journal), 8–10
The Uses of Life (Lubbock), 29

Venkatram, T. K., 91
Vietnam, 114, 116
Visva-Bharati university, 131
Vollers, Karl, 138

Wafd Party, 78
Wallerstein, Immanuel, 7
"We Are All Muslims"
  (al-Bustani), 39
Weiss, Leopold (Muhammad Asad), 9
Weizmann, Chaim, 44, 184n62
White, Hayden, 2
Who Were the Shudras?
  (Ambedkar), 69
Wilkins, Roy, 18
Williams, Monier, 32
World Bank, 162
World Islamic Congress (1931), 40
World War II, knowledge effort
  following, 133–35

The Wretched of the Earth (Fanon), 125
Wright, Richard, 18, 125

Yaghi, ʿAbd al-Rahman, 37
Yemen, 32, 87
Yeola, 69
Yitah, Moshe, 50–51

Zaheer, Sajjad, 117, 146, 147
Zahlan, Antoine, 163
al-Zahra (magazine), 39
Zakaria, Rafiq, 10
al-Zanjani, Abd al-Karim, 71
al-Zayyat, Ahmad Hasan, 19
Ziadeh, Nicola, 152–53, 155–57
Zionism, 13, 38–44, 89–93, 95, 112, 118, 161–62
Zionism, Israel and Asian Nationalism
  (Jansen), 14
Zionist Colonialism in Palestine
  (Sayegh), 165
Zurayk, Constantine, 20, 163
Zureik, Elia, 26–27
Zwemer, Samuel, 59, 60

Founded in 1893,
UNIVERSITY OF CALIFORNIA PRESS
publishes bold, progressive books and journals
on topics in the arts, humanities, social sciences,
and natural sciences—with a focus on social
justice issues—that inspire thought and action
among readers worldwide.

The UC PRESS FOUNDATION
raises funds to uphold the press's vital role
as an independent, nonprofit publisher, and
receives philanthropic support from a wide
range of individuals and institutions—and from
committed readers like you. To learn more, visit
ucpress.edu/supportus.

www.ingramcontent.com/pod-product-compliance
Lightning Source LLC
Chambersburg PA
CBHW021343230426
43666CB00006B/389